Interdisciplinary Contributions to Archaeology

Series editor

Jelmer Eerkens
University of California, Davis
Davis, CA, USA

More information about this series at http://www.springer.com/series/6090

Marieka Brouwer Burg
Hans Peeters • William A. Lovis
Editors

Uncertainty and Sensitivity Analysis in Archaeological Computational Modeling

Springer

Editors
Marieka Brouwer Burg
Department of Anthropology
University of New Hampshire
Durham, NH, USA

Hans Peeters
Groningen Institute of Archaeology
University of Groningen
Groningen, The Netherlands

William A. Lovis
Department of Anthropology
and MSU Museum
Michigan State University
East Lansing, MI, USA

ISSN 1568-2722
Interdisciplinary Contributions to Archaeology
ISBN 978-3-319-27831-5   ISBN 978-3-319-27833-9 (eBook)
DOI 10.1007/978-3-319-27833-9

Library of Congress Control Number: 2016935511

Printed on acid-free paper

This Springer imprint is published by Springer Nature
The registered company is Springer International Publishing AG Switzerland

Preface

This book had its origin in what seemed at the time to be a straightforward question: *Have you done a sensitivity analysis*? Posed by a geologist, this question was directed at an archaeological dissertation involving simulation modeling of hunter-gatherers in Post-Glacial landscapes, a dissertation that was scheduled for defense in just over a month. While not intended to create a fuss, the question was met with equal parts surprise (what exactly constitutes a sensitivity analysis?), trepidation (could a sensitivity analysis be conducted for a complex archaeological scenario?), and worry (could it be done in time?). All of these sentiments were borne out as the lead editor of the present volume began investigating what it would take to devise, implement, and analyze not just one but a series of sensitivity analyses!

Needless to say, once the primary goal of the dissertation defense was accomplished, much time was spent discussing how and when the ensuing sensitivity analysis would be conducted. After a year of research, we (Marieka, Hans, William, Henk Weerts, Kim Cohen, etc.) realized that no straightforward parallel existed for an archaeological simulation involving the combination of unique software programs, coding languages, input parameters and objectives, landscape reconstructions, and behavioral processes. Furthermore, those archaeological computational modelers who have conducted various types of sensitivity analyses have published little on how such techniques are incorporated methodologically or how results impact the modeling development, research design, and execution. Given the lack of any sort of discipline-based protocol for testing our models, or for identifying and isolating sources of error or uncertainty, we convened a forum at the 2014 Meetings of the Society for American Archaeology (SAA) in Austin, Texas, titled "*Error, Sensitivity Analysis, and Uncertainty in Archaeological Computational Modeling*" to more publicly air some of the key issues. The chapters in this volume had their inception as contributions to this forum.

A number of critical modeling issues were brought to the table at this forum, from the selection of scale and repetition to model equifinality and the use of stochastic rather than nonrandom parameters and processes. Perhaps the most repeated of these topics was that of *uncertainty*, the source of most of the errors in our models and the target of sensitivity analysis. It was generally concluded that any computational model, whether statistical, empirical, random, or patterned, should incorporate frequent and systematized procedures for recognizing where and when uncertainty occurs, and how it can be minimized or incorporated. It was also observed that while archaeologists are for most part implicitly aware of uncertainties in a variety of contexts, there have been limited attempts to overtly and systematically face them. The overall aim of this volume, then, is to impress on archaeological modelers (and simulative modelers in particular) the imperative nature of assessing uncertainty at all phases of modeling, from design and construction to execution and post-processing. At a broader scale, all archaeologists can benefit from consideration of uncertainty, especially given that the archaeological record itself is incomplete, biased, and full of unknowns. Furthermore, as many related disciplines (Geology, Geography, Natural Resources, Economics, Risk Management, etc.) regularly engage in and publish the results of sensitivity analyses, this is a methodological procedure we need to incorporate in order for our work to resonate appropriately with non-archaeological colleagues.

Here we present new ways of thinking about and addressing such uncertainty in targeted, context-specific examples. Different approaches to archaeological modeling are presented in case study format, with each chapter contributing a unique perspective on the meta-modeling issues of uncertainty and sensitivity analysis. The case studies are preceded by an introductory chapter that provides an overarching discussion of the theoretical literature on uncertainty and related issues of sensitivity analysis, model calibration, verification, and validation (Brouwer Burg, Peeters, and Lovis) and a chapter that attempts to situate sensitivity analysis in the context of research design (Lovis). The subsequent case studies span the European (Brouwer Burg, Peeters and Romeijn) and North American (Carroll, Watts, White) continents, employ both deductive and inductive procedures, and explore various approaches to research design from a theoretical and methodological perspective. These case studies also engage different approaches to simulation; some involve spatial GIS-based simulations while others apply agent-based simulations in abstract space (also known as agent-based modeling or ABM), both of which operationalize theoretical models of human behavior and decision-making in quantitative form. Topics considered include linear versus nonlinear modeling, scale dependency, differential criteria weighting, as well as parameter relationships. The penultimate chapter considers more overtly the theoretical issues involved with archaeological simulation (Whitley). The final chapter of the volume by van der Leeuw synthesizes the key issues of the preceding chapters with a view toward the future of archaeological computation modeling and the methods required to deal with uncertainty and error.

With the publication of this volume, the editors and other contributors hope that the complex issues of uncertainty and sensitivity analysis are brought to the forefront of archaeological computational modeling and will soon have an explicit role to play across the discipline. However, there is no quick fix: for every model made and run, model designers should consider how and where uncertainty is introduced both theoretically and methodologically, and how this uncertainty impacts model outcome. Formal or computational modeling enables us to investigate uncertainty in an explicit way, but we must bear in mind that underlying ideas about how people behaved in the past are often based on implicit assumptions built on ambiguous archaeological data and/or anthropological analogy. Hence, uncertainty does not stop at the limits of computational approaches, but is also of concern to "traditional" (analogous) models about past human behavior. For this reason, uncertainty assessment should also be applied to implicit ideas and assumptions about the past as well.

Durham, NH, USA — Marieka Brouwer Burg
Groningen, The Netherlands — Hans Peeters
East Lansing, MI, USA — William A. Lovis

Acknowledgments

To achieve our ambitious end, a number of people have contributed to the inception, development, and completion of this volume. We thank, first and foremost, Dr. Henk Weerts (Cultural Heritage Agency of the Netherlands) for his initial inquiry regarding the implementation of sensitivity analyses in archaeological computation modeling. Dr. Kim Cohen (Utrecht University) provided insight and commentary early on in our thought development. We thank the chapter authors for their diligence in observing deadlines and willingness to participate in our round-robin review. External reviewers, many central practitioners in archaeological modeling, were also of critical importance in honing the arguments made in this volume: Drs. Andre Costopoulos (McGill University), Enrico Crema (University College London), Jim Doran (University of Essex), Timothy Kohler (Washington State University at Pullman), Luke Premo (Washington State University at Pullman), Philip Verhagen (University of Amsterdam), and Robert Whallon (University of Michigan). Dr. Sander van der Leeuw (Arizona State University) graciously agreed to read the entire manuscript and provide insight for our final chapter, for which we are enormously grateful. In addition, special thanks to Dr. Michael Barton (Arizona State University) for his invaluable perspective during the SAA Forum, as well as Dr. Kyle Bocinsky (Washington State University at Pullman) for providing insightful and focused commentary on various chapters. Appreciation is also accorded to the two anonymous reviewers who saw potential in the proposal for this volume, as well as our excellent editorial contacts at Springer, Teresa Krauss and Hana Nagdimov.

Contents

About the Editors

Marieka Brouwer Burg (Ph.D. 2011 Michigan State University) is Lecturer of Anthropology in the Department of Anthropology at the University of New Hampshire, New Hampshire, USA. She is interested in the effects of landscape evolution and climate change on human communities, as well as reconstructing decision processes and perceptions of landscape in the past. She uses GIS-based archaeological computational modeling to explore these processes in both Old and New World contexts. Her current research focuses on investigating the spatiotemporal dimensions of ancient Maya mobility and socioeconomic interactions in the central Belize River Valley, Belize.

Hans Peeters (Ph.D. 2007 University of Amsterdam) is Associate Professor of Prehistoric Archaeology at the Groningen Institute of Archaeology, University of Groningen, the Netherlands. His research interests include Hunter-Gatherer Archaeology and Ethnography, Landscape Archaeology, Lithic Technology, Computational Modeling, and Site Formation Dynamics and Fractal Geometry. Peeters' current research projects include Late Glacial and Holocene Hunter-Gatherer Landscape Use of the North Sea Basin, Mesolithic Lithic Technology, Hunter-Gatherer Pyro-Technology, and Dynamics of Intra-Site Spatial Patterning.

William A. Lovis (Ph.D. 1973 Michigan State University) is Professor and Curator of Anthropology in the Department of Anthropology and MSU Museum at Michigan State University, Michigan, USA. His research interests include Hunter-Gatherer Archaeology and Ethnography; The Transition to Horticulture; Applied Theory, Analytic Methods and Research Design; Human–Environment Interactions and Regional Taphonomy; Paleoenvironmental Change; Public Policy including Forensic Archaeology, Law Enforcement Training, and Repatriation; and Great Lakes/Midwest and Europe. Current research projects include archaeological site taphonomy and preservation in the Lake Michigan coastal dunes, Mesolithic regional settlement and mobility in Yorkshire, northern England, and hemispheric climate impacts on Great Lakes coastal dune evolution and activation cycling.

About the Contributors

Jon W. Carroll (Ph.D. 2013 Michigan State University) is Assistant Professor of Anthropology in the Department of Sociology, Anthropology, Social Work, and Criminal Justice at Oakland University, Michigan, USA. His research interests include cultural transmission, social interaction and integration, political and economic organization, social science applications of Geographic Information Systems (GIS), and computer modeling and simulation. Jon is currently working on a research project involving computer modeling of ancient sociospatial dynamics in the Tel Lachish region of Israel using Uninhabited Aerial Vehicle (UAV) remote sensing applications.

Sander van der Leeuw is a Distinguished Sustainability Scientist at the Julie Ann Wrigley Global Institute of Sustainability, Director of the ASU-SFI Center for Biosocial Complex Systems and Foundation Professor in the Schools of Sustainability and Human Evolution and Social Change, Arizona State University, USA. Van der Leeuw is an archaeologist and historian by training, specializing in the long-term impacts of human activity on the landscape. He is recognized as a pioneer in the application of the complex adaptive systems approach to socio-environmental challenges and in this context has studied ancient technologies, ancient and modern man–land relationships, and innovation. A native of Holland who speaks five languages, van der Leeuw has done archaeological fieldwork in Syria, Holland, and France and conducted ethno-archaeological studies in the Near East, the Philippines, and Mexico. In the 1990s, he coordinated for the European Union a series of interdisciplinary research projects on socio-natural interactions and modern environmental problems. This work spans all the countries along the northern Mediterranean rim and used the complex adaptive systems approach to improve understanding of these interactions and their impact on sustainability—the first of its kind. In the 2000s, he codirected an (equally EU-funded) project on invention and innovation from a Complex Adaptive Systems perspective. He is also an External Professor of the Santa Fe Institute (SFI), is a Corresponding Member of the Royal Dutch Academy of Arts and Sciences, and held a Chair at the Institut

Universitaire de France. In 2012, he was awarded the title "Champion of the Earth for Science and Innovation" by the United Nations Environment Programme.

Jan-Willem Romeijn (Ph.D. 2005 University of Groningen) is Professor of Philosophy of Science at the Faculty of Philosophy of the University of Groningen, the Netherlands. His research interests include scientific method, statistical inference, and model selection. Next to doing systematic work in philosophy, he regularly collaborates with scholars from a wide variety of disciplines, most recently also from the humanities.

Joshua Watts (Ph.D. 2013 Arizona State University) is a Postdoctoral Researcher in the Center for Social Dynamics and Complexity at Arizona State University, Arizona, USA. He uses computational modeling methods, including agent-based modeling, to study how human societies integrate with their environment(s) both in the past and the present. For example, he has explored the organization and evolution of prehistoric market-based economies in the Southwest United States and worked with meteorologists on models of modern information networks and individual risk assessments during extreme weather events.

Andrew A. White (Ph.D. 2012 University of Michigan) is Assistant Research Professor in the South Carolina Institute of Archaeology and Anthropology at the University of South Carolina, USA. His research interests include hunter-gatherers, human cultural and biological evolution, complex systems theory, and prehistoric families. Much of his current research is focused on understanding the emergence of social complexity in eastern North America, using a model-based framework to integrate and interpret household- and regional-level archaeological data and address questions about how changes in household-level behaviors and conditions are linked to large-scale, long-term changes in a social system.

Thomas G. Whitley (Ph.D. 2000 University of Pittsburg) is Associate Professor of Anthropology and Director of the Anthropological Studies Center at Sonoma State University, California, USA. He specializes in archaeological applications of GIS and spatial analysis, particularly in the areas of interpreting cognitive landscapes, remote sensing with UAVs, human ecology, complex socioeconomic simulations, and predictive modeling. Recently, he has been developing a digital GIS-based economic simulation of the Helvetii, in Switzerland, during the onset of Caesar's Gallic Wars in 58 BC. He is also working with simulations of coastal hunter-gatherer adaptations and Pleistocene maritime economies on the Pilbara and Kimberley Coasts of Western Australia. His historical archaeological research efforts are in the analysis of institutional and forced labor at penal and industrial locales in both Australia and North America, including mining sites, prisons and camps, mills and factories, as well as homesteads and plantations.

Chapter 1
Introduction to Uncertainty and Sensitivity Analysis in Archaeological Computational Modeling

Marieka Brouwer Burg, Hans Peeters, and William A. Lovis

1.1 Introduction

With the rise of computer use and functionality since the late 1960s, the development of formal computational models executable in a systematic and timely manner in archaeology have witnessed increasing attention within the discipline. However, the role and importance of computational modeling as an investigatory tool is not as widely recognized nor as often implemented by archaeologists as perhaps it could be. This situation does not necessarily pose a methodological problem, just as there are multiple paradigmatic approaches that exist with regard to the research and interpretation of the archaeological contexts we examine. Nonetheless, it is useful to ask ourselves why computational modeling geared at investigating archaeological questions is still considered a "black-box" approach that does not really push the envelope of archaeological theory, research design and inquiry. Making a case for the use of mathematical modeling in archaeological theory building, Read (1990, p. 29) argued that "*the lack of application of mathematical formalism stems from an inadequate understanding of the way mathematics provides not only a language for the expression of relationships, but also a means of reasoning about their*

M. Brouwer Burg (✉)
Department of Anthropology, University of New Hampshire, Durham, NH, USA
e-mail: Marieka.brouwer-burg@unh.edu

H. Peeters
Groningen Institute of Archaeology, University of Groningen, Groningen, The Netherlands
e-mail: j.h.m.peeters@rug.nl

W.A. Lovis
Department of Anthropology and MSU Museum, Michigan State University, East Lansing, MI, USA
e-mail: lovis@msu.edu

M. Brouwer Burg et al. (eds.), *Uncertainty and Sensitivity Analysis in Archaeological Computational Modeling*, Interdisciplinary Contributions to Archaeology, DOI 10.1007/978-3-319-27833-9_1

consequences, hence a language for extending archaeological reasoning." In other words, computational models driven by sound mathematical formulae allow modelers to obtain insight into emerging complexities and theoretical implications of the studied dataset(s). Hence, the problem is not the application of mathematical techniques to data analysis, which archaeologists are well versed at, but rather the construction of natural, social, and behavioral constructs as approximations of a conceived "reality" in the past, and the assessment of model outcomes to evaluate and deepen archaeological theory.

Having introduced the concept of "reality," the next question is what "reality" actually means in archaeology. Is it the reality of the archaeological record as it is observed today, as the product of thousands of years of differential cultural and natural taphonomic processes? Is it the degree to which our presentist conceptions of how people behaved correspond to how people *actually* behaved in the past? Is it what we imagine about the past from our unique ontological perspectives today? These are questions with very different implications, but whatever the answer, if the ultimate aim of archaeology is to increase our understanding of human behavior in the past, we are also confronted with the question of how *confident* we are about the processes that led to the formation of the archaeological record and inferred processes of pattern formation. Or, to put it another way, how do we deal with *uncertainty* in conceiving systemic interrelationships, and the emergence of sociocultural and socionatural structures and subsequent archaeological manifestations, of past behavior? An unknown degree of uncertainty always underlies our interpretations of analytical results, whether one is hypothesizing about how humans behaved in the past based on material culture studies; how patterns in the archaeological record came about with the aid of computational models; or otherwise. Hypotheses cast in archaeological narratives (these are also models) about the behavior of our ancestors generally remain vague when defining systemic interrelationships, the inclusion/role of variables, or attribution of parameter weights, whereas formalized narratives (or computational models) are explicit in their definition of these components. Yet, how confident—if at all—can we be that our model, as a narrative or formalized construct, approximates to some degree the "target system" (which equals reality)? If, for the sake of simplicity, we can gain confidence about the "validity" of models, the next question that arises is how we can determine the performance of those models (i.e., verify that the models do what they are supposed to). In other words, how can we measure degrees of uncertainty implicit in a model in order to evaluate its power relative to the target system?

This question cuts to the central theme of this book: dealing with uncertainty and sensitivity analysis (SA) as a means of model verification and validation. Here, we define model *verification* as a process that identifies if, and how well, a model executes the task it was designed for (e.g., predict soil permeability; see Ngo and See's (2012), Fig. 10.1, reproduced as Fig. 2.1 in Chap. 2). As part of this process, *calibration* aims at tuning and optimizing input parameter values such that they produce model output that can approximate real data. *SA*, which we return to later in this chapter, examines the effects of varying input parameters and values on model output.

Validation of a model involves assessing the degree to which a model produces robust and valid outcomes, and satisfies the outset objectives for the model (Berger et al. 2001; Kleijnen 2005; Ngo and See 2012). For the discipline of archaeological computational modeling, "valid" outcomes are those that approximate reality in the past. Diverse genres of validation are followed in related fields (e.g., geography) and involve process-based, operational, empirical, conceptual, and statistical techniques or, as defined by Zeigler (1976) the three primary methods of replicative, predictive, and structural validation. Generally speaking, the more complex the model, the greater the time and labor will be to undertake verification and validation processes (for an archaeological example, see Murphy 2012). Nevertheless, we argue these steps should become standard for the science of archaeological modeling providing, as they do, critical insight into model strengths, weaknesses, and overall functionality. Our goal in such modeling should be to generate progressively less uncertainty over time, in alignment with the overall goal of science, which is not truth but rather "to get less wrong over time" (Brian Nosek, founder of the Center for Open Science, quoted in Aschwanden 2015). This concept is fundamental because whatever we know now is only our best approximation of the truth, and we must always be vigilant against presuming to have everything right.

Despite the growing body of literature on archaeological modeling and, perhaps surprisingly, computational modeling in particular, the question of uncertainty and model validation is rarely addressed. This scenario stands in stark contrast to modeling in other fields (e.g., geology, physics, biology, engineering), where model validation has become a critical step of the procedure, e.g., in the form of "SA." "Verification" and "calibration," both of which are more commonly referred to in the archaeological literature, are closely related to validation (see above), but represent a step that has very specific methodological implications in connection to the theoretical embedding of models upon which calibration is executed (Morrison 2015). In this chapter, we will take a closer look at the role of computational modeling in archaeology as compared to other disciplines and in particular, the relationship between uncertainty and validation within these models. From a theoretical perspective, we will first outline the differences and similarities in the possibilities of model validation. Next, and in reference to the other chapters in this volume, we will discuss the importance of acknowledgement of uncertainty and the role of SA in archaeological computational modeling, as a means by which to confirm strengths and weaknesses of models.

1.2 The Role of, and Approaches to, Computational Modeling

Referring to a model as "*an imaginary system, represented in language, mathematics, computer code, or some other symbolic medium, that has useful similarities to aspects of a target system in the real world*" and which "*might be viewed as an abstraction, simplification, idealization, or conceptual device*," Kohler and van der Leeuw (2007, pp. 3–4) provide an open and flexible definition. But again, one might wonder what constitutes the "real world" (or reality)? The realities of our world, including the physical world, consist of theories which themselves are based on models and experiments (Morrison 2015). Hence, our observations are not neutral or theory independent. From this perspective then, one approach to the definition of such an imaginary system is as valid as another. Nonetheless, models—computational models in particular—are often believed to be of little use where it comes to the explanation of the observed phenomena. Human systems are generally believed too complex to be cast in simple rules (see, e.g., Clark 2000; Cowgill 2000; Shanks and Tilley 1987). This position, which we challenge (following instead work by Doran 2000; Lake 2004), stems from a perspective that humans are often considered to be the most complex creatures on earth, having free will, their behavior regulated by "independent" and conscious (though not always rational) decision-making.

In our opinion, models form the connective device between theory and the world, which consists of observed phenomena/systems. As such, models have a mediating role (cf. Morrison 1998; Morrison and Morgan 1999) and provide an abstraction or formal specification of some phenomenon/system in terms of an interconnected set of rules that connect variables/parameters, and the behavior of which is compared with the observed counterpart. In order to make any such comparison possible, it is necessary to "activate" a model through simulations and experiments. Simulations can be seen as reconstructions of a target system (model) on the basis of a (mathematical) structure of functions that provides information about the behavioral structure of the target system. Closely connected, experiments can be seen as devices that return data/output that, to some degree, fit/misfit the expected outcomes of the target system, hence providing information about the validity of the model itself.

A number of formal and computational modeling approaches have been applied to archaeological case studies and socionatural questions of human behavior and interactions with other individuals, groups, and the ecological milieu. While formal approaches (including, e.g., linear programming, economic, and game-theory models) have had a lasting impact on archaeological interpretations, computational models involving cellular automata, neural networks, agent-based modeling procedures (ABM) and georeferenced databases have become more popular in this subfield. Here, we focus on the latter two approaches, each of which requires a unique set of assumptions and developmental considerations, and is accompanied by varying strengths and weaknesses (for ABM, see discussion in Epstein 2006; Kohler and Gumerman 2000; Wurzer et al. 2015; and Carroll, Chap. 5, Watts, Chap. 6, and White, Chap. 7 in this volume; for GIS-based approaches, see discussion in Jankowski, et al. 2001; Krist 2001; and Brouwer Burg, Chap. 4 and Peeters and Romeijn, Chap. 3 in this volume). ABM attempts to explain macro-scale behavioral phenomenon through high volume iterations of socionatural dynamics (see, e.g., Axtell et al. 2002). The main advantage of this approach is its recursive nature, which can produce a bandwidth of human–environment interactions given a set of initial parameters, and the range of these processes can be cast against empirical data. Such modeling focuses on varying the behavior of human agents given certain initial or outset conditions, and searches for large-scale patterning that may emerge over successive executions of the model. A primary disadvantage is that oftentimes ABM is carried out in simulated virtual environments that lack grounding in real-world environments.

By contrast, the first and foremost concern of GIS-based modeling of archaeological processes, human behavior, and human–natural interactions is the reproduction of environments in the past. In general, highly detailed geographic, geologic, pedologic, vegetative, and faunal data are harnessed with a powerful geographic information system software (e.g., ArcGIS [the current industry standard], but also IDRISI, GRASS, and others), producing static or dynamic map reconstructions of paleolandscapes that can then be utilized as the foundation upon which decision-chain formulae can be carried out via software-specific functions involving grid-based transformations (Brouwer 2011; Howey 2011; Jankowski et al. 2001; Peeters 2007; Whitley 2000 to name a few). Disadvantages associated with this approach include lack of sufficient or reliable environmental data; a tendency to produce static, "slice-of-time" map surfaces rather than dynamic, open-ended model runs; and the focus on behavior carried out in specific places in time rather than on broad-level behavioral trends that could be applicable in diverse spatiotemporal contexts.

A few mixed-methodology, or "middleware" approaches have also been generated in recent decades, approaches that have coupled or integrated agent-driven simulations of human behavior and socionatural interactions into GISs representing environmental reconstructions (e.g., Brown et al. 2005; Janssen 2009; Lake 2000; see Crooks and Castle 2012 for an overview). Coupling these diverse approaches is a difficult process, as different theoretical concerns, software requirements, and modeling languages are utilized (Gilbert 2008). Lake's (2000) MAGICAL model ran agent-driven decision choices on georeferenced landscapes to explore Mesolithic subsistence systems, but this model was built for a unique spatiotemporal context, a common characteristic of most mixed techniques that has prevented much standardization of coupling techniques for broader contexts in archaeology. It should be noted that this is also the case in the field of geography, from which these methods were initially conceived (Crooks and Castle 2012, p. 221). The two primary techniques developed so far involve either the coupling of two distinct geospatial and agent-based systems via data transfer (Westervelt 2002); or the embedding and integration of the systems such that one system is subsumed under the other predominant systems (Maguire 2005). For example, GIS-centric systems would run agent-based scripting language on georeferenced gridded layers, such as has been done by Brown et al. (2005) with the ABM extension Agent Analyst in ArcGIS. Simulation-centric systems would tie iterative results of socionatural behavioral outputs to georeferenced surfaces using GIS functionality. A number of open source simulation toolkits now exist that can facilitate such demands (e.g., Swarm, MASON, and NetLogo; see Crooks and Castle 2012: Tables 12.3–12.5 for individual attributes, and Verhagen and Whitley 2012, p. 88 for applications to archaeology), although far more exploration and experimentation is needed.

While such coupled or integrated approaches allow modelers to tether questions of socionatural interactions to georeferenced natural backgrounds—ostensibly the overall goal of all computational archaeological modeling—the drawbacks of such models are similarly compounded, resulting in highly complex, multi-component and multi-phased projects that necessarily involve compounded uncertainties and associated error. However, we believe this paired or mixed-methodology linking GIS-based environmental reconstructions to ABM approaches is ultimately the manner in which archaeologists will be able to obtain the clearest views into human–environment interactions in the past. The current challenge, then, is to establish field-wide "best practices" for identifying error and uncertainty in our models. Such best practices can be disseminated at regular forums held at yearly meetings and via online venues that encourage archaeological modelers to communicate, learn, and build upon the work of their peers. Websites such as Open ABM (https://www.openabm.org), part of the Network for Computation Modeling for SocioEcological Science (CoMSES Net) is a big step in the right direction, yet one that must become more widely publicized and engaged in by all modelers working in this field of research.

1.3 Certainty About Uncertainty and Model Validation

When speaking about models, simulations, and experiments, one has to address issues of uncertainty and model validation, which leads to the question of how models can be compared to, and provide information about, target systems in the real world (Morrison 2015, p. 20). Archaeologists find themselves in a rather difficult situation in this respect. Archaeological "reality" consists of a record which results not only from human behavior in the past, but also from a myriad of natural and anthropogenic processes that have transformed initial patterns in terms of composition and distribution of observable phenomena (see Lovis, Chap. 2), as well as theoretical conceptions of what is of archaeological relevance and the addition of methodological constraints. Hence, there are many uncertainties surrounding the interpretive possibilities of the archaeological record and subsequent construction of narratives and formal models about human behavior. Of course, these problems are largely acknowledged within the field and have triggered much of the paradigmatic discussion since the 1960s (see Evans 2012 for an interesting discussion of how uncertainty and error is introduced and dealt with in the related field of geography, and Refsgaard et al. 2007 for an overview with regard to environmental modeling). Indeed, this is also the context within which archaeological computational modeling took off, and much has been achieved. However, issues of uncertainty and model validation have remained in the background, which suggests that we take this fact for granted (and carry on), or that the issue is too delicate to handle (but we carry on anyway). So how have other disciplines dealt with this issue?

1.3.1 Uncertainty in Geoscientific Modeling

As both archaeologists and geoscientists tend to collect their basic data from sedimentary deposits—many geologists consider archaeological remains simply as sedimentary composites—it is perhaps useful to start our brief overview here. In various ways, geoscientific modeling aims at problems that compare well to archaeological ones. A lot of work is concerned with prediction and assessment of resource potential (what? where? how much?), or the effects of geophysical dynamics on landforms (what happens under changing conditions?). We will illustrate both contexts with an example.

Prediction and assessment of resource potential for commercial purposes typically aims at error reduction and has to deal with four sources of uncertainty[1]: (1) model properties; (2) boundary conditions; (3) ground-truthing; and (4) computing. In the case of reservoir (e.g., hydrocarbons, groundwater) modeling for instance, computing-related uncertainties are relatively easy to account for, as bandwidths of error can be calculated from earlier results. The other sources of uncertainty are analyzed by means of running models for a large number of slightly varying sets of values. In the context of reservoir modeling, parameters such as permeability and porosity need to be connected to lithological models, which express the geostatistical properties of the reservoir's spatial characteristics. Parameter values are measured on core samples and/or experimentally determined. The use of geostatistical approaches enables the quantification of model outcomes and statistical uncertainty information about individual grid cells. From these data an "average" model with an "average" uncertainty distribution can be calculated. The range of models can be tested against real data in order to identify the "best fits"; in consideration of known or estimated bandwidths of error, this can result in hundreds of equiprobable model results within a set of boundary conditions (more on equifinality follows below in Sect. 1.3.4). As these boundary conditions are also subject to uncertainty, these settings have to be varied as well within reasonable limits. When tested against real data, a considerable number of model results are usually classified as unrealistic, leaving a smaller set of model results (with known uncertainties) that are more or less probable. Clearly, ground-truthing is important to gauge the model properties and boundary conditions. But the question remains: how much ground-truthing is needed (one case, two cases, etc.), and how many matches between model outcomes and reality must be obtained to warrant model validation? This is plainly a matter of cost-benefit experience. Any set of "real data" is incomplete and may not be fully representative. This implies that model results that do not completely fit with ground truth are not necessarily wrong. Therefore, a limit of maximal divergence from ground truth has to be set; the less ground truth is available, the larger the limit. Model runs that fall within this limit are accepted; model runs that fall outside this limit are rejected.

[1] We owe this example to Dr. Henk Weerts of the Cultural Heritage Agency of the Netherlands.

Modeling the effects of geophysical dynamics on landforms primarily focuses on the alteration of earth surface characteristics under changing conditions of erosion and sedimentation; in short, dynamic landscape process modeling. In this context, the researcher also has to deal with multiple sources of uncertainty, which are largely the same as in the previous example. But instead of building a model on a geostatistical basis in connection to the spatial distribution of a resource, dynamic landscape process modeling builds on equations that describe physical terrain properties in connection to a number of variables/parameters.[2] Evans (2012) outlines the following sources of uncertainty that occur throughout the life cycle of any simulation model: uncertainty associated with input data; model choice; model mechanics; and output. Input data can introduce uncertainty through various means, such as data measurement error, overlooking data, and choosing inappropriate sample sizes or inappropriate discretization measures. Some of these issues will become obsolete as data gathering and processing technologies continue to improve in accuracy. Others (such as sample size and sample binning) must be carefully problematized by model builders during model design and construction. Model choice can also introduce uncertainty in various ways: most notably in the selection of appropriate variables, scale, parameters, and formulae or mathematical transformations. Calibration and SA are especially useful in this phase to determine the necessity and impact of various model components. During the running of models, error is unavoidably generated as either "model-fix" errors (related to model elements not present in the real world) or "process fix" errors (related to simplification of complex elements in the real world; see van der Sluijs et al. 2003 for further explanation). In addition, the modeling code may contain mistakes, leading to model "bugs" (Evans 2012, p. 330). Code-checking programs and forums for modelers to view, edit, and revise one another's code can help in this regard (see Galán et al. 2009 for advice). Finally, the output uncertainty of any model must be assessed to satisfy model verification and validation. Various mathematical and statistical calculations can be applied to model output at this point and is usually done in the form of sensitivity testing. In the discipline of geography, Monte Carlo Sensitivity (MCS) testing is commonly applied, in which a number of model iterations are run with different input data, variable, and parameter combinations. Bayesian models are also commonly used to sample varying distributions of parameter weights and explore overall impacts on uncertainty.

In addition, there is random error to account for, which creeps into models due to "noise," an elusive term defined by Evans as "variation in our variables of interest around the values we expect to represent their 'true' or 'important' value" (Evans 2012, p. 310). Such noise can generally be explained via stochastic modeling that randomly tests the range of outcomes of a given model and uses Monte Carlo sampling to identify the most probabilistić outcomes based on more frequent occurrences in the random sampling. Error and bias, separate concepts in traditional

[2] An example is the dynamic landscape evolution model LAPSUS developed at Wageningen University.

modeling, are often conflated in more complex models as both concepts generally arise from inaccuracies of the data, the modeler, or both.

The above examples particularly line up with archaeological modeling in the context of Cultural Resource Management. As we have seen in the previous paragraph, GIS-based predictive modeling is concerned with questions of what to expect where and in what quantities; hence, it is about spatial distributions of archaeological phenomena/sites. However, the approach to uncertainty in and validation of predictive models in archaeology cannot be the same as in the geosciences due to differences in the nature and reliability of data. Typically, recent statistics-based studies on the performance of correlative and sampling-based models have shown that these are quite unsuccessful if validation relies on the archaeological record (see, e.g., Verhagen 2007). In contrast, predictive models of archaeological site survival which are based on dynamic landscape process modeling may prove more successful, as validation can, at least partly, be based on the same principles as in the geosciences.

1.3.2 Uncertainty in Ecosystem Modeling

As mentioned earlier, the initial formation of the archaeological record is directly related to human behavior in the past. How did or was the daily behavior of (groups of) individuals affected by the environment and vice versa, and to what extent were people resilient to changes in the environment? The study of the interaction between living species and their environment is typically the subject of behavioral ecology, as it is in archaeology, and is a research field that has an influential and long tradition in (computational) modeling. Perhaps May's (1973, 1976) work on model ecosystems can be cited as one of the most influential studies in the exploration of self-organizing systems and complexity.

A lot of early research in ecosystem modeling is characterized by simple models that focus on the understanding of ecological diversity, stability, and complexity in particular. Typically, these simple models tend to show nonlinear (stochastic) behavior with a sensitive dependence on initial conditions, which makes clear that one has to deal with inherent uncertainty in models where interdependence of dynamic system components (populations, environments) is central. Over time, however, models have become more complex, making it increasingly difficult to deal with the uncertainty that is compounded in these models, due to the many uncertainties on input distributions. Recent studies have tried to find solutions to this problem, and have come to the conclusion that expert estimates (expert judgment) of input distributions as approximations to describe model precision may be more useful than quantitative analysis (e.g., McElhany et al. 2010). SA (output responses to systematically varied changes in input) and error estimation (closeness of model output to measurement) as part of the modeling process is increasingly considered to evaluate uncertainty for model selection (Snowling and Kramer 2001).

In discussing animal (including humans) movement as an important topic of investigation, Viswanathan et al. (2011, p. 12) note that data-centric approaches to this issue primarily focus on comparison of model outputs with empirical data in order to find out which model fits the data best. However, they state that it is more important to bear in mind that models make assumptions, and that these lead to predictions that are not necessarily supported by a model's outcome. This, then, can lead to theoretical considerations with regard to the underlying assumptions. An interesting example is provided by Raichlen et al. (2014) who explored search patterns among Hadza hunter-gatherers in northern Tanzania, and found that about one half of foraging movement can best be described as Lévy walks, which are often considered to correspond to "optimal" search patterns for scarce and randomly distributed resources (Brown et al. 2007; Viswanathan et al. 1999), and reflects environmental complexity (de Jager et al. 2011, but see Jansen et al. 2012). Raichlen et al. (2014), however, have found little evidence for this, as differences in resources brought back to each camp are not associated with major differences in the use of Lévy walks. Furthermore, they found that Brownian walks, which describe random search patterns, occur less frequently than composite Brownian walks, which share similarities with Lévy walks (de Jager et al. 2012).

Hence, it becomes clear that systematically occurring foraging patterns may be related to the underlying complexity of foraging environments, which may carry implications for Optimal Foraging Theory. In this context, the use of abstract mathematical models rooted in physics help to disentangle and clarify patterns of distribution and movement. It forces us to think about the complexity of environments and the way animals use them. In the case of archaeology, it may reveal deeper insights about site distribution patterns relative to environmental factors, which are too often conceived of in terms of coarse-grained models and as such, do not do justice to issues of scale and environmental diversity.

1.3.3 Uncertainty in Social Modeling

In this last example, we will take a brief look at uncertainty in the modeling of social systems, where interaction among (groups of) individuals is central. How did interactions among (groups of) individuals impact daily behavior, and how were these interactions affected by changes in the socioeconomic/-political/-cultural/-technical, and -ecological environment?

A basic social science fact holds that the more people interact, the more alike they become in their cultural features (beliefs, behaviors, attitudes, etc.; Axelrod 1997, p. 203). However, this tendency toward convergence is usually halted before complete homogeneity is achieved between individuals and groups; a result of the inevitable development of a few culturally distinct and stable units. Axelrod (1997) has demonstrated just how these processes can occur with a numerically based agent-based model that can facilitate calculation of multiple dimensions of culture, although the model becomes more complex to execute with each cultural feature added and consequently the possibility of introducing error also increases. Culture is conceived of as a number of shared features (e.g., language or belief systems) that have alternating traits representing different expressions of these features (different languages and different belief systems). The more frequently an individual or cultural group interacts with a peer group, the more likely the two entities will become, until all cells in the model have converged under a few larger, "polarized" stable cultural regions (Axelrod 1997, p. 220).

While the initial starting or outset conditions of this model are extremely simple, and in so being, rather elegant, there are a number of uncertainties that are also manifested. First, this model is based on a very abstracted notion of culture as easily separable components that can be described in increasingly detailed categories of attributes (the example of "belt color" is used in the article). Thus, uncertainty arises when the modeler is forced to select a few features from the array of cultural features that make up any cultural system, thereby decreasing the diversity of the system. While the model is successful in yielding insight into large-scale cultural processes, it is consequently unable to describe the nuanced relationships and complexities that exist between cultural features and the entities that comprise them. Second, the model does not support movement between agents (sites or individuals) and thus we cannot learn anything about how human migration or mobility might impact interaction between individuals or groups, which is certainly not representative of human reality today or in the past. Third, agents can only interact with their adjacent neighbors, again an imposed characteristic of the model that does not reflect human reality, in which people move around and engage with other individuals and groups in varying sized spheres from a home base or other anchoring location. Fourth, established mechanisms affecting culture change are not incorporated, such as cultural drift and attractiveness, terrain and geographic variation, status, or technological change. All of these factors lead to uncertainty, and it is perhaps not surprising that when the model outcomes are cast against real-world instances of cultural interaction, no match is found (see discussion in Axelrod 1997, p. 220; also, Bettinger 2008; Bettinger and Eerkens 1999; Eerkens and Lipo 2005).

Other models of social complexity, such as those focused on the evolution and dynamics of cities, have in recent decades shifted toward bottom-up, organic approaches to development and behavior, the driving mechanism of equilibrium or homeostasis traded for those of catastrophe, chaos, and bifurcation (Batty 2012, p. S9). Scholars have noted that social units scale according to fractal patterning, in which self-similar patterns and processes are replicated, with small but regular variation, at both small and large iterations (Batty and Longley 1994). Spatial interaction effects between individuals and groups can also be described by these fractal structures, defining the manner in which segregation, diffusion, and/or "emergences" of social units occur (Batty 2008; Bonner 2006). Such models are incredibly useful for understanding large-scale dynamics of supra-individual social interactions; however, these models are oftentimes abstracted to such a degree that modelers lose sight of individuals and their lived realities. While conceptualizing human spatial dynamics in geometric terms is elegant and seemingly parsimonious, it is only an approximate metaphor. Making the outset assumption that all humans and human groups will act in an identical manner over time and space—multiplying and spreading over their territories in geometrically uniform configurations—sets up the system to fail if modeling *reality* is the overall goal, especially given the enormous spatial diversity present in human land-use decisions (tied in part to environment, economics, subsistence and settlement systems, technologies, ideologies, etc.). While many theories of geometric growth, gravitational pulls, and rank-size ordering of settlements can approximate some human spatial behavior, the modeler must know that variations and exceptions to the patterns will manifest in any real-time system. Additionally, these patterns are developed upon and best approximate spatial behaviors among first-world societies; a person has only to fly over a third-world country to realize that settlement expansion into virgin forests or uninhabited desert appears far from fractal in nature.

Another concern of city systems and the theories that attempt to define spatial processes of city formation is the lack of coherence or interconnection between approaches (a concern for archaeological computational modelers as well; see discussion above). As discussed by Batty (2012), the concepts of gravitation, diffusion/segregation, and rank-size relationships are not nearly as isolated as the literature would have you believe; rather, these processes are all "entangled" and the current challenge to urban geographers modeling urban systems is to weave together theories and approaches that can accommodate each of these concepts. The successful interweaving of these concepts will undoubtedly benefit archaeological modeling. Additionally, as the science of city systems transitions toward an approach in which models are used to inform rather than predict human spatial behavior, or its outcomes, archaeological modelers may find corollary verification and validation techniques that can greatly assist in the modeling of past human systems that cannot be accurately ground-truthed.

1.3.4 A Word on Equifinality and Uncertainty

Another important auxiliary concern for all modelers working to reproduce some reality (whether in the past or present) is the question of *equifinality*. This issue has been dealt with for some time now in the literature on systems and systemic analytic approaches, as well as the literature on general archaeological topics and the more specific subject of archaeological modeling. This is due in large part to the clear contribution of equifinality to uncertainties of interpretation, or outcome. As commonly configured in contemporary parlance, and recognizing that there are minor nuances in definition, equifinality is a reference to the fashion in which open systems can achieve the same or similar outcome states from different starting points, and/or through different historical processes or trajectories [Premo 2010, p. 31 for a similar definition; see Lyman 2004, who attributes the initial coining of the definition to von Bertalanffy (1949, 1956), and its introduction to archaeology by Hole and Heizer (1969)].

Since as archaeologists we deal with the patterning of material remains as proxy for the behaviors that created them and the processes that may have altered them in the period intervening between behavioral formation and archaeological observation, equifinality inserts a strong dose of uncertainty at several points in archaeological modeling—initial or starting state characteristics, is there one or potentially are there several?; procedural or decision-making logics over the time durations of interest from initial starting states, and the information and parameters that drive them; and potential alterations in the material signatures of behavior (taphonomic processes); among others. For some equifinality is viewed as a theoretically rooted phenomenon (Lyman 2004; Premo 2010; Rathje et al. 2013). Equifinality looms large for those primarily processual archaeologists who engage with middle range theory (MRT) and who conceptualize the material remains of human behaviors as the outcome of open system interactions (i.e., networks) (Cordell et al. 1994; Cunningham 2003). Some suggest that the problem of equifinality may not be uniformly solvable even with high level theory, but rather may well be more constrained and case specific (see M.B. Schiffer in Rathje et al. 2013, p. 36, particularly the discussion of proximate and limited causation). In certain instances, actualistic experimentation, as MRT, has the potential to reduce input uncertainty and understandings of outcome variability.

In archaeological modeling, this forces the recognition of multiple initial states in, potentially, different "environments," whether technologically, archaeologically, mentally, socially, etc. While often recognized at an abstract level, there are few directed attempts on the part of archaeological modelers to insert the uncertainty associated with equifinality into their work, although there are some important examples from which to draw insight (e.g., Graham and Weingart 2015; Premo 2010; see also Hodder 1976 for an early exploration). Of particular interest is the notion that simple replication of archaeological signatures through computational modeling is not necessarily sufficient for validation of either the starting state, or the historical processes that may have resulted in it, both of these in large degree being modeler's choices, albeit informed ones. This has significant import for models that only attempt to reproduce the archaeological record, leading to notions of more exploratory, experimental and heuristic use of approaches such as ABM (see, e.g., Premo 2010, in what is characterized as a "Postpositivist archaeology"), with one goal being to reduce "underdetermination among alternatives" (Premo 2010 citing Richardson 2003), and another being to disabuse us of emulative approaches. Ultimately, this altered perspective on and application of computational modeling should result in reduced uncertainty across multiple modeled dimensions, variables, and parameters.

1.4 Sensitivity Analysis and Determining Model Strength/Weakness

SA assesses how models respond to change in inputs and input values (van Groenendaal and Kleijnen 2002; Vonk Noordegraaf et al. 2003, p. 434), but does not include calculation of the probability of change as risk analyses do (van Groenendaal and Kleijnen 1997). Utilized most frequently in the earth sciences

(Lenhart et al. 2002; van Griensven et al. 2006) and behavioral ecology (Happe et al. 2006; Vonk Noordegraaf et al. 2003), SAs are particularly useful for verifying meta-model functionality and for validating output simulations in cases where such simulations cannot be tested against a robust set of empirical data (Kleijnen 2005). SAs can also reveal where uncertainty is introduced into a model, and which inputs must be accorded special attention in modeling design and execution. One of the main drawbacks of SA involves the requirement of being able to simulate reality, often an impossible task in archaeological modeling but much more reasonable for a geologist modeling an underground reservoir of water. Furthermore, fuzzy assumptions are unavoidable in modeling of past landscapes and behaviors, making quantitative analysis through statistical means a complicated procedure. However, without incorporation of verification techniques (described here in the form of SAs), archaeological modelers risk producing "just so" stories of the past, rather than systematically tested hypotheses about socionatural systems.

Various approaches to SA may be employed, including one-way analysis (e.g., the "one-at-a-time" or OAT design; Happe et al. 2006; Vonk Noordegraaf et al. 2003, p. 434), two-way or multiway analysis, or probabilistic analysis (Saltelli 2005; Taylor 2009). One-way analyses are useful for simple models with few inputs, as only one parameter or variable is changed per model run. While straightforward in its implementation, one-way analysis fails to account for interactions that may occur between inputs on account of varying input dependencies, and risks development of models that are overly crude (Vonk Noordegraaf et al. 2003, p. 434). Additionally, most simulation modeling involves a number of either social or natural inputs that are linked in hierarchical or cascading model structures. Multiway SAs are widely considered to be better suited to the task at hand (Taylor 2009; Happe et al. 2006), especially because they can reveal information regarding nuanced interactions between inputs.

The utility of multiway SAs for simulation modeling may appear obvious; however, implementation of multiway SAs comes with an important proviso: the more inputs are incorporated, the less feasible it becomes to thoroughly evaluate all input combinations. In fact, the majority of social and natural simulation models published in the recent past can be characterized as *over-parameterized*, with more than ten input parameters. In such instances, a multiway SA becomes complex and difficult to evaluate, as the researcher will ideally want to investigate every combination of parameters, leading to, for example, 10! number of combinations (3,628,800 unique combinations). Such uncritical over-parameterization can lead to large amounts of uncertainty production and should be avoided through careful selection of key factors (Doran 2008).

SA can be a useful tool to determine which potential factors should be retained and which can be removed to improve model efficiency and accuracy. In behavioral ecology, researchers often apply the statistical techniques of Design of Experiments (DOE) and meta-modeling in order to reveal significant information about the behavior of the model as well as the programing logic, and to determine which inputs have the greatest impact on the model (Happe et al. 2006; Kleijnen 2005; see Brouwer Burg, Chap. 4 for an archaeological application). A subset of inputs that are assumed to strongly influence the model are chosen, and a limited range of input, or factor, settings are chosen to define the low, default, and high value settings for each selected input. This approach to SA is easy to generate and analyze using regression statistics and can yield important information regarding the effects of particular inputs as well as how inputs interact with each other. A similar streamlining strategy is referred to in the statistical literature as extreme SAs (Taylor 2009), or "corner testing" (Gilbert 2008), a technique that also sets selected inputs to their highest or lowest value (or best/worst case scenario) to determine the outer limits or boundaries of a parameter space in which all possible parameter values fall.

Probabilistic techniques are also very useful for analyzing the sensitivity of parameters on the model output (Taylor 2009). In such cases, each parameter is assigned a probability value. With each iteration of the model, one random value within the distribution for that parameter is selected. Over many model iterations, many random values are chosen. Analysis of the outcomes of the model iterations reveal their statistical properties and provide an indication of the sensitivity to the selected parameter.

1.5 Summary and Chapter Overviews

The overall goal of this volume is to problematize the issues of uncertainty, error, and SA, and discuss methods for identifying and dealing with these issues in archaeological computational modeling. Each of the contributing authors comes at this question from a unique spatiotemporal and methodological perspective, revealing just how diverse a long-awaited "solution" or best practice protocol will be. In Chap. 2, Lovis explores the role of SA and other methodological concerns of archaeological modeling for research design and theory building. Coming at the subject as a relative outsider, he provides a unique perspective on the merits and shortcomings of SA, and weighs in on how to make this practice a worthwhile component of archaeological computational research. From a more epistemic perspective, Peeters and Romeijn describe a priori and post hoc approaches to confronting uncertainty in Chap. 3. They suggest that choosing particular families of models that yield highly variant or invariant outcomes are best for robust hypothesis testing. In Chap. 4, Brouwer Burg examines GIS-based methods for exploring archaeological dynamics, in comparison to ABM approaches. Brouwer Burg references a case study of Mesolithic hunter-gatherers in the Netherlands to illustrate the complexities of designing and executing SAs for her Hunter-Gatherer Land Use Model (HGLUM). In Chap. 5, the capability of agent-based models to explore nonlinear behavioral patterning (such as cultural transmission) is presented by Carroll. SA is applied to the Intercommunity Cultural Transmission Model (ITCM) for the Late Prehistoric Great Lakes Period of North America. Watts tackles the question of scale and repetition for model validation in Chap. 6, and investigates how scale-dependent variables can impact model outcomes, referencing a model designed to simulate Hohokam economic transactions in central Arizona. In Chap. 7, White also investigates the impact of varying model parameters, this time focusing on demographic inputs and their effects on hunter-gatherer population stabilizing mechanisms. Whitley discusses current issues that have arisen with increased computational power and database management systems, calling for more attention in the field to theoretical development in Chap. 8. Finally, in Chap. 9 van der Leeuw draws together the preceding chapters in this volume and discusses issues of uncertainty and SA in the context of a wider perspective on how archaeological perceptions of the past introduce ontological uncertainty, and how the interpretative choices we make are influenced by the path-dependency of model construction procedures. He concludes that formal modeling approaches that allow us to explore structure-specific decisions and their consequences (even unintended ones) in the present can greatly enhance understandings of socio-natural processes in the past, a move away from reductionist and evolutionary schemas that van der Leeuw sees as critical to the advancement of the field.

References

Aschwanden, C. (2015). *Science isn't broken. Five ThirtyEight newsletter*. ESPN. Retrieved from www.fivethirtyeight.com/features/science-isnt-broken/.

Axelrod, R. (1997). The dissemination of culture: A model with local convergence and global polarization. *Journal of Conflict Resolution, 41*(2), 203–226.

Axtell, R., Epstein, J. M., Dean, J. S., Gumerman, G. J., Swedlund, A. C., Harburger, J., et al. (2002). Population growth and collapse in a multi-agent model of the Kayenta Anasazi in Long House Valley. *Proceedings of the National Academy of Sciences of the United States of America (PNAS), 99*(3), 7275–7279.

Batty, M. (2008). The size, scale, and shape of cities. *Science, 319*(5864), 769–771.

Batty, M. (2012). Building a science of cities. *Cities, 29*, S9–S16.

Batty, M., & Longley, P. A. (1994). *Fractal cities: A geometry of form and function*. San Diego, CA: Academic.

Bettinger, R. L. (2008). Cultural transmission and archaeology. In M. J. O'Brien (Ed.), *Cultural transmission and archaeology: Issues and case studies* (pp. 1–9). Washington, DC: SAA Press.

Bettinger, R. L., & Eerkens, J. (1999). Point typologies, cultural transmission, and the spread of bow-and-arrow technology in the prehistoric Great Basin. *American Antiquity, 64*, 231–242.

Berger, T., Goodchild, M., Janssen, M. A., Manson, S. M., Najlis, R., & Parker, D. C. (2001). Methodological considerations for agent-based modeling of land-use and land-cover change. In D. C. Parker, T. Berger, & S. M. Manson (Eds.), *Agent-based models of land-use and land-cover change*. Report and review of an international workshop. Irvine.

Bonner, J. T. (2006). *Why size matters: From bacteria to blue whales*. Princeton, NJ: Princeton University Press.

Brouwer, M. E. (2011). *Modeling mesolithic hunter-gatherer land use and post-glacial landscape dynamics in the central Netherlands*. Ph.D. Thesis, Department of Anthropology, Michigan State University.

Brown, C. T., Liebovitch, L. S., & Glendon, R. (2007). Lévy flights in Dobe Ju/'hoansi foraging patterns. *Human Ecology, 35*, 129–138.

Brown, D. G., Riolo, R., Robinson, D. T., North, M. J., & Rand, W. (2005). Spatial process and data models: Toward integration of agent-based models and GIS. *Journal of Geographic Systems, 7*(1), 25–47.

Clark, J. E. (2000). Toward a better explanation of heredity inequality: A critical assessment of natural and historic human agents. In M. A. Dobres & J. E. Robb (Eds.), *Agency in archaeology* (pp. 92–112). London: Routledge.

Cordell, L. S., Kelley, J. H., Kintigh, K. W., Lekson, S. H., & Sinclair, R. M. (1994). Toward increasing our knowledge of the past: A discussion. In G. J. Gumerman & M. Gell-Mann (Eds.), *Understanding complexity in the prehistoric southwest* (Proceedings, Vol. 16 (Book 16). Santa Fe Institute studies in the sciences of complexity, pp. 149–191). Boulder, CO: Westview Press.

Cowgill, G. E. (2000). "Rationality" and contexts in agency theory. In M. A. Dobres & J. E. Robb (Eds.), *Agency in archaeology* (pp. 51–60). London: Routledge.

Crooks, A. T., & Castle, C. J. E. (2012). The integration of agent-based modeling and geographic information for geospatial simulation. In A. J. Heppenstall, A. T. Crooks, L. M. See, & M. Batty (Eds.), *Agent-based models of geographical systems* (pp. 219–252). New York: Springer.

Cunningham, J. J. (2003). Transcending the "Obnoxious Spectator": A case for processual pluralism in ethnoarchaeology. *Journal of Anthropological Archaeology, 22*, 389–410.

de Jager, M., Weissing, F. J., Herman, P. M. J., Nolet, B. A., & van de Koppel, J. (2011). Lévy walks evolve through interaction between movement and environmental complexity. *Science, 332*, 1551–1553.

de Jager, M., Weissing, F. J., Herman, P. M. J., Nolet, B. A., & van de Koppel, J. (2012). Response to comment on "Lévy walks evolve through interaction between movement and environmental complexity". *Science, 335*, 918d.

Doran, J. E. (2000). Trajectories to complexity in artificial societies: Rationality, belief and emotions. In T. A. Kohler & G. J. Gumerman (Eds.), *Dynamics in human and primate societies: Agent-based modeling of social and spatial processes* (pp. 89–144). New York: Oxford University Press.

Doran, J. (2008). Review of "the model-based archaeology of socionatural systems". *Journal of Artificial Societies and Social Simulation, 11*, 1–4.

Eerkens, J. W., & Lipo, C. P. (2005). Cultural transmission, copying errors, and the generation of variation in material culture and the archaeological record. *Journal of Anthropological Archaeology, 24*, 316–334.

Epstein, J. M. (2006). *Generative social science: Studies in agent-based computational modeling*. Princeton, NJ: Princeton University Press.

Evans, A. (2012). Uncertainty and error. In A. J. Heppenstall, A. Crooks, L. M. See, & M. Batty (Eds.), *Agent-based models for geographical systems* (pp. 309–346). Dordrecht, The Netherlands: Springer.

Galán, J. M., Izquierdo, L. R., Izquierdo, S. S., Santos, J., del Olmo, R., López-Paredes, A., et al. (2009). Errors and artifacts in agent-based modeling. *Journal of Artificial Societies and Social Simulation, 12*(1), 1. Retrieved from http://jasss.soc.surrey.ac.uk/12/1/1.html.

Gilbert, N. (2008). *Agent-based models*. London: Sage.

Graham, S., & Weingart, S. (2015). The equifinality of archaeological networks: An agent-based exploratory lab approach. *Journal of Archaeological Method and Theory, 22*, 248–274.

Happe, K., Kellerman, K., & Balmann, A. (2006). Agent-based analysis of agricultural policies: An illustration of the agricultural policy simulator AgriPoliS, its adaptation, and behavior. *Ecology and Society, 11*(1), 49.

Hodder, I. (1976). *Spatial analysis in archaeology*. Cambridge, England: Cambridge University Press.

Hole, F., & Heizer, F. (1969). *An introduction to prehistoric archaeology* (2nd ed.). New York: Holt, Rinehart, and Winston.

Howey, M. C. L. (2011). Multiple pathways across past landscapes: Circuit theory as a complementary geospatial method to least cost path for modeling past movement. *Journal of Archaeological Science, 38*, 2523–2535.
Jankowski, P., Andrienko, N., & Andrienko, G. (2001). Map-centered exploratory approach to multiple criteria spatial decision making. *International Journal of Geographical Information Science, 15*(2), 101–127.
Jansen, V. A. A., Mashanova, A., & Petrovskii, S. (2012). Comment on "Lévy walks evolve through interaction between movement and environmental complexity". *Science, 335*, 918c.
Janssen, M. A. (2009). Understanding artificial Anasazi. *Journal of Artificial Societies and Social Simulation, 12*(4). Retrieved from http://jasss.soc.surrey.ac.uk/12/4/13.html.
Kleijnen, J. P. C. (2005). An overview of the design and analysis of simulation experiments for sensitivity analysis. *European Journal of Operational Research, 164*, 287–300.
Kohler, T. A., & Gumerman, G. J. (2000). *Dynamics in human and primate societies: Agent-based modeling of social and spatial processes. Santa Fe Institute, studies in the sciences of complexity*. New York: Oxford University Press.
Kohler, T. A., & van der Leeuw, S. E. (2007). Introduction. Historical socionatural systems and models. In T. A. Kohler & S. E. van der Leeuw (Eds.), *The model-based archaeology of socionatural systems* (pp. 1–12). Santa Fe, NM: SAR Press.
Krist, F. J. J. (2001). *A predictive model of paleo-indian subsistence and settlement*. Ph.D. Thesis, Department of Anthropology, Michigan State University.
Lake, M. W. (2000). MAGICAL computer simulation of mesolithic foraging. In G. J. Gumerman & T. A. Kohler (Eds.), *Dynamics in human and primate societies: Agent-based modeling of social and spatial processes* (pp. 107–143). New York: Oxford University Press.
Lake, M. W. (2004). Being in a simulacrum: Electronic agency. In A. Gardner (Ed.), *Agency uncovered: Archaeological perspectives on social agency, power and being human* (pp. 191–209). London: UCL Press.
Lenhart, T., Eckhart, K., Fohrer, N., & Frede, H.-G. (2002). Comparison of two different approaches of sensitivity analysis. *Physics and Chemistry of the Earth, 27*, 645–654.
Lyman, R. L. (2004). The concept of equifinality in taphonomy. *Journal of Taphonomy, 2*(1), 15–26.
Maguire, D. J. (2005). Towards a GIS platform for spatial analysis and modeling. In D. J. Maguire, M. Batty, & M. F. Goodchild (Eds.), *GIS, spatial analysis and modeling*. Redlands, CA: ESRI Press.
McElhany, P., Steel, E. A., Jensen, D., Avery, K., Yoder, N., Busack, C., et al. (2010). Dealing with uncertainty in ecosystem models: Lessons from a complex salmon model. *Ecological Applications, 20*, 465–482.
Morrison, M. S. (1998). Community and coexistence: Kant's third analogy of experience. *Kant-Studien, 89*(3), 257–277.
Morrison, M. S., & Morgan, M. S. (1999). Models as mediators: Perspectives on natural and social science. In *Ideas in context* (p. 52). Cambridge, England: Cambridge University Press.
Morrison, M. S. (2015). *Reconstructing reality: Models, mathematics, and simulations*. New York: Oxford University Press.
Murphy, J. T. (2012). Exploring complexity with the Hohokam water management simulation: A middle way for archaeological modeling. *Ecological Modelling, 241*, 15–29.
Ngo, T. A., & See, L. (2012). Calibration and validation of agent-based models of land cover change. In A. J. Heppenstall, A. Crooks, L. M. See, & M. Batty (Eds.), *Agent-based models for geographical systems* (pp. 181–198). Dordrecht, The Netherlands: Springer.
Peeters, J. H. M. (2007). *Hoge Vaart-A27 in context: Towards a model of Mesolithic-Neolithic land use dynamics as a framework for archaeological heritage management*. Ph.D. Thesis, Department of Archaeology, University of Amsterdam, Amsterdam.
Premo, L. (2010). Equifinality and explanation: The role of agent-based modeling in postpositivist archaeology. In A. Costopoulos & M. Lake (Eds.), *Simulating change, archaeology into the twenty-first century* (Foundations of archaeological inquiry, pp. 28–37). Salt Lake City, UT: The University of Utah Press.

Raichlen, D. A., Wood, B. M., Gordon, A. D., Mabulla, A. Z. P., Marlowe, F. W., & Pontzer, H. (2014). Evidence of Lévy walk foraging patterns in human hunter-gatherers. *Proceedings of the National Academy of Sciences, 111*(2), 728–733.

Rathje, W. L., Shanks, M., & Witmore, C. (2013). *Archaeology in the making, conversations through a discipline*. New York: Routledge.

Read, D. W. (1990). The utility of mathematical constructs in building archaeological theory. In A. Voorrips (Ed.), *Mathematics and information science in archaeology: A flexible framework* (Studies in modern archaeology, Vol. 3, pp. 29–60). Bonn, Germany: Helos.

Refsgaard, J. C., van der Sluijs, J. P., Etejberg, A. L., & Vanrollegham, P. A. (2007). Uncertainty in the environmental modeling process—A framework and guidance. *Environmental Modeling and Software, 22*, 1543–1556.

Richardson, K. A. (2003). On the limits of bottom-up computer simulation: Towards a nonlinear modeling culture. In R. H. Sprague (Ed.), *Proceedings of the 36th Hawaiian international conference on system sciences* (pp. 1–9). Los Alamitos, CA: IEEE Computer Science Press.

Saltelli, A. (2005). Global sensitivity analysis: An introduction. In K. M. Hanson & F. M. Hemez (Eds.), *Sensitivity analysis of model output* (pp. 27–43). Los Alamos, NM: Los Alamos National Laboratory.

Shanks, M., & Tilley, C. (1987). *Re-constructing archaeology*. Cambridge, England: Cambridge University Press.

Snowling, S. D., & Kramer, J. R. (2001). Evaluating modeling uncertainty for model selection. *Ecological Modelling, 138*(1), 17–30.

Taylor, M. (2009). What is sensitivity analysis? In *What is ...? series*. Hayward Medical Communications, a division of Hayward Group Ltd. Retrieved from www.whatisseries.co.uk Accessed June 13, 2012.

van der Sluijs, J. P., Risbey, J., Kloprogge, P., Ravetz, J. R., Funtowicz, S. O., Quintana, S. C., et al. (2003). RIVM/MNP guidance for uncertainty assessment and communication. Retrieved from http://www.nusap.net/downloads/detailedguidance.pdf.

van Griensven, A., Meixner, T., Grunwald, S., Bishop, T., Diluzio, M., & Srinivasan, R. (2006). A global sensitivity analysis tool for the parameters of multi-variable catchment models. *Journal of Hydrology, 324*, 10–23.

van Groenendaal, W. J. H., & Kleijnen, J. P. C. (1997). On the assessment of economic risk: Factorial design versus Monte Carlo methods. *Journal of Reliability Engineering and System Safety, 57*, 91–102.

van Groenendaal, W. J. H., & Kleijnen, J. P. C. (2002). Deterministic versus stochastic sensitivity analysis in investment problems: An environmental case study. *European Journal of Operational Research, 141*, 8–20.

Verhagen, P. (2007). *Case studies in archaeological predictive modeling* (p. 14). Leiden, The Netherlands: Archaeological Studies Leiden University.

Verhagen, P., & Whitley, T. G. (2012). Integrating archaeological theory and predictive modeling: A live report from the scene. *Journal of Archaeological Method Theory, 19*, 49–100.

Viswanathan, G. M., da Luz, M. G. E., Raposo, E. P., & Stanley, H. E. (2011). *The physics of foraging. An introduction to random searches and biological encounters*. Cambridge, England: Cambridge University Press.

Viswanathan, G. M., Buldyrev, S. V., Havlin, S., da Luz, M. G. E., Raposo, E. P., & Stanley, H. E. (1999). Optimizing the success of random searches. *Nature, 401*, 911–914.

Vonk Noordegraaf, A., Nielen, M., & Kleijnen, J. P. C. (2003). Sensitivity analysis by experimental design. *European Journal of Operational Research, 146*, 433–443.

von Bertalanffy, L. (1949). Problems of organic growth. *Nature, 163*, 156–158.

von Bertalanffy, L. (1956). General system theory. *General Systems, 1*, 1–10.

Westervelt, J. D. (2002). Geographic information systems and agent-based modeling. In H. R. Gimblett (Ed.), *Integrating geographic information systems and agent-based modeling techniques for simulating social and ecological processes* (pp. 83–104). Oxford, England: Oxford University Press.

Whitley, T. G. (2000). *Dynamical systems modeling in archaeology: A GIS approach to site selection processes in the greater Yellowstone region*. Ph.D. Thesis, Department of Anthropology, University of Pittsburg, Pittsburg.

Wurzer, G., Kowarik, K., & Reschreiter, H. (2015). *Agent-based modeling and simulation in archaeology* (Advances in geographic information science). Vienna, Austria: Springer.

Zeigler, B. P. (1976). *Theory of modeling and simulation*. New York: Wiley.

Chapter 2
Is There a Research Design Role for Sensitivity Analysis (SA) in Archaeological Modeling?

William A. Lovis

2.1 Introduction

The 2014 Society for American Archaeology Forum devoted to sensitivity analysis (SA), for which this more extended essay was originally prepared, largely derived from observations made by several of us that the testing of predictive models and simulations in archaeology is largely accomplished in the absence of systematic evaluation of model design or structure, internal operation and decisions, and parameter spaces common in other disciplines both social and natural scientific, and in the latter particularly the earth and environmental sciences. This appears to be the case regardless of modeling goal, that is explaining or replicating a suite of archaeological observations at different scales, or exploring the degree to which theory and model might or might not be in accord.

To a degree, I come to this discussion as an impartial outside observer. While not an active modeler, I regularly work with modelers, bringing quantitative spatial analytic insights largely derived from geography to bear on problems of spatial decisions and mobility among archaeological hunter-gatherers. My intention here is not necessarily to convince the reader to undertake SA, but rather to explore the various roles SA might play in research design, under different modeling goals, and how these considerations might link with theoretical underpinnings and considerations.

W.A. Lovis (✉)
Department of Anthropology and MSU Museum, Michigan State University, East Lansing, MI, USA
e-mail: lovis@msu.edu

M. Brouwer Burg et al. (eds.), *Uncertainty and Sensitivity Analysis in Archaeological Computational Modeling*, Interdisciplinary Contributions to Archaeology, DOI 10.1007/978-3-319-27833-9_2

In this light, my first serious exposure to SA came via a single paragraph in a book review in *JASSS* by Doran (2008). To wit:

> Both these studies are sophisticated archaeologically, but perhaps less so as regards ABSS method. There seems to be an uncritical assumption that the more detail that is included, the better the model. There is little evidence that the authors are familiar with the attempts of the ABSS community to clarify such matters as validation, sensitivity analysis and parameter space exploration, and the critical task of choosing an appropriate level of abstraction (or granularity) for a model.

Several years later, in an important volume on archaeological simulation, there remained almost no mention of SA (Costopoulos et al. 2010), an event replicated recently in a compendium specifically addressing agent-based modeling (ABM) in archaeology (Kurzer et al., 2015), and in stark contrast to its prevalence in a prominent volume on geographic ABM (Heppenstall et al. 2012). The question at hand, then, is whether archaeological modelers/simulators should engage in such activities (more) regularly as a means of both refining theory and models, and providing increased confidence in and use of our outcomes both within and, perhaps more importantly, among modelers in other disciplines with overlapping, parallel, or similar goals. Here I provide an exploratory peregrination through various facets of archaeological research design that bears directly on this question. I synoptically explore where model uncertainty might lie, particularly in terms of archaeological data quality, as well as the compilation and evaluation of aggregated historical data in the effort to define variables and their parameters. How SA is positioned relative to larger social theory and more pertinently Middle Range Theory (MRT) is related to the examination of uncertainty, and how such uncertainty is situated and assessed in the larger schema of research design logic is a primary focus (see Ioannidis 2005 for a broader discussion of this issue in research). Providing a primer in the details and variable approaches to how to do or apply SA is not, although various approaches will be found in the presentations following this essay. While ultimately I may not provide immediately tangible outcomes or solutions, the several arenas focused upon to my mind warrant more concerted analytic thought.

SA is often associated with predictive computational models including ABMs, although it is arguable that it may be most strongly tied to theory-driven models engaged in exploration of system dynamics (Kyle Bocinsky, personal communication), as well as being a central component of decision allocations and outcomes in Artificial Intelligence (AI). It is one component of several verification processes situated early in most research design and which collectively result in model validation. Procedures for SA are well known and summaries are readily available (e.g., Hamby 1994). Such verification and validation processes are central to contemporary modeling, which renders SA's apparent absence among archaeological modelers particularly curious. Predictive models in archaeology have had a long and bumpy disciplinary history (Clarke 1970; Doran 1970; see Costopoulos et al. 2010; Doran 2011; Lake 2014 for recent historical overviews). They are most often reality driven, and problem or question directed, the form of the latter framed largely by the theoretical umbrella under which an investigator is situated (and potentially focused on theory itself rather than observed "realities"). Depending on researcher goals, archaeological models may range from fundamentally exploratory to explanatory, or even replicative, with most attempting to incorporate information held to be current state of knowledge on the problem at hand. By their nature, and related to the recognition of incomplete knowledge, models are not intended to be precise representations, but rather are abstract *simulacra* (*sensu* Renfrew 1981) that accommodate as much as feasible of the known information.

2.1.1 Error, Uncertainty, and Sensitivity Analysis

Evans (2012, pp. 309–346) among others provides a useful summary of potential sources of uncertainty and error in ABM—one that illuminates the importance of SA in archaeological model design. Evans arrays these potential sources in several sequential arenas.[1] Of particular interest, however, are: (1) input data errors including (a) measurement and transcription error, (b) sample size issues, (c) missing data, and (d) classification error; (2) what is termed "model choice" including (a) choice of variables, (b) model structure or operation, (c) model scale, and (d) model parameters (i.e., "fitting"); and (3) potential fits to known input–output data, all of which results in some range of output uncertainty from multiple potential sources each with potentially different sensitivities. It is in this arena that the rationale for SA is most commonly framed. Readers are referred to Evans (2012) for useful detail. I will return to an illustrative archaeological exemplar of these issues in Sect. 2.6.

2.2 Resolution and Scale in Model Choice

While this discussion will weave across the boundaries between general computational and ABMs, there are in fact some significant distinctions that should be kept in mind, and which at least in part reflect changes in goals and approaches that have evolved across the last half century in a variety of disciplines more central than archaeology to the development of modeling. According to some, the distinctions may be cast as contrast sets, such as that in Table 2.1 (from Bernard 1999, reproduced in Crooks and Heppenstall 2012, p. 95, Table 5.1). Regardless of whether or not there is individual agreement with this contrastive characterization, and while admittedly such itemized categorical dyads diminish detail, it is clear that choice of approach is goal oriented, and that in terms of archaeology such choice impacts several important factors; the nature of "environment" and how it is treated, the relative resolution of "space" as bounded units of area, and the potential to proliferate parameters of interest, or not. And while cast as oppositional dyads, such modeling enterprises form *something* of a continuum (albeit not

[1] For my purposes, here I will ignore the various limitations of machine computing addressed by Evans (2012) as they might impact error and uncertainty.

Table 2.1 Differences in modeling techniques between ABM and traditional modeling

Traditional modeling	Agent-based modeling
Deterministic (one future)	Stochastic (multiple futures)
Allocative (top-down)	Aggregative (bottom-up)
Equation-based formulas	Adaptive agents
Do not give explanations	Explanatory power
Few parameters	Many parameters
Spatially coarse	Spatially explicit
Environment given	Environment created
You react to them	You learn from them

From Bernard (1999), reproduced in Crooks and Heppenstall (2012, p. 95), Table 5.1

literally) across the boundaries, that is as ABM dimensional grain coarsens the outcomes become less explanatory. On its face, the fact that much archaeological inquiry is by nature of its data embedded in coarser spatial scales would suggest that ABM might be less desirable and advantageous as an approach, although there are some counterintuitive outcomes of ABM spatial modeling to suggest this generalization might not necessarily hold at least as it relates to analytic cell size (see discussion and examples in Stanilov 2012, p. 261). Likewise, issues of temporal scale may also loom large in this decision, since temporal resolution for ABMs is likewise central to decision-making. Both the spatial and temporal resolution and scale of models in disciplines such as geography are substantially more refined than most archaeological data sets allow. This in turn impacts significantly on the utility of SA as a routinized component of research design, particularly in various kinds of proxy reconstructions (from my environmental focus this appears to be the case), perhaps less so for ABM/ABSS (Agent Based Social Simulation), and this latter analytic category may remain an open question.

2.3 The Context

As Hegmon notes, a model may be "a dynamic description of a specific case," in contrast to a mathematically "dynamical" model with its changing variables and relationships (Hegmon 2003, p. 229). To achieve Hegmon's broader end, the other type of models apply the information derived from such case specific and pattern recognition exercises as either input or output parameter definitions for application in multi-iteration simulations, and as has already been noted most recently in simulations acted out by fictive "agents" making decisions within or based upon these parameters. The latter avenue's recent growing popularity has been attributed by some to the theoretical inroads of the post-Processual discourse (Verhagen and Whitley 2012, p. 60), while others envision the same post-Processual debate as inserting an inhibiting factor into the growth of such analyses (Costopoulos et al. 2010). Those working in nonlinear systems have varying views on the role of such theory on the development of practice (see contributions in Beekman and Baden 2005). The future of ABM's widespread archaeological adoption has also been met by some skepticism (Doran 1999; Hegmon 2003, p. 229).

That said, ABM in a variety of different forms, employing agents with different capabilities and modeling contexts (i.e., all agents are *not* created equal!) is often used both deductively and heuristically by archaeologists, and in fact such disparate application reflects the primacy attributed by different schools of theoretical thought to different explanations and emphases on different prevailing causal variables, and potentially vastly different goals between theory driven and reality-driven models. As noted, such procedures can be applied to both the anthropological "present" (as in behavioral and evolutionary ecology, largely played out among hunter-gatherer populations), or the archaeological past of human groups of interest, however defined (see Lake (2014) for a similar perspective on evolutionary archaeology). Presumably, the mutual goals of these various approaches regardless of theoretical persuasion are to gain a better understanding of past human behaviors, particularly the parameters that condition what we ultimately observe as outputs in the archaeological record and the accuracy of the inferences we make about them.

While the foregoing summary can admittedly be accused of being somewhat reductionist, it is nonetheless revelatory of several facets of modern archaeological research design—research design situated in a theoretical milieu which no longer hews as closely to the deductive and environmentally focused line of strict early processualism (Hegmon 2003; but see Verhagen and Whitley 2012, p. 50). As archaeologists, we collectively work from the premise that our empirical knowledge of the past, as viewed through residues of past behavior, is both incomplete and may likely be biased. Early on in decisions about the structure of research design, there is the recognition that a problem of interest can potentially be approached using predictive/simulation models. The internal relationships of different model variables, and the nature of their interaction, can generally be defined as a multivariate suite of linked hypothesized "if:then" statements. The internal model structure can therefore *sometimes* be couched as inferential hypotheses, but most often these are inductively originated exploratory devices querying the effects of changes in one or more characteristic (variable) of a system on another, that is operationalizing the exploratory model as a heuristic device. Of note is that it is precisely this issue that SA addresses.

Questions subsequently arise about what data are or might be appropriate as input for the simulation exercise: variable definitions, relationships, resolution, and parameters. This stage of research design formulation regularly entails a key decision: should or can one engage in the series of exercises that have collectively become known as "data mining" (Andres 2010), that is the extraction of existing data from multiple sources, the synthesis of these data into a comprehensive "knowledge set" or "knowledge space," and the consequent evaluation of its potential utility through a variety of means. Or will it be necessary to engage in either data supplementation, or data collection *de nouveau* because existing data of sufficient quality (type, quantity, resolution, scale) are not available? New data collection may not, as some naïvely believe, necessarily result in enhanced outcomes (see case study in Sect. 2.5) although data collection specifically directed at a problem has a higher probability of yielding useful results, for example, in refining individual variable parameters. Meta analyses of existing data coupled with consequent evaluation may well result in startling outcomes about both the original studies, the derivative use of original data in subsequent studies, and may even at times result in new, different and even exciting insights and outcomes (e.g., Anonymous 2013; Myhrvold 2013).

2.4 Middle Range Theory

As others (e.g., Gilbert 2008) have already correctly asserted most simulations, which I here characterize as dynamically interactive sets of probabilistic/predictive statements, occupy the niche of MRT *sensu* Merton (1949). Both definitionally and operationally they may not necessarily be restricted to the several internal archaeological conceptions of MRT well known to (early) processual archaeologists (cf. Binford 1978; Schiffer 1976; Raab and Goodyear 1984), whether implemented with decisions that are keyed to ecosystemic variables, or coupled with the decision-making behavior and consequences of either individual agents or group processes. There are also significant evolutionary theoretic implications that derive from this distinction.[2]

In contemporary practice, and with respect to MRT, computational models in archaeology ABM or otherwise, largely span two primary arenas (but see Costopoulos et al. 2010; and Costopoulos and Lake 2014). One is fundamentally specific problem or case directed empirically mining large data sets and manipulating nested sets of variables statistically to assess evident multivariate regularities pertinent to understanding a range of past or present human behaviors. This is fundamentally an inductive pattern recognition process, and can often serve as a means of identifying relevant or essential variables, their potential parameters, and their relative redundancy relationships with or to other variables. The categories of information derived from data mining are often fundamental to SA. This issue is further addressed in Sect. 2.5. The second is more deductive and overtly theoretically directed and often used as a heuristic device (see Premo 2010).

Importantly, for middle range models there may be no quantitative outputs that are useful to the prediction, but rather may more readily gravitate towards

[2] This distinction to a degree replicates a long-standing debate in evolutionary theory between the primacy of individual and group selection (i.e., Darwin vs. Wynn Edwards; Borello 2005), as well as the role of information and its potentially differential distribution and access within the system (Whallon 2006, 2011). This distinction has also been recognized by Doran (1999) in his evaluation of "Agent Based Modeling in Archaeology," and the differences between what he terms "individual cognition" and "group cognition," although there are nuances of this distinction that cannot be afforded space here. Likewise, they may be variable in scale, being broadly applicable or narrowly so; the latter keyed to the individual case rather than the broader arena of like cases (recognizing that even simulation analyses keyed to individual cases may explain more than the case of interest).

expectations of qualitative similarities or matches (Gilbert 2008). We archaeologists are, perhaps too concerned with attempting to identify quantitative regularities that exactly replicate and predict the outcomes of the social behaviors we explore (sometimes known as *facsimile models*). In other words, what we think we are doing may not necessarily be in accord with our expectations of what we want to do or are actually doing. As Andres (2010) correctly observes about the origins of SA in environmental risk research: "Consequently, the methods of SA were developed to deal with deterministic computer models where experiments can be reproduced exactly, and both inputs and outputs are known with high precision." One of the session participants (Carroll 2016) opined in an early review of this chapter "I've mostly seen SA used by our geography friends to assess deterministic environmental models that operate under much less fuzzy assumptions."

Can archaeological simulations claim such precision? More often than not, the answer is "No." High precision inputs, and the empirical basis against which to cast simulated outputs against, are difficult to achieve in archaeology. If I am correct in this observation, these disjunctions have potentially major implications for the archaeological application of SA, and require further discussion and exploration—perhaps, as Kyle Bocinsky notes (personal communication), through exploration of "sensitivity to imprecision." I will return to this point with some examples further along in this essay.

2.5 Multicriteria Decision-Making (MCDM), Exploratory Data Analysis (EDA), and Knowledge Discovery in Databases (KDD)

In part, such exploration can revolve around a couple of key observations about how we go about actually undertaking analysis, rather than the way in which analysis should ideally be done. Herein lies a healthy dose of pragmatism. While not comprehensive, this section presents several in an array of potential techniques increasingly employed at the front end of many modeling exercises, quite specifically to engage with accumulated and compiled data that requires what is now referred to as "hygiene" or cleaning. It is this process that presumably results in data that is ascertained to be accurate by some criterion, possesses the appropriate information for problem, and is sufficiently robust to generate some modicum of confidence. The uncertainty contained in this end product, which is unavoidable and inherent in any such data, is embedded in the input for the remainder of the modeling exercise.

Much of what we do archaeologically has a spatial component, at times but not always replicated over multiple time points, that is, $t_{0,}$ t_1, t_2, … , t_n. This being the case, it behooves us to look at an example in the spatial domain. In their discussion of map-centered exploratory approaches to multicriteria decision-making (MCDM) Jankowski et al. (2010) espouse exploratory use of existing data employing what they refer to as complex extensions of standard exploratory data analysis (EDA) (see, e.g., Baxter 1994 on exploratory multivariate analysis). They make the important case, which is certainly true for archaeology, that what they term a process of "reduction of the cognitive complexity…" of outcomes and understanding the relationships among criteria (variables, dimensions) is achievable with "standard statistical procedures." They go on, however, to allow that where users are not statistically well versed they rely strongly on the application of data mining techniques designed to "detect regularities, dependencies, or trends, and to draw generalized descriptions of data features and relationships" (Jankowski et al. 2010, p. 106). In this endeavor, they rely on procedures operationalized (or perhaps more accurately characterized) by Fayyad et al. (1996) as knowledge discovery in databases (aka KDD).

As the preceding authors reveal, while to a degree KDD are designed to simplify interpretation of complex internal data structures, the approach nonetheless employs statistical techniques for categorization, prediction via regression, grouping via clustering, dependency analysis, etc. some of which require appropriate training to employ and interpret effectively. These are all pattern recognition approaches with underlying implicit models, for example, linearity and mutual exclusivity. In an archaeological world, we would like these patterns to reflect a past reality of agent-derived decision outcomes as reflected in the archaeological record. We also know that for various reasons the archaeological record may not be an accurate record of such outcomes (see for a recent exposition Bevan and Wilson 2013, p. 2416), and that even this imperfect observable record may be produced via multiple and even disparate trajectories—the ever present issue of *equifinality* (Premo 2010).

Among the alternative and/or tandem solutions to the problems associated with embedded uncertainties in model parameters, the latter including inputs and their ranges of variation, is the application of stochastic modeling. Here, it is acknowledged a priori that our variable and parameter inputs are imprecise, that is, that they contain unknown uncertainties, and that we likewise might not possess sufficient control over the behavioral processes involved in a decision made on such input information, that is, input and choice logic imprecisions may not necessarily allow regularity of model outputs. The use of random inputs across multiple iterations to a certain level of confidence means that any variation of outputs is actually a probability statement, where any given output state has an attached probability. The use of such randomization approaches in archaeology has substantial time depth, and it would appear that in the context of current modeling endeavors and a posteriori evaluation via SA that their role may become increasingly important.

2.6 The Archaeological Record and Uncertainty

A pertinent example of this problem is what I term *The Problem of Small Scale Systems* (see Peeters and Romeijn 2016 this volume on a similar view). Under the best conditions, an archaeological modeler will have access to a robust archaeological record through which to operationalize a problem-oriented modeling exercise—a well preserved and representative record with sufficient numbers of observations at the appropriate scale, temporal control, and resolution for accurate variable identification and parameter definition. As the adequacy to problem of any of these dimensions diminishes individually or collectively, there is a commensurate increase in relative uncertainty. Presumably, but system dependent, is the question of whether increased adequacy of any single dimension will reduce uncertainty. In the case of small-scale systems, it is the issue of sample size and relative confidence that occupies considerations of uncertainty across other dimensions. And, this does not *ipso facto* imply that larger scale and potentially more complex systems do not themselves suffer from uncertainty. While it can be readily argued that archaeological modeling is not sufficiently unique to categorically eschew the routine use of SA for all modeling exercises, it is precisely in the context of increased uncertainty that SA is most warranted, since input uncertainties tend to be retained and potentially even enhanced (propagation processes) through various phases of the model and ultimately expressed as outcomes.

For facsimile models attempting to replicate specific observed archaeological patterns, there is an additional danger—that of the output data driving the evaluation of parameter spaces to achieve known ends. For some, this would amount to tautology, although such exploration can readily be defended as a heuristic exercise, that is, understanding which variables and parameter spaces best account for the observed outcomes may well result in a replicative pattern.

My own research engages with northern latitude hunter-gatherers, and such uncertainty becomes particularly salient as one is confronted by human systems with high levels of mobility and shorter duration stays over large spaces by small(er) numbers of people, often in highly dynamic environments. Coupled with highly portable technologies, oftentimes physically expressed at behavioral loci as low-density residues, the resultant archaeological signal is difficult to accurately detect, resulting in marginal compliance with all of the desirable characteristics for model input enumerated. It is worth noting that several of the chapters in this volume address precisely these kinds of contexts in their modeling and posterior evaluations [cf. Peeters and Romeijn (Chap. 3), Brouwer Burg (Chap. 4), Carroll (Chap. 5), all this volume].

Insertion of *The Problem of Dynamic Environments* poses additional, and at times intractable, considerations. For example, drawing from my collaborative paleoenvironmental research as a case study, coastal site preservation in the extensively and intensively researched northern Lake Michigan basin of the Great Lakes (USA) is variable over both space and time—ultimately a taphonomic consequence of coastal dune activation cycles and the effects of isostatic rebound or isostasy (aka uplift) and lake level variations in the northern portions of the study region (Lovis et al. 2012a, b), with the former possibly keyed to hemispheric effects of local climate (Monaghan et al. 2013).

An example of the impacts of such variable site preservation is the fact that archaeological sites in the active coastal zone are well preserved around the peak of the so-called Medieval Warm Period/Holocene Climatic Optimum (~AD 950–1250), and are almost absent on either side of this period. Our potential output reference points for SA are therefore grossly flawed, which begs the question about whether those output points collectively would be appropriate empirical observations with which to attempt facsimile modeling, let alone assess model performance. Additional field research, and indeed the ability to perform ground truthing, would be neither productive nor cost-effective despite the probability of "discovering" an anomalous case. *Apropos* of the latter is that some occupation sites are buried under 20 m of eolian sediment (Lovis et al. 2012a). The potential solution would be to focus the model on one or more rather discrete time periods where the empirical data might be (relatively more) complete, for example, a few centuries around the peak of the Medieval Warm Period/Holocene Climatic Optimum, although this would not solve the truthing issue, nor would the results necessarily apply to time segments preceding or following the modeled period. Thus, our goals would be substantially limited by the variable nature of the empirical record, and not address the more general and spatiotemporally dynamic case.

As we are aware, any predictive model inputs/processes are the hypothetical statements (aka arguments) we believe are responsible for our observations of outcome regularities and which we manipulate in various ways to assess how closely our hypotheses can replicate our empirical observations at various scales and resolutions. Importantly, many of our model inputs are defined in terms of resolution, scale, and parameters on the basis of incomplete data garnered from parallel data mining procedures as we employ for understanding the archaeological record. In the Lake Michigan, USA case above, for example, there are ethnohistoric documents that might inform model inputs (e.g., Jochim's 1976 use of Rogers's 1962 Round Lake Ojibwa ethnographic data in his modeling of Late Glacial German hunter-gatherers), and more broadly based information on hunter-gatherers or marginal horticulturalists, but which may not provide sufficient information on the parameter spaces of the derived input variables, whether they be decision based, or the inputs that are being evaluated by agents in the process of making decisions, for example, resources and social variables. The limitations of uniformitarian principles on environmental modeling are addressed by Brouwer Burg (Chap. 4). On a cautionary note, the use of ethnographic analogy can suffer in a parallel fashion.

This prior set of observations, however, provides a platform forcing archaeologists who are building behavioral models of any sort to systematically break down embedded decisions into their constituent logical units. Such precision as it relates to social behavioral rules can subsequently in turn be employed as bridging for the formation processes of the archaeological record and how that record will be manifested, that is, expectations of what the archaeological record should look like without background "noise."

2.7 Modeling Environment and Modeling Behavior: Tandem Exercises

In fact, paleoenvironmental modeling and (socio)behavioral modeling can be viewed as two independent corollary or tandem tasks that need to coincide at an advanced point in a research program (see Brouwer Burg 2016 this volume for additional insights). This is particularly true in ABM where the simulated or modeled "landscape" under certain circumstances provides the information input for both

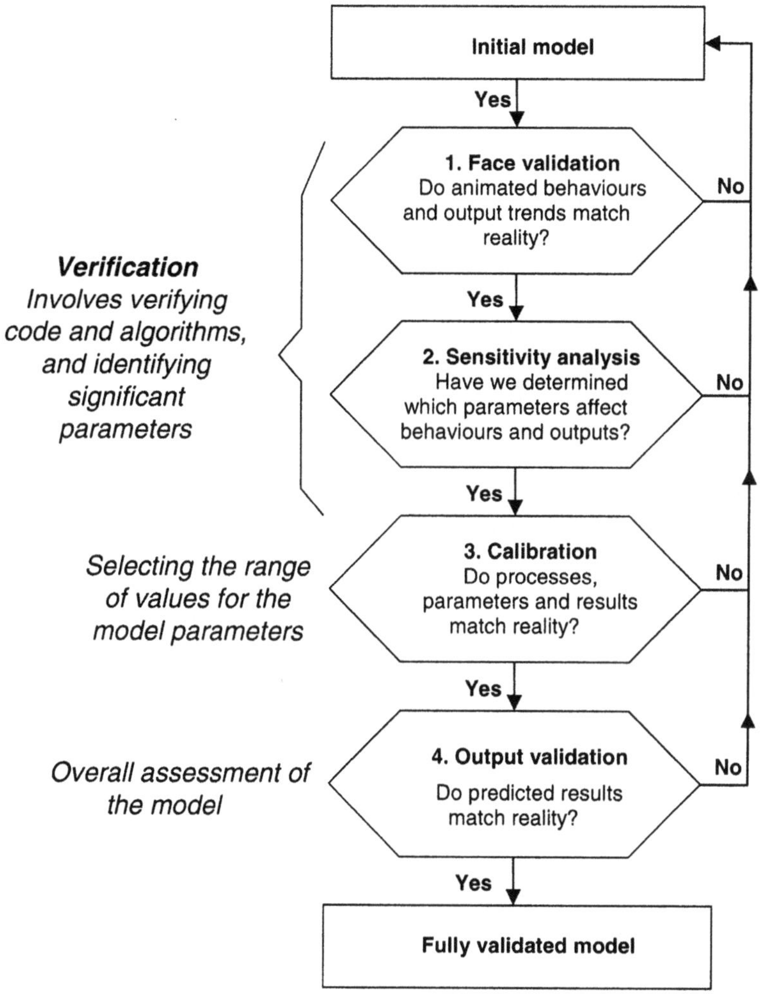

Fig. 2.1 General validation process of an ABM (reproduced from Ngo and See (2012, p. 183), Fig. 10.1)

learning and decision-making by individuals or groups. Of particular interest is that the environmental simulation is precisely the kind of context in which SA is applied well and regularly. Take, for example, the process of model validation presented in Fig. 2.1 for an ABM study of land cover change (reproduced from Ngo and See 2012, p. 183, Fig. 10.1), which presents a clear sequential context for SA in the larger process of ABM model validation within the research design. Of interest is the critique that accompanies this discussion, which argues that much of the validation process is normally not addressed explicitly—only the output validation (Ngo and See 2012, p. 183); an observation consistent with the Semantic Conception as articulated by Henrickson and McKelvey (2002) (i.e., ontological vs. analytical adequacy).

Archaeologists may be confronted with a potentially unresolvable conundrum. First, because most of our models and simulations are complex (some would argue overly so), at both ends of the process it is difficult to tease out interactions among and between variables at either the input or the output stage. Second, the fact that the inputs may possess unacceptable levels of uncertainty limits our ability to evaluate the outputs. When inputs have such characteristics, they should technically, albeit reluctantly, be removed from analysis. Moreover, it is essential to maintain independence of both inputs and expected outputs to minimize or eliminate tautologies. At its most overt, we can't employ the same archaeological input data as we expect to predict as an outcome, even if we think the archaeological information is unbiased or representative. Bevan and Wilson (2013, p. 2416), who do employ SA in their point pattern model evaluation, make the interesting case for strategically withholding segments of the available data (aka cross-validation) as a means of avoiding this problem and allowing appropriate cyclic assessment of model or multiple model accuracy. A luxury, however, that only accrues to large(r) archaeological data sets, sufficient that the investigator is confident of its being representative, is the drawing and analysis of iterative random samples and the subsequent use of a variety of standard manipulative techniques (see Hamby 1994, pp. 141–146). And, while I very much like the systematics of their analysis of peer polity centers in Bronze Age Crete, I also agree with Bevan and Wilson's self-insights into the effects of archaeological observational biases in the generation of simulated site location suites as well as the use of multiple models with different primary inputs as measures of fit (Bevan and Wilson 2013, pp. 2423–2425). Of particular interest in this regard is the suggestion to undertake Monte Carlo simulation as a means by which to engage in "a more subtle treatment of the uncertainty" associated with site ages, sizes, and locations, as well as directly addressing via modeling the biases in recovery and information resolution resulting in "patchy" data (Bevan and Wilson 2013, pp. 2423–2424). This is a useful method to deploy in (primarily deterministic) modeling situations with the input uncertainty we might find in archaeological and past behavioral contexts.

2.8 Finally—Sensitivity Analysis

Archaeologists who engage in high-level computational modeling of any sort do not suffer from the quantitative phobias that might accompany avoidance of SA in model evaluation. Thus, the continued lack of systematic and routine SA application remains curious (see, e.g., Kurzer et al. 2015). I say this with full recognition that in current applications model dynamics and responses are regularly evaluated systematically relative to parameter values, but rarely with formal recourse to SA. SA is a controlled experiment, put into operation with systematic procedure and appropriate method, normally quantitative (see White 2016, Chap. 7 for a clear systematic application). SA is actually an embedded experimental design that provides a posteriori evaluation that can be employed as feedback for input variable and parameter space definition and evaluation. The question asked by SA is, on its face, simple: What is the influence of model input on model response? At the level of individual input variables and their parameters answering this question provides, among other information, insight into which model variables should be retained or discarded (but see below), the relative influence of variables on the output, identification of those that might be imprecisely defined and those that might well be accurate output predictors. Under any conditions, this is important information to extract from an analysis. And while the specific analytic path and quantitative approach one takes might vary, it is difficult to argue lack of utility or even necessity.

In terms of larger issues of research design, it is possible to invoke notions of analytic concordance—that is, the clarity of relationship between theory and the primacy it places on specific dimensions and variables as causally explanatory, the behavioral questions that derive from and which should be in accord with the theoretical underpinnings, the relationship between those questions and dimensions and the units of observation one chooses to employ, the methodological assumptions that both underlie and link those observations to specific forms of manipulation, etc. (see Carr 1985a, b, for further clarification). In fact, it is arguable whether any analysis, including modeling designed to replicate observed outcome states (i.e., reality-based models), is devoid of some theoretical underpinnings *whether they are explicitly stated or not*. SA has the potential to cast in stark profile ontological and observational inadequacies and inconsistencies.

It is likely that the real issue at hand here is not necessarily the overt absence of SA in archaeological modeling, but that we may be trying to do more with our models and modeling than our data most often allow. That said, the coarsest spatial and temporal resolutions employed by most spatial modelers are far finer than is attainable by archaeological data. We proliferate input data with numerous variables and high levels of parameter uncertainty, asking questions that beg the nature of the interactions among those uncertain inputs and which we may not be able to assess, and we have limited/incomplete or biased observable output parameters against which we cast our results. The latter is currently, at least, a death knell to facsimile models.

Perhaps the best lesson that may be learned from this is that if we are to employ SA regularly, and I believe archaeological modeling should move in that direction, that it must be engaged with clear ground rules. We need to simplify our expectations and our models, both. We should employ the most robust information at both the input (variables, parameters, and scale) and outputs even if the result is coarser resolution—a hard lesson but one already learned by our geography colleagues. As the analytic adage holds, one can't make coarse data finer, but one can aggregate fine data to coarser scales and resolutions. SA may well assist in the latter process, whether in model development and evaluation, or in facsimile modeling.

Acknowledgments I owe deep thanks to Kyle Bocinsky for his insightful comments into an earlier draft of this chapter, and for pointing me to some critical literature. Henk Weerts was the catalyst that prodded our research group to collectively consider the application of sensitivity analysis to archaeological modeling. Jim Doran provided multiple thought provoking observations that resulted in a much better product, but likely still with flaws of my own making and responsibility.

References

Andres, T. (2010). Sensitivity analysis. In N. J. Salkind (Ed.), *Encyclopedia of research design* (pp. 1340–1341). Thousand Oaks, CA: Sage.

Anonymous. (2013). A bone to pick. The *Economist*, Dec 21, 2013. Retrieved February 10, 2016 from http://www.economist.com/news/science-andtechnology/21591837-enthusiastic-amateur-suggests-work-how-dinosaurs-grew-wrong-bone

Baxter, M. J. (1994). *Exploratory multivariate analysis in archaeology*. Edinburgh, England: Edinburgh University Press.

Beekman, C. S., & Baden, W. W. (Eds.). (2005). *Non-linear models for archaeology and anthropology*. Burlington, VT: Ashgate.

Bernard, R. N. (1999). *Using adaptive agent-based simulation models to assist planners in policy development: The case of rent control. Working paper 99-07-052*. Santa Fe, NM: Santa Fe Institute.

Bevan, A., & Wilson, A. (2013). Models of settlement hierarchy based on partial evidence. *Journal of Archaeological Science, 40*, 2415–2427.

Binford, L. R. (1978). *Nunamiut ethnoarchaeology*. New York: Academic.

Borello, M. (2005). The rise, fall and resurrection of group selection. *Endeavour, 29*(1), 43–47.

Brouwer Burg, M. (2016). GIS-based modeling of archaeological dynamics: Strengths, weaknesses, and the utility of sensitivity analysis. In Brouwer Burg, H. Peeters, & W. A. Lovis (Eds.), *Uncertainty and sensitivity in archaeological computational modeling*. New York: Springer.

Carr, C. (1985a). Perspective and basic definitions. In C. Carr (Ed.), *For concordance in archaeological analysis, bridging data structure, quantitative technique and theory* (pp. 1–17). Prospect Heights, NY: Waveland Press.

Carr, C. (1985b). Getting into data: Philosophy and tactics for the analysis of complex data structures. In C. Carr (Ed.), *For concordance in archaeological analysis, bridging data structure, quantitative technique and theory* (pp. 18–44). Prospect Heights, NY: Waveland Press.

Carroll, J. (2016). In M. Brouwer Burg, H. Peeters, & W. A. Lovis (Eds.), *Uncertainty and sensitivity in archaeological computational modeling*. New York: Springer.

Clarke, D. L. (1970). *Models in archaeology*. London: Methuen.

Costopoulos, A., & Lake, M. W. (Eds.). (2010). *Simulating change: Archaeology into the twenty-first century, foundations of archaeological inquiry*. Salt Lake City, UT: University of Utah Press.

Costopoulos, A., Lake, M. W., & Gupta, N. (2010). Introduction. In A. Costopoulos & M. Lake (Eds.), *Simulating change: Archaeology into the twenty-first century (foundations of archaeological inquiry)* (pp. 1–8). Salt Lake City, UT: University of Utah Press.

Crooks, A. T., & Heppenstall, A. J. (2012). Introduction to agent-based modeling. In A. J. Heppenstall, A. T. Crooks, L. M. See, & M. Batty (Eds.), *Agent-based models of geographical systems* (pp. 85–108). New York: Springer.

Doran, J. (1970). Systems theory, computer simulations, and archaeology. Special issue: Analysis. *World Archaeology, 1*(3), 289–298.

Doran, J. (1999). Prospects for agent based modelling in archaeology. *Archeologia e Calcolatori, 10*, 33–44.

Doran, J. (2008). *Review of: The model based archaeology of socionatural systems*. In T. A. Kohler & S. E. van der Leeuw (Eds.), *Socializing complexity: Approaches to power and interaction in archaeological discourse*. In S. Kohring & S. Wyne-Jones (Eds.), *Journal of Artificial Societies and Social Simulation*. Retrieved March 19, 2014, from http://jasss.soc.surrey.ac.uk/11/3/reviews/doran.html.

Doran, J. (2011). *Review of: Simulating change: Archaeology into the twenty-first century (foundations of archaeological inquiry)*. In A. Costopoulos & M. W. Lake (Eds.), *Journal of Artificial Societies and Social Simulation*. Retrieved December 02, 2014, from http://jasss.soc.surrey.ac.uk/14/4/reviews/2.html.

Evans, A. (2012). Uncertainty and error. In A. J. Heppenstall, A. T. Crooks, L. M. See, & M. Batty (Eds.), *Agent-based models of geographical systems* (pp. 309–346). New York: Springer.

Fayyad, U., Piatetsky-Shapiro, G., & Padhraic, S. (1996). From data mining to knowledge discovery in databases. *Journal of Artificial Intelligence, 11*(3), 37–53.

Gilbert, N. (2008). *Agent based models*. Thousand Oaks, CA: Sage Research Methods.

Hamby, D. M. (1994). A review of techniques for parameter sensitivity analysis of environmental models. *Environmental Monitoring and Assessment, 32*, 135–154.

Hegmon, M. (2003). Setting theoretical egos aside: Issues and theory in North American archaeology. *American Antiquity, 68*, 213–243.

Henrickson, L., & McKelvey, B. (2002). Foundations of "New" social science: Institutional legitimacy from philosophy, complexity science, postmodernism, and agent-based modeling. *Proceedings of the National Academy of Sciences, 99*(Suppl. 3), 7288–7295.

Heppenstall, A. J., Crooks, A. T., See, L. M., & Batty, M. (Eds.). (2012). *Agent-based models of geographical systems*. New York: Springer.

Ioannidis, J. P. (2005). Why most published research findings are false. *PLOS Medicine*. doi:10.1371/journal.pmed.0020124.

Jankowski, P., Andrienko, N., & Andrienko, G. (2010). Map centered exploratory approach to multiple criteria spatial decision making. *International Journal of Geographical Information Science, 15*(2), 101–127.

Jochim, M. (1976). *Hunter-gatherer subsistence and settlement: A predictive model*. New York: Academic.

Kurzer, G., Kowarik, K., & Reschreiter, H. (Eds.). (2015). *Agent based modeling and simulation in archaeology*. New York: Springer.

Lake, M. W. (2014). Trends in archaeological simulation. *Journal of Archaeological Method and Theory, 21*, 258–278.

Lovis, W. A., Arbogast, A. F., & Monaghan, G. W. (2012a). *The geoarchaeology of Lake Michigan Coastal Dunes. Environmental research series no. 2*. East Lansing, MI: Michigan Department of Transportation, Michigan State University Press.

Lovis, W. A., Monaghan, G. W., Arbogast, A. F., & Forman, S. L. (2012a). Differential temporal and spatial preservation of archaeological sites in a great lakes coastal zone. *American Antiquity, 77*(3), 591–608.

Merton, R. K. (1949). On sociological theories of the middle range. In R. K. Merton (Ed.), *Social theory and social structure* (pp. 39–53). New York: Simon & Schuster/The Free Press.

Monaghan, G. W., Arbogast, A. F., Lovis, W. A., & Kowalski, D. (2013). Millennial-scale cycles of coastal dune formation during the Late Holocene, Lake Michigan. North-Central GSA Section Meeting. *Abstracts with Programs, 45*(4), 67.

Myhrvold, N. P. (2013). Revisiting the estimation of dinosaur growth rates. *PLOS ONE, 16*, 2013. doi:10.1371/journal.pone.0081917.

Ngo, T. A., & See, L. M. (2012). Calibration and validation of agent-based models of landcover change. In A. J. Heppenstall, A. T. Crooks, L. M. See, & M. Batty (Eds.), *Agent-based models of geographical systems* (pp. 181–198). New York: Springer.

Peeters, H., & Romeijn, J.-W. (2016). Uncertainty in exploratory computational modeling in archaeology: A case study between theory and practice. In M. Brouwer Burg, H. Peeters, & W. A. Lovis (Eds.), *Uncertainty and sensitivity in archaeological computational modeling*. New York: Springer.

Premo, L. S. (2010). Equifinality and explanation: The role of agent-based modeling in postpositivist archaeology. In A. Costopoulos & M. Lake (Eds.), *Simulating change: Archaeology into the twenty-first century, foundations of archaeological inquiry* (pp. 28–37). Salt Lake City, UT: University of Utah Press.

Raab, L. M., & Goodyear, A. C. (1984). Middle-range theory in archaeology: A critical review of origins and applications. *American Antiquity, 49*, 255–268.

Renfrew, C. (1981). The simulator as demiurge. In J. Sabloff (Ed.), *Simulations in archaeology* (pp. 283–306). Albuquerque, NM: The University of New Mexico Press.

Rogers, E. (1962). *The Round Lake Ojibwa. Occasional paper 5.* Toronto, ON: Royal Ontario Museum, University of Toronto.

Schiffer, M. B. (1976). *Behavioral archaeology*. New York: Academic.

Stanilov, K. (2012). Space in agent-based models. In A. J. Heppenstall, A. T. Crooks, L. M. See, & M. Batty (Eds.), *Agent-based models of geographical systems* (pp. 253–269). New York: Springer.

Verhagen, P., & Whitley, T. G. (2012). Integrating archaeological theory and predictive modeling: A live report from the scene. *Journal of Archaeological Method and Theory, 19*, 49–100.

Whallon, R. (2006). Social networks and information: Non-"utilitarian" mobility among hunter-gatherers. *Journal of Anthropological Archaeology, 25*, 259–270.

Whallon, R. (2011). An introduction to information and its role in hunter gatherer bands. In R. Whallon, W. A. Lovis, & R. K. Hitchcock (Eds.), *The role of information in hunter-gatherer bands* (Ideas, debates and perspectives 5, pp. 1–28). Los Angeles, CA: Cotsen Institute of Archaeology, University of California.

White, A. (2016). In M. Brouwer Burg, H. Peeters, & W. A. Lovis (Eds.), *Uncertainty and sensitivity in archaeological computational modeling*. New York: Springer.

Chapter 3
Epistemic Considerations About Uncertainty and Model Selection in Computational Archaeology: A Case Study on Exploratory Modeling

Hans Peeters and Jan-Willem Romeijn

3.1 Introduction

Uncertainty is an integral aspect of all scientific models in any field of application: we are mostly unsure which hypothesis is adequate as a means of predicting, representing, or reconstructing the system of interest. In quantitative research, the problem of uncertainty is often tackled by statistical means. Archaeological spatial modeling of human behavior is no exception to this: uncertainty is largely approached from a statistical perspective (e.g., Verhagen 2007). The available data allow us to test and choose among hypotheses, using classical statistical tools, or else to establish a probability assignment over a given range of hypotheses by Bayesian means. It is common to both classical and Bayesian methods that the model precedes any such treatment of uncertainties. Hence, the uncertainty that pertains to the model itself does not normally come into view in these statistical approaches. It is precisely the model uncertainty that is at stake in our paper.

In spatial models of human behavior, the sources of model uncertainty are numerous and compounded. The different input components of the model each come with their own uncertainty (e.g., paleolandscape models, assumptions about past human behavior, biased datasets). Moreover, owing to the complexity of the models, the modeling results become critically sensitive to misspecifications, so mistakes in the modeling assumptions have comparatively large effects on the model output. Finally,

H. Peeters (✉)
Groningen Institute of Archaeology, University of Groningen, Groningen, The Netherlands
e-mail: j.h.m.peeters@rug.nl

J.-W. Romeijn
Department of Philosophy, University of Groningen, Groningen, The Netherlands
e-mail: j.w.romeijn@rug.nl

M. Brouwer Burg et al. (eds.), *Uncertainty and Sensitivity Analysis in Archaeological Computational Modeling*, Interdisciplinary Contributions to Archaeology, DOI 10.1007/978-3-319-27833-9_3

the data that are used to determine the best fit within a statistical model are often also used to motivate particular modeling choices. In other words, the hypotheses we confront with the data were constructed on the basis of those very data. Apart from the fact that such seemingly double use of the data is subject to methodological criticism (e.g., Worrall (2010), but see Steele and Werndl (2013) for a nuanced response), model specifications and output thus rely heavily on the assumption that the—often scarce—data are somehow representative of the target system. In short, model uncertainty is a serious problem for computational modeling in archaeology.

In this paper, we look into the consequences of model uncertainty in this context. Specifically, we consider a case study of computational modeling for exploratory purposes, and we identify two distinct ways in which uncertainties are dealt with. We then generalize from the case study and provide a broader discussion on model evaluation and construction. In this abstract re-description of the case study we disentangle different notions of uncertainty that computational modelers grapple with, we indicate that robustness analysis is central to our dealings with uncertainty in exploratory use of computational models, and we sketch how such an analysis may lead to modeling improvements. We believe a thorough discussion of the case study will help the appreciation of the general discussion later on in the paper. But before we get to this, let us turn to a general outlook on computational modeling in archaeology and lay out the specifics of our case study.

3.2 Target Systems and Modeling Goals

Before we consider model uncertainty and the tools and methods that may control for it, we clarify some of the goals that model-building archaeologists have (see Kohler and van der Leeuw 2007). This will set the stage for a proper appreciation of the problems and sharpen the focus of our paper.

Developing a computational model of some system involves the definition of starting points, and making choices about which variables to include, which interactions between variables to define, and how to weigh parameters. The definition of starting points is directly connected to the purpose or goal of models: prediction, reconstruction, and exploration. A predictive model outputs a set of expectations that can be tested against the data that define the target system. A reconstructive model offers an abstract structure that resembles some target system on certain salient features. An explorative model, finally, occasions insight into the generative rules that underlie the structure or the workings of the target system, thereby establishing, or at least hypothesizing, certain properties of the system, for example, the band-widths of system variability.

Within this context, a modeling approach has to be chosen. In archaeology, quite a number of them have been practiced (see, e.g., van Leusen and Kamermans 2005) and can be captured under the labels "correlative," "generalized behavior," and "system-based." Correlative approaches primarily investigate statistical relationships between variables (mostly aspects of landscape) and archaeological site occurrence and are frequently used in the context of cultural resource management (CRM). Approaches based on generalized behavior are built on "known" and

	Correlative	Generalized behavior	System-based
Prediction	●	○	
Reconstruction		●	
Exploration		○	●

Fig. 3.1 Generalized relationship between modeling approaches and purpose/goal. *Black dots* represent a certain prevalence of one approach over another

assumed aspects of what people have been doing within a particular socioeconomic setting. Both approaches are mostly using geographical information systems (GIS) as the modeling environment. System-based—including agent-based—approaches primarily focus on the emergence of patterns (of variability) through mathematically defined processes, and rules of interaction (e.g., between individuals or groups/populations) in a more abstract modeling environment. These broad "families" of approaches are not exclusive to one particular purpose of modeling, although some prevalence may be noted (Fig. 3.1).

The choice for a particular approach has implications for the selection of model variables and definition of relationships between them. At this point, prior knowledge and conditional factors are fed into the model system, hence introducing constraints (boundary settings) and varying sources and degrees of uncertainty. Clearly, this will be of influence on model returns, but what this actually means for the performance (or quality) of the model is not easy to establish (see, e.g., Kamermans et al. 2009). As yet, the assessment of model uncertainty by means of sensitivity analysis has received limited attention, despite the availability of approaches (Bayesian Theory and Dempster-Shafer Theory) that explicitly incorporate uncertainty as a modeling factor (but see Finke et al. 2008; van Leusen et al. 2009). Moreover, different modeling goals will require different approaches to the uncertainties in the models: a data-oriented statistical technique that assists reliable prediction might lead to models that do badly on the count of reconstruction.

Out of the three modeling goals sketched above, the present paper is focused on the goal of exploration, and for which the role of statistical analysis is not very prominent. And this entails a particular take on the uncertainties at issue. Instead of looking at ways to remedy the uncertainty in the models—weighing parameters and adapting them on the basis of data—our goal is to gauge and control for the uncertainty in the starting points and modeling choices, in the hope that we can use the models for exploration, despite the uncertainties. In particular, we focus on exploration aimed at clarifying the model content and generating hypotheses. As will be seen, this has consequences for the kind of analysis of uncertainty that is appropriate.

3.3 Starting Points and Modeling Choices: A Case Study

We will approach the question of model uncertainty on the basis of an explorative model of postglacial hunter-gatherer landscape use (Peeters 2007). The study area—the Flevoland Polders in the Netherlands—is characterized by a low accessibility and visibility of archaeological phenomena, as these are generally buried under several meters of sediment, and mostly consist of scatters of flint artifacts, and less frequently fragments of (charred) bone and pottery. Excavations do, however, demonstrate that the average preservation of remains is good, thus making their scientific value high. Despite these insights, the study area is basically a black box where it comes to an understanding of postglacial hunter-gatherer behavioral variability.

As indicated, we will consider the use of computational models for the development of hypotheses and more generally for the gradual buildup of a coherent qualitative picture of the target system at hand. The models in Peeters' study were designed to explore the potential of the study area for landscape use by hunter-gatherers after the last glacial, using an approach based on generalized (not agent-based) behavior. Central to the modeling approach was the idea that the area had undergone far reaching environmental changes (in terms of composition and geography) due to structural sea-level rise between 7000 and 4000 BP, and that these changes affected the possibilities of landscape use in a qualitative (what?) and quantitative sense (to what extent?). Hence, the models had to integrate environmental and behavioral parameters, which in combination resulted in a GIS-based assignment of values to individual grid cells.

3.3.1 Environmental Parameters

Despite the availability of a large body of geological (bore-hole) data, it was decided not to reconstruct landscape change from these data—for example, because of the lack of chronological control, and issues of spatially variable histories of sedimentation and erosion, as well as sample density—but instead to develop a computer model of landscape change to ascertain a consistent environmental framework. For this purpose, environmental variables had to be selected and parameters set (summarized in Table 3.1), in order to build such a framework. These were fed into an iterative set of "if-then" rules to create a time-series (one century interval) of landscape maps with a spatial resolution of 500×500 m (Fig. 3.2).

3.3.2 Behavioral Parameters

Central to the approach is that "cost/benefit" rules—[Characteristic] of/by/to [Constraint] is/are [Qualification] for [Goal]—lead to a "perceived" value of landscape units for any sort of "behavior" (or activity if one likes). In this way,

Table 3.1 Environmental variables, parameters, and parameter settings of the landscape model

Environmental variable	Parameter	Setting
Elevation of the early Holocene surface	Top of Pleistocene surface	Geostatistically interpolated (block kriging; 500 × 500 m grid-cell setting)
(Ground)water level	(a) Sea-level rise	(a) Reconstructed sea-level at time t_x in 100-year intervals between 7000 and 4000 BP
	(b) Capillary groundwater rise	(b) Fixed % groundwater table increase (difference between water level at time t_x and grid-cell elevation) with a maximum of 1 m
Vegetation	Dominant vegetation zone	Six vegetation zones relative to (ground)water table
		One open water zone
		Boolean categories
Altering surface elevation	*Sedimentation*	
	(a) Increase of surface elevation through peat accumulation	(a) Fixed % of the difference between surface elevation and (ground)water level at time t_x in wetland vegetation zones
	(b) Increase of surface elevation through clay accumulation	(b) Fixed % of the difference between surface elevation and water level at time t_x in zones where water levels are above surface elevation
	Erosion	
	(c) Decrease of surface elevation during two regionally documented events	(c) Fixed % in zones where water levels are above surface elevation

environmental information was connected to "behavior" through a set of "if-then" decision statements. Based on archaeological data from the study area and generalized knowledge about hunter-gatherer behavior, a range of "behaviors" was defined in connection to the virtual environments. Although the focus was primarily on some aspects of food resource acquisition and dwelling (examples summarized in Table 3.2), any sort of "behavior"—including ritual—could potentially be defined and fed into a similar framework, provided a connection can be made to the dimensions of our virtual world. Similarly, any defined "behavior" can be as simple or complex as one would like it to be. Drawing from the examples provided in Table 3.2, such cost/benefit rules can for instance be formulated as:

> [high densities] of [large mammals] are [beneficial] for [hunting]
> [proximity] of [open water] is [beneficial] for [traveling]
> [presence] of [dense woodland] is [problematic] for [traveling]
> [absence] of [open water within 500 m] is [unfavorable] for [dwelling]

Perception values for each grid cell in the spatial model were calculated on the basis of "perception weights" assigned to the parameters included.[1] As such, the maps

---

[1] Weight values range from 0 (bad/low density/costly) to 1 (good/high density/beneficial). For more details on procedures, see Peeters (2007) (available from http://dare.uva.nl/document/42380).

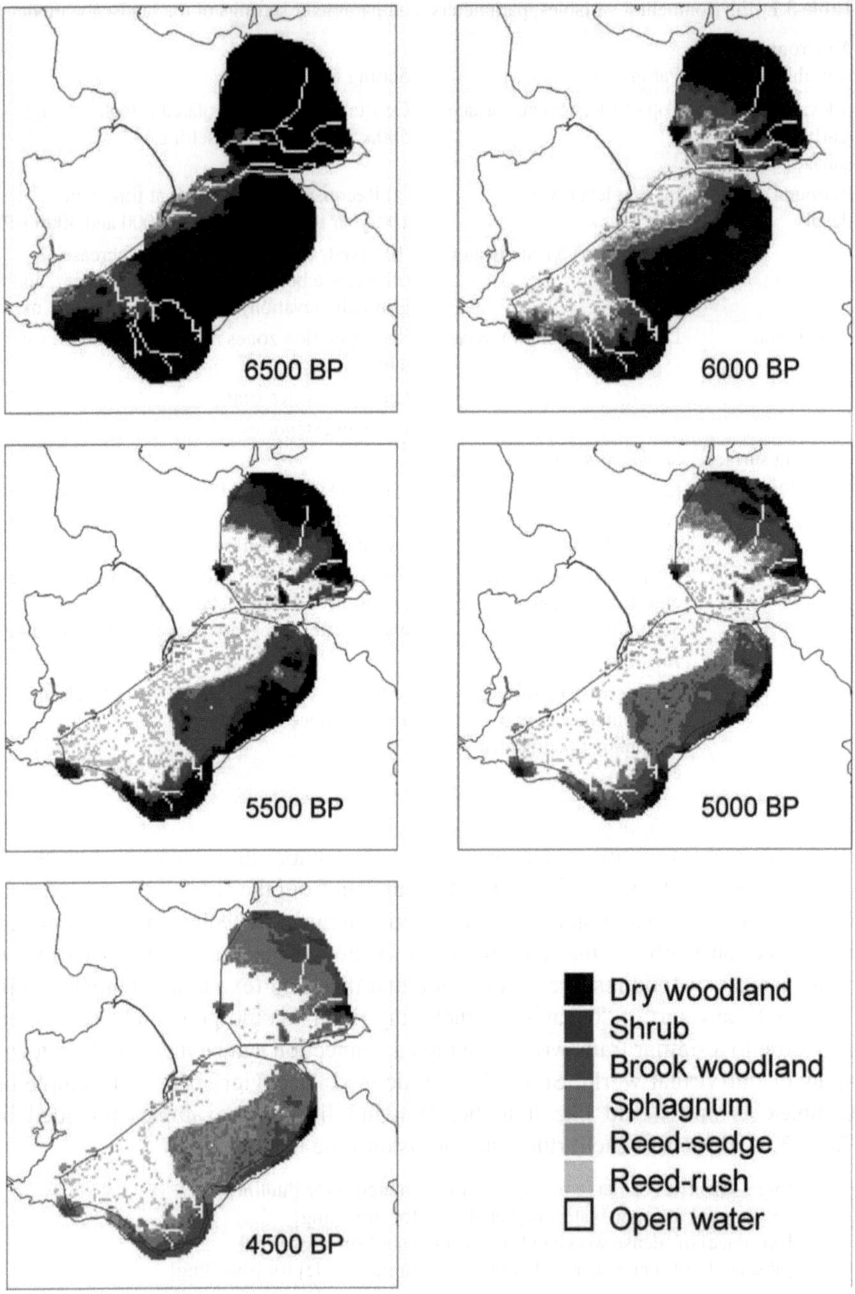

Fig. 3.2 Time-series of paleogeographical reconstructions based on the Flevoland environmental model with clay accumulation set at 20 % (see Table 3.1). Grid cells measure 500×500 m (from Peeters 2005, Fig. 4, p. 156)

Table 3.2 Example "behaviors" and their model parameters

Behavior/activity	Parameter
Large mammal hunting	Large mammal encounter probability
	Overland traveling possibility
	Overwater traveling possibility
	(Overland and overwater traveling determine "traveling weight")
Dwelling	Overland traveling possibility
	Overwater traveling possibility
	Soil moisture
	Presence of water within 500 m

produced for each time slice represent "perception surfaces" (cf. Whitley 2000) instead of predictions of site location (Fig. 3.3). Where and when certain types of behavior actually occurred cannot be predicted, as this depends on decisions that were made on the basis of many factors at the "ethnographic scale" (e.g., occurrence of game, hunter's experience, perceived gain and needs). These factors were in constant fluctuation at a temporal and spatial scale that is unattainable in the specific model environment outlined above (already our 100-year time slices easily include three generations of hunter-gatherers). Indeed, the problem of temporal resolution provides a major factor of uncertainty with regard to the understanding of the archaeological record (Bailey 2007; Holdaway and Wandschnider 2008), and one that can only be approached through computational modeling as a means to build a link between "ethnographic" and "archaeological" time.

3.4 What to do with Uncertainty?

The above broad outline of starting points and modeling choices makes clear that the modeling work in this case study involves a myriad of sources of uncertainty, each of which having their own problems. The environmental part introduces simplifications of landscape dynamics, whereas the behavioral part brings in biased assumptions about how prehistoric hunter-gatherers may have "perceived" some possibilities of landscape use. On the other hand we have to bear in mind the goal of the modeling work at hand. In this case, the modeling primarily serves an explorative purpose: a heuristic device that helps to ask questions and interrogate the archaeological record, and in addition—through inclusion of an erosion map—helps to sort out at a regional scale which areas are likely to bear the best preserved archaeological resources. To some extent this is a predictive use of the model in question, but the most prominent use of the models remains that they invite hypotheses about the nature of sites potentially present in some geographical space rather than directly supporting, for example, CRM decision making.

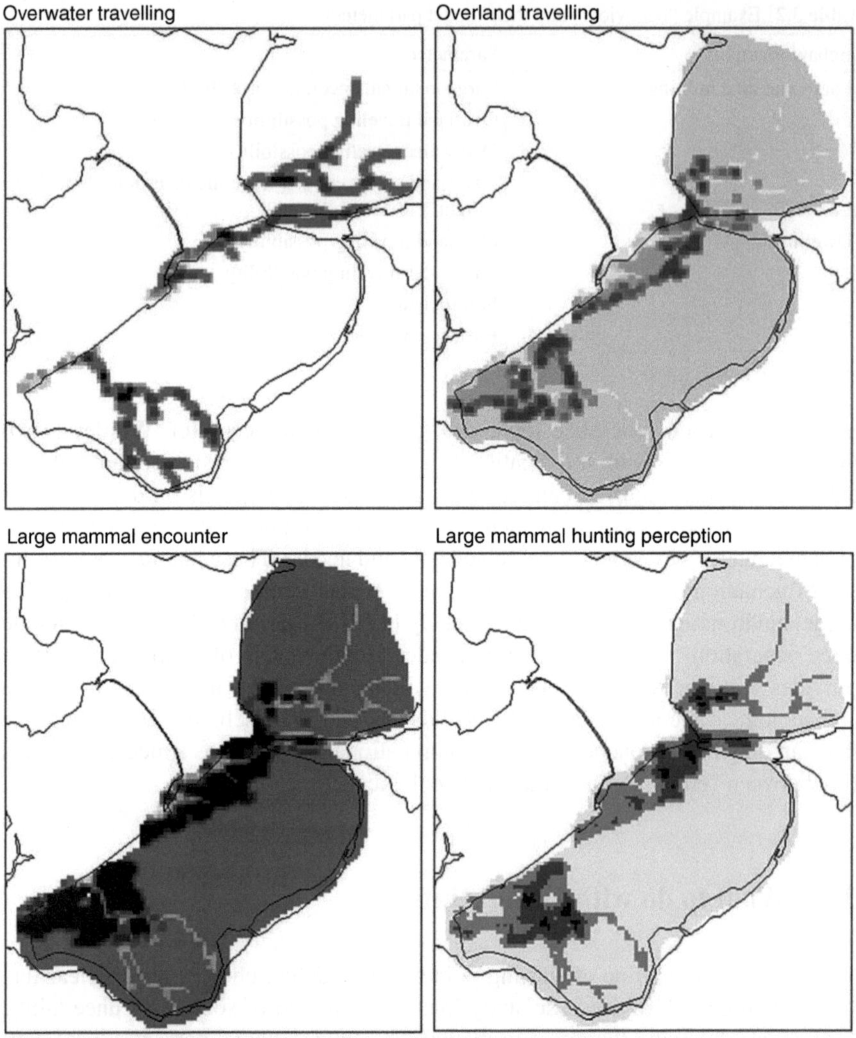

Fig. 3.3 Example of the large mammal hunting model for the 6500 BP time slice (from Peeters 2005, Fig. 8, p. 160). The environmental model for this time slice is shown in Fig. 3.2 (*top left*). *Top left*: cost/benefit surface for overwater traveling (dark = good; light = bad); *top right*: cost/benefit surface for overland traveling (dark = good; light = bad); *bottom left*: large mammal encounter probability (dark = high; light = low); and *bottom right*: perception surface for large mammal hunting (dark = good; light = bad)

In view of the many difficulties to evaluate or "ground-truth" the outcome of these models—for example, due to the very problems of detecting and assessing sites in the study area altogether—it seems to us that posterior analysis of model uncertainty may add little. The data are so sparse that they will hardly help to reduce overall uncertainty. Of course specific parts of the model may be improved by relying on data. The landscape modeling part, for instance, could be evaluated against bore-hole data, as the model was not based on reconstructions from these very data. The "virtual stratigraphy" of grid cells emerging from the modeled landscape dynamics appeared to fit the actual sequences recorded in bore-hole columns rather well, which provides at least some confidence that there exists concordance between the computational and the empirical model. In fact, this aspect lends itself for statistical calibration, an approach common to modeling in the geosciences (Brouwer Burg et al., Chap. 1). The behavioral part of the model is another matter of course, and one that does not lend itself very easily for calibration on the empirical facts. Across the board, we encounter many uncertainties that do not seem amenable to a standard statistical treatment.

This, then, brings us to the issues that are central here. How problematic are the uncertainties when it comes to the exploratory use of models? Can we control for uncertainties at the front end of model building, in order to safeguard the quality of the model output? And if so, what would be the best way to do this? Specifically, we are asking how the uncertainties in the computational models just described impact on the role of the models as catalysts of theorizing and hypothesis formation. The idea is that potentially adverse effects of the uncertainties can be controlled for by employing specific statistical tools: we can perform a sensitivity analysis, otherwise known as a robustness analysis, of the models and hence determine the reliability of the conclusions we draw from them. To flesh this out, we will first return to the case study and see some exploratory use of the computational model at work. In the light of this we identify two kinds of uncertainties, one within statistical models and one about such models. After this we will discuss the ways in which uncertainty may be controlled for in the case at hand, and which may be employed more broadly in computational archaeology. In the final part of the paper, we will then suggest how these techniques, once suitably developed, lead to better models in computational archaeology.

3.5 Back to the Model

In our case study, the model of hunter-gatherer landscape use is further explored in terms of interactions between environmental and behavioral parameters. More specifically, we ask how sensitive the model outcomes are to changes in environment–behavior interactions. In order to hold grip on the effects of parameter settings and model outcome, we will look at one single factor: the increase of surface elevation through clay accumulation.

In this model clay accumulation only affects landscape zones in which the surface is below groundwater level (reed-sedge, reed-rush, and open water). In the initial model, clay accumulation was set at 20 % relative to water depth. When varying the accumulation rate between 0 and 100 % in steps of 10 % (Fig. 3.4), it can be noted that no clear changes occur between 0 and 30 %. However, from 40 % onwards, major fluctuations in the relative importance of open water and the reed-rush zone

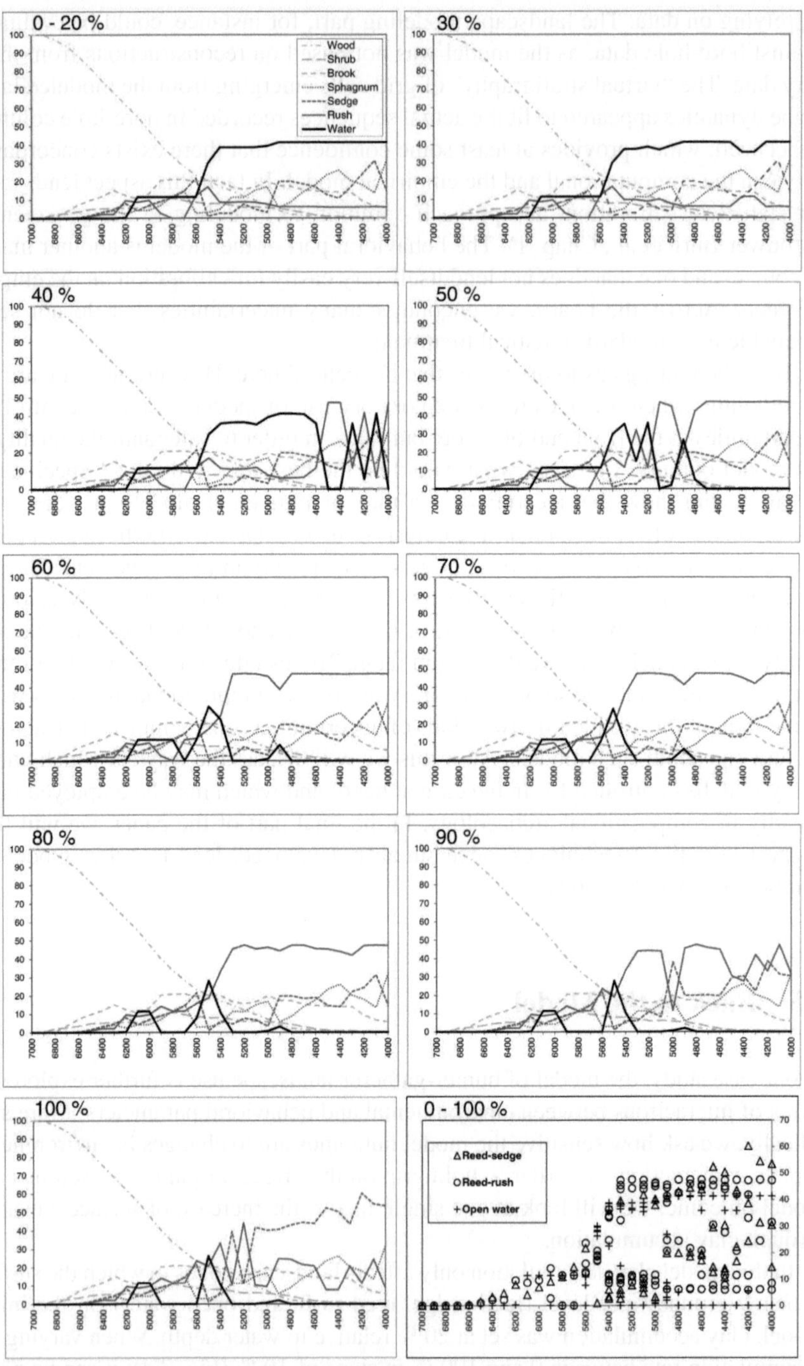

Fig. 3.4 Relative importance (percentage on the *vertical axis*) of vegetation zones for different rates of clay accumulation in 100-year time lags (age BP on the *horizontal axis*). The *lower right* graph plots all values obtained for those vegetation zones which are affected by clay accumulation, with a clay accumulation setting between 0 and 100 % in 10 % lags

occur. Open water and reed-rush are in competition, and eventually reed-rush becomes dominant over open water. Between 80 and 90 % of clay accumulation, reed-rush and reed-sedge get in competition, while the relative importance of open water is further reduced.

In view of the deterministic definition of the landscape zones in Boolean categories, these trends are to be expected: with the decrease of water depth due to increasing clay accumulation, vegetation types that favor more shallow water will gain importance. Nonetheless, there are some surprising patterns to note. The differences in the relative importance of open water and reed-rush between 30 and 40 % clay accumulation become quite substantial but were expected to be gradual. However, when increasing clay accumulation with only 1 %, it appears that a rather abrupt "turn-over" occurs from 37 to 38 %, initiating increasing fluctuations in the course of time (Fig. 3.5). A somewhat comparable, yet less marked shift occurs from 84/85 to 86 %, when the relative importance of reed-rush starts to fluctuate strongly compared to the rather stable situation at lower clay accumulation rates (Fig. 3.5). So apparently, even a simple deterministic linear model like this can produce unforeseen outcomes, suggesting some degree of nonlinear behavior.

The question here is: how do such changes to the relative importance of inundated landscape zones affect modeled human behaviors that are somehow connected to these zones. To explore this further, we will look at the "large mammal hunting" behavior summarized in Table 3.2. The calculation of perception values for large mammal hunting involved the following transformations:

$$\begin{aligned} TW_c &= {}^{avg}LT_{\sum c1...c9} + {}^{avg}WT_{\sum c1...c9} \\ HP_c &= TW_c * LM_c \end{aligned} \tag{3.1}$$

where TW_c is the traveling possibility weight of the target grid cell; ${}^{avg}LT_{\sum c1...c9}$ the average overland traveling possibility weight of the target grid cell, including neighboring grid cells; ${}^{avg}WT_{\sum c1...c9}$ the average overwater traveling possibility weight of the target grid cell, including neighboring grid cells; HP_c the hunting perception weight of the target grid cell; and LM_c the animal encounter possibility of the target grid cell.

The only parameter influenced by the effects of clay accumulation on the landscape is "overwater traveling possibility," set (on a scale from 0 to 1) at 0.25 for the reed-sedge zone, 0.5 for the reed-rush zone, and 1 for open water (non-inundated zones clearly have 0 overwater traveling possibility). With the decrease of open water in the advantage of reed-rush and eventually reed-sedge, overall overwater traveling possibilities are reduced. However, as overwater (WT) and overland traveling (LT) are complementary in the calculation of traveling weights in the original model, the overall effects are buffered by TW_c and LM_c, none of which are affected by clay accumulation. Hence, HP_c is indifferent in connection to varying clay accumulation settings. This, then, leads us to a theoretical reconsideration of the front-end modeling choices.

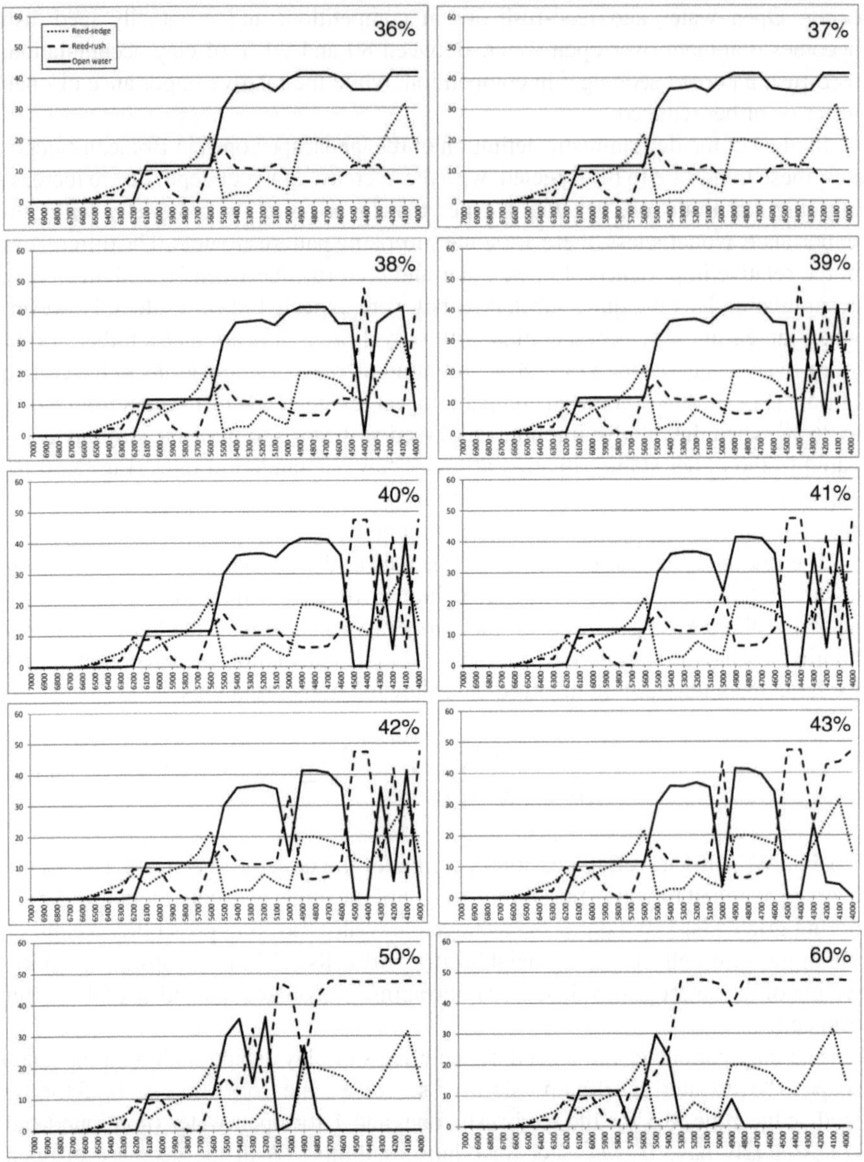

Fig. 3.5 Relative importance (percentage on the vertical axis) of vegetation zones that are affected by clay accumulation in 100-year time lags (age BP on the horizontal axis). The graphs show the abrupt transition from a relatively stable situation up to 37 % of clay accumulation, towards an unstable situation between 38 and 50 % of clay accumulation. This unstable phase is followed by a stable phase between 60 and 84/85 % of clay accumulation, after which new fluctuation sets in

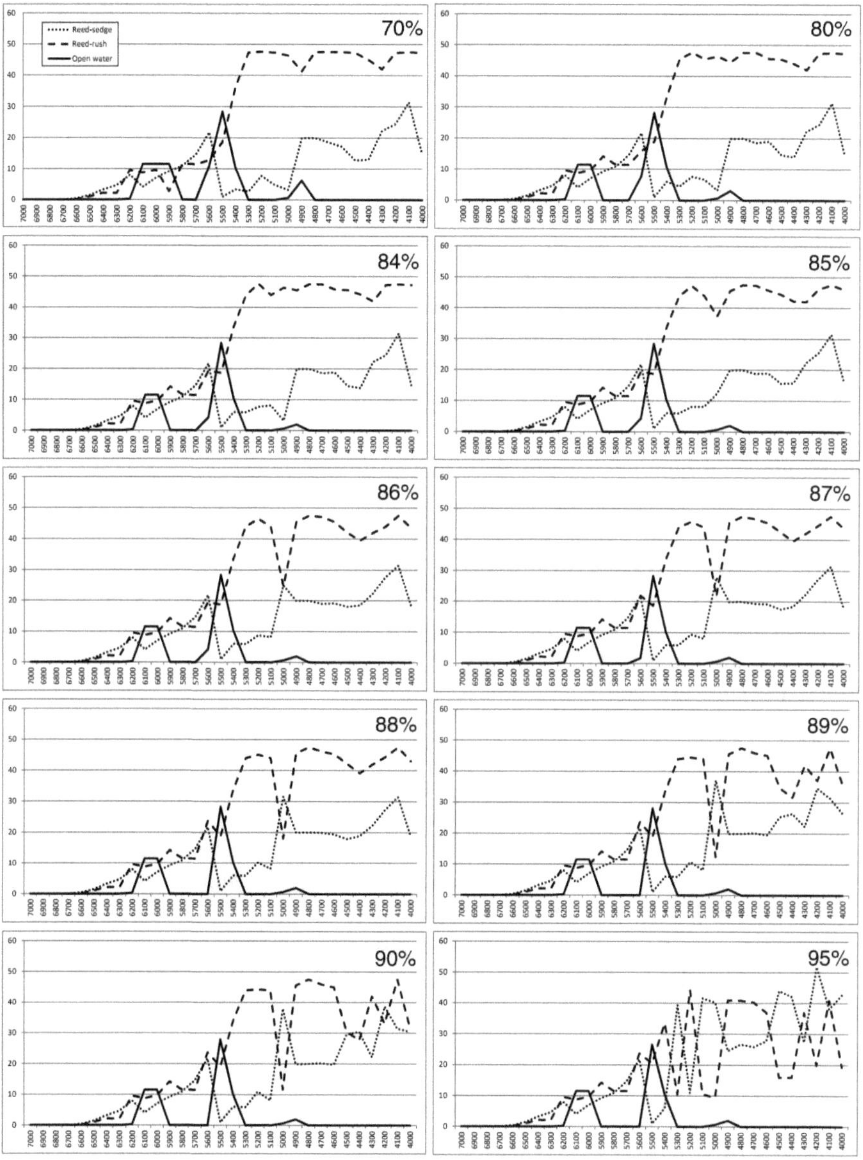

Fig. 3.5 (continued)

We have seen that the simple, deterministic landscape model composed of Boolean categories is sensitive to—occasionally minor—changes in an environmental parameter. In this example, clay accumulation influences the relative importance of open water, reed-rush vegetation, and reed-sedge vegetation. The modeled hunting perception that involves the relation between traveling possibilities and encounter possibility of large mammals is, however, not influenced by these landscape changes. In other words, the modeled behavior is insensitive to changes in the environmental parameter "clay accumulation." One cause of this indifferent model outcome may lay in the strict Boolean definition of vegetation categories (Table 3.1) relative to (ground) water level, which creates hard divisions in weight values of behaviors connected to these zones. Using fuzzy categories with overlapping boundaries will certainly provide better proxies of "natural" variability (cf. Arnot and Fisher 2007). Another cause may lie in the applied buffering distance of neighboring grid cells to calculate TW_c. This distance was set at one grid cell, which implies that TW_c only changes if the average possibility values of WT and LT for the nine grid cells taken into account had been affected.

Here we get to the key issue for the computational model: the influence of an environment changing at the local level (i.e., the target and neighboring grid cells) on the potential behavior within the target grid cell is only felt if changes occur within the neighboring grid cells. Now, the modeled behavior in our example of large mammal hunting is particularly bound to non-inundated vegetation zones, which are normally bordered by a reed-sedge/rush zone as soon as (ground) water levels reach the land surface. The replacement of open water by reed-rush in the landscape model is in fact occurring at some distance (more than one grid cell) from non-inundated land. This implies that the average possibility values of WT are not affected in the context of the large mammal hunting model. Consequently, WT will only have a noticeable effect on HP_c, if TW_c is considered over larger distances (more than one grid cell).

If the calculation of HP_c indeed should include grid-cell values over larger distances, we also have to conclude that a "remote evaluation" or grid-based evaluation of target grid cells is maybe not such a good way to proceed. Our large mammal hunters were not flying over the landscape, nor were they parachuted onto a grid cell to evaluate its hunting potential: they moved through the landscape. And when traveling overwater, they had to find their way through reed vegetation, which varied in spatial extent and density. This is probably what will have influenced decisions of where to go, to find routes, and see where good possibilities—not necessarily the best or most optimal—for a successful hunt would be. In other words, our hunters, and their targets, are (decision-making) agents.

This negative conclusion might lead us to believe that our case study misses the mark, but we don't think so. The exercise demonstrates strengths (the landscape model) and weaknesses (parameter connections) in the computational model, and brings certain sensitivities of parameter settings, or lack thereof, into focus. We believe that our illustration of exploratory model use is in fact rather informative on how model uncertainties are often dealt with, and on what problems we run into when doing so. We show that exploring model outcomes under variation of front-end modeling choices—sensitivity analysis—offers a means to reconsider the theoretical basis that, in this case, defines environment–behavior interactions. Notably, the usual format of a sensitivity analysis is that variations over model input lead to particular, often qualitative patterns in the outcome variables, so that these patterns can be concluded from the model despite the uncertainties over input. Our case study is unusual in that, for us, the lack of response in the outcome variables invites a theoretical advance; we will return to this below. At this point, we simply note that this is a theoretical advance and hence a fruitful exploratory use of the model nonetheless.

Returning to the above case, we have to conclude that HP_c in this particular model setup is insensitive to WT. The inclusion of WT is not "wrong" per se, but in this case it is ineffective in the posteriorly defined model settings. At the same time we feel that a leap forward can be made when a spatial modeling environment, like the one presented here, is combined with an agent-based approach. In doing so, the abstract "environment" in which digital agents usually operate in the context of ABM approaches (but see Danielisová et al. 2015; Janssen and Hill 2014) is replaced by a modeled environment that can, however, be validated (even statistically) on the basis of empirical data. In this way, the modeling environment and approach permit to build exploratory frameworks that help to increase our understanding of the archaeological record in dealing with issues of time perspectivism.

3.6 Statistical Uncertainty

With our case study firmly in place, we now turn to a more systematic discussion of the kinds of uncertainties involved, and the methods used to control for them. We discuss statistical uncertainty in this section and model uncertainty in the next one, focusing mostly on sensitivity or robustness analysis in both. We end by briefly considering, in the penultimate section, if uncertainties can be resolved by invoking theoretical criteria for models. It will be seen that the two sections following this one are more important for the paper as a whole but we nevertheless believe that some insight into ordinary statistical uncertainty is needed first: we hope that it reminds the reader of standard dealings with uncertainty and it introduces the idea of robustness analysis in a, more or less, familiar context.

As we said, the dominant response to uncertainties in scientific modeling is to deploy statistics. Statistical techniques can be used whenever the hypotheses that we entertain express expectations about empirical facts that are cast in terms of probabilities rather than certain facts. Rather than predicting the presence of a settlement with certainty, a hypothesis might for instance determine that a settlement here is more probable than there or more specifically that the chances of finding a settlement are only 20 %, and so on. Standard statistical methods allow us to confront such hypotheses with data, for example, records of excavations that have or have not laid bare settlements, and subsequently lead to a choice among the available hypotheses.

We can illuminate an important distinction within statistics by focusing on the kind of choice the statistical tools allow us to make. Classical statistical methods offer categorical choices among available hypotheses. We test a hypothesis, possibly against an alternative, and then decide to go along with it or not. Or else we estimate a parameter and so choose the hypothesis with the parameter value that makes the data come out maximally probable. By contrast, Bayesian statistics outputs a probability distribution over the hypotheses under consideration, as an expression of our opinion about the hypotheses. The choice among hypotheses is not categorical but by degree, for example, we might end up assigning a probability of 90 % to the hypothesis that the chance of finding a settlement in a particular area is 20 %. Bayesian statistics thus regulates how data impact on our opinions over hypotheses.

In order for Bayesian statistics to output such verdicts concerning hypotheses, a modeler needs to input a so-called prior probability at the outset: a probability distribution over the hypothesis that expresses her initial opinions about them. This aspect of Bayesian statistics is often lamented, because it introduces a subjective starting point into the statistical analysis. It is not always clear what can motivate the probability over hypotheses. However, the input component might also be considered an entry point for opinions that researchers already have about the subject matter, for example, insights based on experience with the subject matter that may be brought to bear on the model. In evaluating archaeological hypotheses, the elicitation of expert judgments can be a welcome addition to the empirical data, which is often scarce and contested. Moreover the formal treatment of opinions over hypotheses, as offered by Bayesian statistics, may help to streamline the theoretical debate and evaluate arguments in it. In other words, the Bayesian methods may have an edge over classical ones.

We can easily make this concrete by reference to the case study. In the landscape model, an important role was played by the parameter that accounts for clay accumulation. Of course the accumulation rate will vary over place and time, but the modeler will typically have an idea of what range of values will be appropriate, and might even be able to provide a probability distribution over rates that expresses her expectations. A statistical analysis of the landscape model using bore-hole data may benefit greatly from the prior opinions of an expert, and the Bayesian framework offers ways to accommodate these in the analysis.

Recall that this paper focuses on the exploratory use of models, for which the role of statistical analyses is not very prominent. However, it turns out that there are other uses of probability assignments over model parameters, uses that do not involve data but that fit very well with the goal of model exploration. Returning to the case study, we saw that the clay accumulation rate influenced what the model predicts about the landscape. In certain regions of the parameter the dependence of the vegetation on accumulation rate is critical: a small rate change might result in substantial changes in vegetation. In other regions, the vegetation patterns remained more or less stable. Assuming that this is not an artifact of the model's use of binary variables, the uncertain expert opinion may thereby play a crucial role. If, according to the expert, the range of probable values includes such a critical region, then the model predictions vary wildly. But this is not the case if the expert excludes such critical regions from an established range of values. The probability assignment over parameter values, delivered by the expert, thus determines whether or not the model predicts unstable vegetation patterns.

The suggestion here is that the use of probability assignments over model parameters, as an expression of expert opinion, may provide robust qualitative conclusions, and thereby support the exploratory use of models. By dealing with the uncertainty concerning the model parameters in a particular way, we manage to bring out what the model tells us about the target system, despite the statistical uncertainties that surround the model. To draw robust conclusions of that sort, we rely on the model as an adequate representation of the target system, and we assume that the uncertainty about model parameters is adequately captured by the expert opinions, that is, by the probability assignments. Accordingly, a model may be improved by reformulating it in such a way that experts have a better grip on the uncertainties.

To illustrate, we return to the case study. The Flevoland model introduced earlier seems to be rather unfit for a direct evaluation of the hypotheses in the model, by computing their fit with the data or the posterior probabilities. Although a statistical approach may suit the environmental dimension of the framework in view of the vast body of data available, the behavioral dimension causes problems, as the archaeological data interpretable to a specific level of behavior are particularly few. Of course, if one would accept a strong environmental dependency of hunter-gatherer behavior, one could argue that a reduction of uncertainty in the environmental dimension implies the same in the behavioral dimension. However, despite the subsistence-focused examples provided, we do not support such purely deterministic lines of reasoning. Not only do hunter-gatherers also take decisions on the basis of cosmologically inscribed factors (Descola 1999; Lavrillier 2011; Nadasdy 2007), there is furthermore a "sociohistorical" aspect to the use of landscapes based on, for instance, acquired information through sharing of knowledge and movement along paths (Aporta 2009; Lovis and Donahue 2011; Mlekuž 2014).

The aspects of behavioral complexity may, however, offer an opening to employ robustness analysis. Candidate models of various context of behavior, that include diverse ranges of parameters—bear in mind that theoretically any factor one would like can be included—can be analyzed to identify invariances. As invariant features of modeled behavior are less sensitive to variations in the starting points, such features can be expected to leave an archaeological echo, in contrast to features that return high degrees of variance. In this way it may become possible to identify patterns in model outputs that can be "tested" against archaeological data that are more of a qualitative than a quantitative nature, as in the case of our example area. Robustness analysis, then, may provide insight into the sensitivity of model parameters to differences in starting conditions, and—without the neglect of uncertainty—give way to the definition of models that return "perception surfaces" that, in a way, get closer to the "active landscape" as it was used by hunter-gatherers than the "neutral landscapes" in Peeters (2007) exploratory playground.

3.7 Model Uncertainty and Exploratory Modeling

One presupposition is central to both classical and Bayesian statistics and is highly relevant to our present concerns: all statistical approaches to uncertainty require that we choose a set of hypotheses, or theoretical possibilities, over which the experts, and perhaps the data, then produce a verdict. In statistics, this range of hypotheses is often called a model. The basis for a model is typically a set of causal relations, perhaps a mechanism, or some other structure, in which salient quantities and their qualitative relations are determined, without fully specifying the parameter values that are associated with them. The foregoing exposition on landscape use offers a good example. For our purpose, it is important to notice that the model serves as a presupposition for the statistical treatment of uncertainties: we cannot express any statistical uncertainty if we do not, at the outset, come up with a set of hypotheses or parameter values.

What to do when we are uncertain about the quantities and relations that need to be included in the model? The usual application of statistics is not appropriate when the uncertainty pertains to the very conceptual structure that is used to control for uncertainties, so the uncertainty that pertains to the statistical model itself. Looking at the case study, we see that exploration of the model led to a criticism of the way in which environmental and behavioral models were connected, or more precisely, the way in which behavioral responses to the environment were conceptualized. The uncertainty here is fundamental. It does not concern the value of some parameter or other, it rather concerns the way in which agents and their relations to the environment are conceived within the model. In other words, it concerns the entire model setup. And it is to this kind of uncertainty that we now turn. Although there are at least as many approaches to the issue of model uncertainty as there are uses of models, our present goal is quite specific: we want to control for the detrimental impact that model uncertainty has on the use of models for exploratory purposes. We consider three approaches: statistical model selection, robustness analysis, and in the next section the use of measures of informativeness and surprise.

A first and rather natural response is to partially remove the uncertainty by fitting the models to data. In other words, we convert model uncertainty into statistical uncertainty and repeat the statistical procedures on the level of models. We are then in the business of statistical model selection: the models are taken as hypotheses, and evaluated according to their respective fit with the data, or according to other data-related quality criteria. Several classical approaches to adjudicating between models are on offer, all based on their own formalization of model quality. And there are also model selection tools along Bayesian lines. For one, we may express our opinions concerning the candidate models by assigning probabilities to them, and then compute the so-called posterior model probabilities, on the basis of the data and the prior probabilities. The development of such model selection tools for the archaeological context provides an interesting avenue to explore.

It seems clear, however, that statistical model selection cannot be the only answer to the issue of model uncertainty, certainly not when the use of models for exploratory purposes is at stake. Dealing with model uncertainty in the afore-mentioned manner will not align with the exploratory purposes of modeling for at least three reasons. First, the application of such selection tools requires the availability of ample data, whereas exploratory modeling often happens when little data are available. Moreover, off-the-shelf model selection tools are based on idealizations that are typically not met in the archaeological context, while advanced tools that may be applicable in this context are less well established and hence prone to technical and interpretive problems. Finally, and most importantly, if we select a single model in response to model uncertainty, or average over a number of models, we seem to cover up something that may in fact be highly informative, namely that the models have certain qualitative features in common. Some features of the models might be constant, despite the uncertainty over them.

We submit that, in the case at hand, we can better deal with model uncertainty by focusing on these commonalities among the models, rather than to opt for one of them to the exclusion of others, or to average over the models. The idea is, in other words, that we deal with model uncertainty by selecting those results and insights that are invariant, or robust, under a wide range of models. This is a reiteration of the robustness analysis explained in the preceding section. Statistical and computational methods can be employed to identify such invariances, namely by supporting a systematic search of the parameter spaces of several models and charting the range of predictions that the models then generate. Such an exercise presents a view of the theoretical possibilities that the models under consideration offer and connects these to the potentially observable consequences of the different modeling assumptions. In short, an exercise like that gives the modeler a feel for the system she is modeling.

It may be viewed with some suspicion that the modeler does not have full command over the model she has built and so needs simulations and statistics to trace the role of the assumptions that have gone into it. Surely, it may be thought, the role of those assumptions should be in plain sight! But the practice of computational modeling is just not like that. Often models are highly complex, involving a multitude of parameters that are densely interlinked. It is generally not visible how such models relate to the empirical facts that they are supposed to account for. In fact modelers may well be surprised by the stringency or flexibility that a model offers in this respect. Investigating the spread of predictions relative to variations in the starting points, as done in robustness analysis, is a natural way of exploring the nature and contents of the models under scrutiny.

Looking again at our case study, we can quickly see that the analysis does not fit the mold of a robustness analysis. So what approach to model uncertainty is taken in the case study then? Recall that the uncertainty at stake is one about the entire model setup, and in particular about the connections between the environmental and the behavioral model. How should agents be conceptualized in the first place, and how do we relate them to their environment? The insight obtained from the exploratory use of the model was that agents and environment are independent where they should not be; the appropriate coupling of the environmental and behavioral model is missing. The behavior of the modeled agents appeared to be robust under substantial environmental variation, flying in the face of widely shared ideas about the relations between agents and environment. In other words, in our case study a faulty robustness casts doubt on modeling assumptions and so invited substantial revisions of the model.

From a distance, the inferential pattern that emerges is similar to the robustness analysis sketched before. Researchers will normally harbor intuitions about relations that should manifest between the variables that characterize their system of interest, in this case: a causal relation between vegetation and hunting opportunities.

By simulating the impact of variations in one such variable on other variables, researchers can check if their model adequately captures their intuitions. So where robustness analysis helps to find salient invariances, the analyses here help to check systematic covariation.

3.8 Theoretical Criteria

This last point connects to a rather speculative aspect of the view we have developed so far. Researchers check models for their robust properties but they also check them against numerous items of background knowledge, often tacitly. Good computational modeling offers researchers a grip on these background checks and allows them to make the checks explicit. So when it comes to the quality of models for the purpose of exploratory use, researchers will consider highly theoretical aspects of the models. They might ask what model will generate interesting hypotheses, what model presents surprising theoretical possibilities, or what model will be most informative. In the case study at hand, the model was judged to be defective because it failed to show dependencies that are expected on the basis of background knowledge of the system under scrutiny, that is, theoretical background knowledge of hunting behavior.

Speaking more generally, in the face of uncertainty over models researchers might select their favorite model not on the basis of how well it fits with available data but rather on these highly theoretical aspects. A model that passes specific checks against background knowledge is preferable, even if there are no empirical data that can be used to make those checks empirical. Or, more theoretical still, a model might be preferred because of the checks that it occasions, the insights that it might deliver, because of surprising predictions it might offer, or because of the opportunity it gives to formulate testable hypotheses, all of this quite independently of the data. Such theoretical aspects of models are very hard to formalize and quantify. But we are optimistic that some progress can be made in this direction, primarily by adapting and refining extant model selection tools. The informativeness of a model is naturally related to the specificity of a model, and so is the surprisingness, although in a different manner. And in turn, model selection tools provide a handle on the specificity (cf. Romeijn et al. 2012). We believe that a conceptual clarification of these theoretical criteria for models will be beneficial to a wide range of sciences, including archaeology, and we think that a formalization and quantification will contribute to this clarification.

Leaving aside these speculations on formalizing the theoretical virtues of models, we hope that the foregoing has made clear that model uncertainty is a serious methodological concern, and one that cannot be tackled by standard statistical means. We have shown that statistical model selection will typically not provide resolution, whereas robustness analysis and model comparison on the basis of theoretical criteria may present fruitful, certainly in the context of the exploratory use of models.

3.9 Conclusion

We hope to have made clear that model uncertainty needs proper attention but also that it is a methodologically complex problem that cannot be dealt with in a standard and straightforward fashion. The case study presented here makes very clear how important it is to critically (re)consider the relationships to be built in models from a theoretical perspective. It occurs to us that, generally speaking, models of human behavior and that of hunter-gatherer behavior in particular, are difficult—if not impossible—to calibrate through validation on empirical facts. Although Bayesian approaches could be very useful to explicitly deal with model uncertainty through assignment of prior probabilities to parameter settings and candidate models, the frequent lack of unambiguous data obstructs computation of posterior model probabilities. However, in an exploratory context of modeling purposes, we think it seems better to deal with sources of uncertainty at the front end of model building, and apply techniques such as robustness analysis and work on the development of systematic selection tools that rely on theoretical criteria, as sketched above. Such tools cannot aim at the selection of "a best" model but will help to identify families of models which return invariant or—conversely—highly variant outcomes, hence providing a basis to choose among those models which seem to offer the best possibilities for hypothesis testing. And it is exactly this possibility that will help to improve the acceptance of computational modeling as a useful tool for archaeology, a position that is not generally shared among archaeologists. With a critical approach to model uncertainty and model selection from an epistemic perspective, we believe that the research program of computational modeling in archaeology is engaged in a process of continuous self-improvement. This self-correcting character is reason for optimism about the viability of models in archaeology, which is much in line with the more general views expounded in Henrickson and McKelvey (2002) with regard to agent-based modeling in the social sciences.

References

Aporta, C. (2009). The trail as home: Inuit and their pan-Arctic network of routes. *Human Ecology, 37*, 131–146.

Arnot, C., & Fisher, P. (2007). Mapping the ecotone with fuzzy sets. In A. Morris & S. Kokhan (Eds.), *Geographic uncertainty in environmental security* (pp. 19–32). Dordrecht, The Netherlands: Springer.

Bailey, G. (2007). Time perspectives, palimpsests and the archaeology of time. *Journal of Anthropological Archaeology, 26*, 198–223.

Danielisová, A., Olševočová, K., Cimler, R., & Machálek, T. (2015). Understanding the Iron Age economy: Sustainability of agricultural practices under stable population growth. In G. Wurzer, K. Kowarik, & H. Reschreiter (Eds.), *Agent-based modeling and simulation in archaeology* (pp. 183–216). New York: Oxford University Press.

Descola, P. (1999). Des proies bienveillantes. Le traitement du gibier dans la chasse amazonienne. In F. Héritier (Ed.), *De la violence* (Vol. II, pp. 19–44). Paris: Odile Jacob.

Finke, P. A., Meylemans, E., & van de Wauw, J. (2008). Mapping the possible occurrence of archaeological sites by Bayesian inference. *Journal of Archaeological Science, 35–10*, 2786–2796.

Henrickson, L., & McKelvey, B. (2002). Foundations of "new" social science: Institutional legitimacy from philosophy, complexity science, postmodernism, and agent-based modeling. *Proceedings of the National Academy of Sciences, 99* (Suppl.3), 7288–7295.

Holdaway, S., & Wandschnider, L. (2008). Time in archaeology: An introduction. In S. Holdaway & L. Wandschnider (Eds.), *Time in archaeology: Time perspectivism revisited* (pp. 1–12). Salt Lake City, UT: University of Utah Press.

Janssen, M. A., & Hill, K. (2014). Benefits of grouping and cooperative hunting among Ache hunter-gatherers: Insights from an agent-based foraging model. *Human Ecology, 42*, 823–835.

Kamermans, H., van Leusen, M., & Verhagen, P. (Eds.). (2009). *Archaeological prediction and risk management. Alternatives to current practice*. Leiden, The Netherlands: Leiden University Press.

Kohler, T. A., & van der Leeuw, S. E. (2007). Introduction. Historical socionatural systems and models. In T. A. Kohler & S. E. van der Leeuw (Eds.), *The model-based archaeology of socionatural systems* (pp. 1–12). Santa Fe, New Mexico: School for Advanced Research Press.

Lavrillier, A. (2011). The creation and persistence of cultural landscapes among the Siberian Evenkis: Two conceptions of 'sacred' space. In P. Jordan (Ed.), *Landscape and culture in northern Eurasia* (pp. 215–231). Walnut Creek, CA: Left Coast Press.

Lovis, W. A., & Donahue, R. E. (2011). Space, information, and knowledge: Ethnocartography and North American boreal forest hunter-gatherers. In R. Whallon, W. A. Lovis, & R. K. Hitchcock (Eds.), *Information and its role in hunter-gatherer bands* (pp. 59–84). Los Angeles, CA: The Costen Institute of Archaeology Press of UCLA.

Mlekuž, D. (2014). Everything flows: Computational approaches to fluid landscapes. In G. Earl, T. Sly, A. Chrysanthi, P. Murrieta-Flores, C. Papadopoulos, I. Romanowska, & D. Wheatley, D. (Eds.), *Archaeology in the digital era, volume II: e-Papers from the 40th annual conference of computer applications and quantitative methods in archaeology (CAA), Southampton, 26–29 March 2012* (pp. 839–845). Amsterdam, The Netherlands. Retrieved from http://dare.uva.nl/aup/en/record/500958.

Nadasdy, P. (2007). The gift in the animal: The ontology of hunting and human–animal sociality. *American Ethnologist, 34*(1), 25–43.

Peeters, H. (2005). The forager's pendulum: Mesolithic–Neolithic landscape dynamics, land-use variability and the spatiotemporal resolution of predictive models in archaeological heritage management. In H. Kamermans & M. van Leusen (Eds.), *Predictive modeling for archaeological heritage management: A research agenda* (pp. 149–168). Amersfoort (Nederlandse Archeologische Rapporten 29).

Peeters, J. H. M. (2007). *Hoge Vaart-A27 in context: Towards a model of Mesolithic-Neolithic land use dynamics as a framework for archaeological heritage management*. Amersfoort.

Romeijn, J. W., van de Schoot, R., & Hoijtink, H. (2012). One size does not fit all: Derivation of a prior-adapted BIC. In D. Dieks, W. Gonzales, S. Hartmann, F. Stadler, T. Uebel, & M. Weber (Eds.), *Probabilities, laws, and structures* (pp. 1–28). Berlin, Germany: Springer.

Steele, K., & Werndl, C. (2013). Climate models, calibration, and confirmation. *British Journal for the Philosophy of Science, 64*(3), 609–635.

van Leusen, P. M. & Kamermans, H. (Eds.). (2005). *Predictive modeling for archaeological heritage management: A research agenda*. Amersfoort.

van Leusen, P. M., Millard, A. R., & Ducke, B. (2009). Dealing with uncertainty in archaeological prediction. In H. Kamermans, P. M. van Leusen, & Ph. Verhagen (Eds.), *Archaeological prediction and risk management. Alternatives to current practice* (pp. 123–160). Leiden.

Verhagen, P. (2007). *Case studies in archaeological predictive modeling* (p. 14). Leiden, The Netherlands: Archaeological Studies Leiden University.

Whitley, T. G. (2000). *Dynamical systems modeling in archaeology: A GIS evaluation of site selection processes in the Greater Yellowstone region*. Unpublished Ph.D. Dissertation, Pittsburgh.

Worrall, J. (2010). Error, tests, and theory confirmation. In D. G. Mayo & A. Spanos (Eds.), *Error and inference: Recent exchanges on experimental reasoning, reliability, and the objectivity and rationality of science* (pp. 125–154). Cambridge, England: Cambridge University Press.

Chapter 4
GIS-Based Modeling of Archaeological Dynamics (GMAD): Weaknesses, Strengths, and the Utility of Sensitivity Analysis

Marieka Brouwer Burg

4.1 Introduction

Archaeologists are often faced with a difficult task: How can we reconstruct a narrative about past human societies and lives, and the mechanisms driving behavioral change or continuity, from the incomplete and oftentimes scant empirical data we recover from the archaeological record? For many, the answer has been to collect more data with more precise instruments and interpret this data with more detailed and nuanced models and theories. However, the "more" solution does not necessarily function as a panacea for mitigating the extreme variations present in the archaeological record because more data does not necessarily translate into better-informed inferences about the past. In fact, more data can potentially generate more and different questions, introduce more uncertainty and error into a model, and ultimately detract from constructive hypothesis testing and theory building.

One way around this problem is to use available data in more creative ways, shifting from data-centric, bottom-up, inductive approaches to theory-driven, top-down, deductive approaches that test hypotheses of human socionatural processes drawn from contemporary or semi-contemporary understandings of historic, ethnographic, demographic, and environmental trends (sources of information not without their own complications; see Section 4.3). Both formal and computational modeling approaches have gained popularity in the field as important deductive strategies for revealing patterns that can be tested with existing albeit incomplete and sometimes biased data. A variety of computational modeling genres have been developed over the years to carry out such deductive and exploratory approaches to

M. Brouwer Burg (✉)
Department of Anthropology, University of New Hampshire, Durham, NH, USA
e-mail: Marieka.brouwer-burg@unh.edu

M. Brouwer Burg et al. (eds.), *Uncertainty and Sensitivity Analysis in Archaeological Computational Modeling*, Interdisciplinary Contributions to Archaeology, DOI 10.1007/978-3-319-27833-9_4

archaeological questions and along with advances in computing power and spatial modeling, this newer mode of working with archaeological data is becoming an irreplaceable tool in the archaeologists' tool kit. Agent-based modeling (ABM) is perhaps the most well-known variety of computational modeling applications; see Chaps. 1, 5, and 6 for a fuller discussion.

Another variety of computational modeling applications has focused more overtly on the spatial aspects of human socionatural dynamics, which I refer to here as geographic information systems (GIS)-based modeling of archaeological dynamics (GMAD), and which has been referred to in other disciplines as "map centered exploratory approaches to multi criteria decision making" (e.g., Jankowski et al. 2001). Such models are focused on displaying the geographic "decision space" of initial socionatural hypotheses, and while they do not readily facilitate recursive processual outcomes on the scale of ABM, their incorporation of empirically based paleoecological reconstructions can yield useful and complementary data to the former approach. In fact, the formal integration of graphical spatial analytics with ABM has been an ongoing exercise among geographers and has been applied by several archaeologists as a robust tool for understanding human socionatural dynamics in the past (some current examples include Barton et al. 2012, pp. 42–53; Lake 2000; Rogers et al. 2012, pp. 5–14; for difficulties of merging such tools, see Gilbert 2008, p. 68). This chapter explores the weaknesses and strengths of using non-iterative GMAD, especially with regard to the propagation of uncertainty and error, and examines the utility of sensitivity analysis (SA) from the perspective of a case study of hunter-gatherer land use.

4.2 The Hunter-Gatherer Land-Use Model (HGLUM)

The Hunter-Gatherer Land-Use Model (HGLUM) is a multi-tiered, multi-criteria decision model developed to investigate socionatural dynamics among temperate and boreal forest foragers (Brouwer Burg 2013; Fig. 4.1). HGLUM was applied to Early Holocene foraging processes in the central river valley of the Netherlands, but versions of the model are now also being applied to the Younger Dryas (ca. 10,950–10,000 years BP[1]) in the Province of Flevoland, the Netherlands (van den Biggelaar et al. 2014). The model is geared toward exploration of group processes, the assumed behavioral reactions of hunter-gatherer bands as a whole to external stimuli and internal motivations. The basal tier of the model inductively generates ecological (or "total landscape"; Brouwer Burg 2013) models of the past landscape from a rich database of empirical geophysical data. The superseding tier explores the differential suitability of the landscape given a range of past behavioral processes, informed by ethnographic data from boreal and temperate forest hunter-gatherers. Similar procedures have been developed for other parts of the Netherlands

[1] All dates from here are reported as uncalibrated radiocarbon dates.

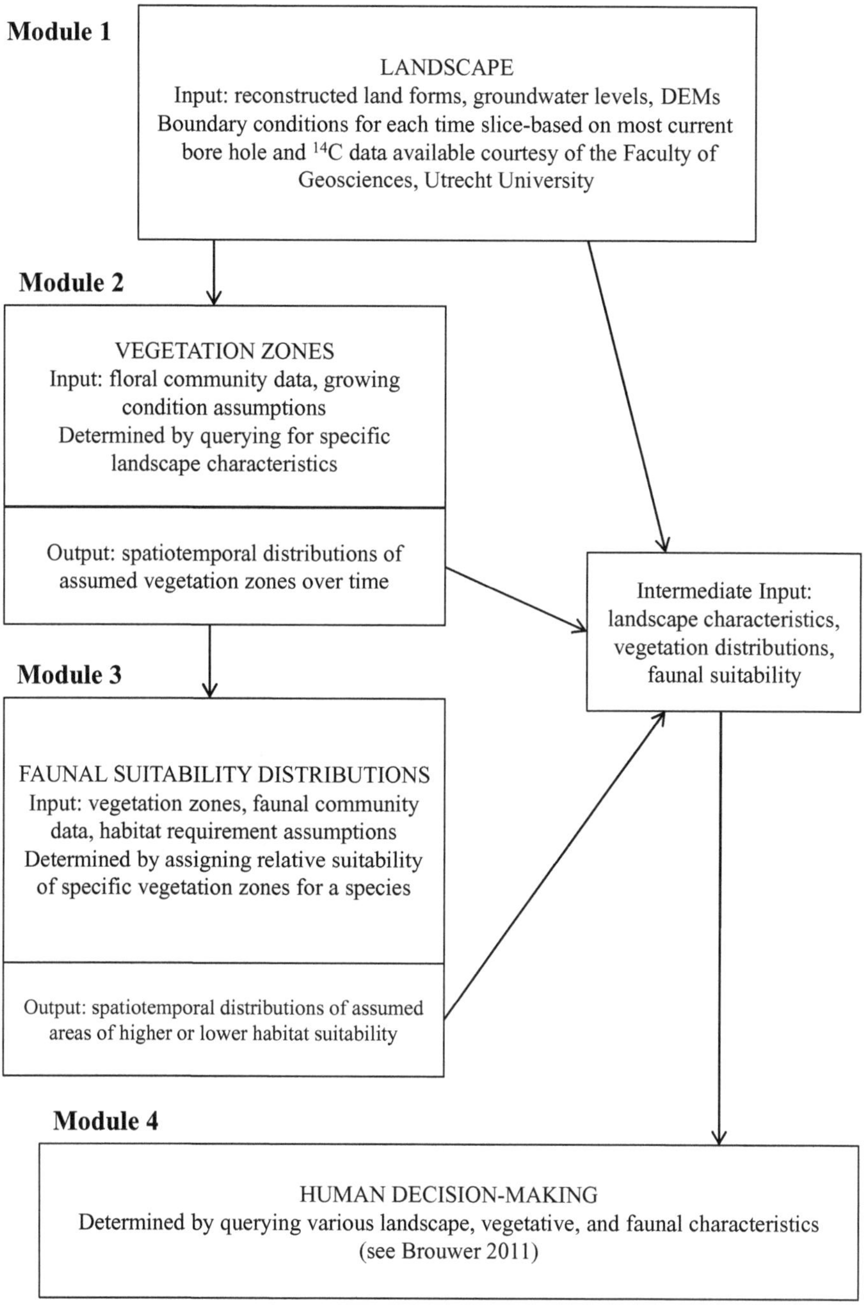

Fig. 4.1 HGLUM flowchart (from Brouwer, 2011, p. 350)

Table 4.1 Initial rankings for attainment of minimum resources within a residential resource use strategy (model large game)

	Red deer	Roe deer	Wild boar	Aurochs	Beaver	STMs	PEV[a]
Red deer	1	5	3	5	7	9	0.47
Roe deer	1/5	1	1/2	1	2	4	0.12
Wild boar	1/3	2	1	2	4	6	0.20
Aurochs	1/5	1	1/2	1	2	5	0.12
Beaver	1/7	1/2	1/4	1/2	1	2	0.06
STMs	1/9	1/4	1/6	1/4	1/2	1	0.03

[a]PEV = Principle eigenvector value

(i.e., Peeters 2007, and currently under development van den Biggelaar et al. 2014); the Czech Republic (Danielisová and Pokorný 2011); in Wyoming, Georgia and in Michigan, USA (Krist 2001; Whitley 2000, 2005; Whitley et al. 2009). HGLUM is a non-iterative model, meaning that no elements of ABM were incorporated; however, there are certain benefits of employing detailed and highly accurate paleoecological maps, striking a balance between accuracy in the ecological sphere and generality in the behavioral sphere.

Ecological models of topography, hydrology, and floral and faunal distributions were generated for three 25 × 25 km study areas over a 4000-year time span, in 500-year intervals (for details, see Brouwer Burg 2013). This spatial scale falls toward the smaller end of the spectrum of territory size for ethnographically documented boreal/temperate hunter-gatherers, which ranges from approximately 320 km^2 for the Berens River Ojibwa (Rogers 1967, 1969) to 4870 km^2 for the Waswanipi Cree (Laughlin 1980; Rogers 1967, 1969; for further comparisons, see Kelly 1995, Table 4.1). The time span chosen allows the model to yield information concerning landscape evolution and behavioral change during the entire Mesolithic (Postglacial) period in northwest Europe. The spatial results of the model consist of square-shaped raster surfaces (also known as grids). A resolution of 1:10 was chosen, meaning that each grid cell represents 0.1 × 0.1 km, with a total of 62,500 cells per raster. This modeling scale is considered to be rather coarse for the purpose of human land-use decision-making; however, the scope of the model is largely dictated by the quality and resolution of the underlying geographic data. Further, a resolution that can facilitate many recursive executions of the model is an important consideration; for this model, raster grids consisting of 62,500 cells are chosen because they have the capacity to provide sufficient granularity for data mining and analysis but also do not impose significant time and computing power restrictions to the modeling process.

Topographic and hydrological reconstructions are derived from a high-volume coring database housed in the Geosciences Department at Utrecht University. Vegetation zones and faunal suitabilities are calculated based on known habitat distribution and ethological preferences, and are used to determine potential hunter-gatherer encounter rates between, for example, red deer, wild boar, beaver, etc. at a given locations and time periods.

From this foundational understanding of what has been termed the "total" landscape (Brouwer Burg 2013), different hypothesized land-use strategies of hunter-gatherers were applied as a way to explore spatial patterning, ecosystem use, and cognitive perceptions of the landscape. These counterposed land-use strategies were situated at opposite ends of the hunter-gatherer subsistence–settlement spectrum (e.g., Binford 1980; Kelly 1995): from foraging to collecting strategies. These strategies were subdivided further to distinguish between residential and logistical settlement patterns, as well as between targeted resource groups: large game, generalized (broad-spectrum) foraging, and wetlands. Such partitioning allowed the modeler to prioritize certain parameters for each type of subsistence–settlement strategy and resource focus.

The overall goal of HGLUM was not to produce a facsimile model of past social–natural circumstances, but rather to heuristically investigate the many different natural and cultural parameters that consciously and unconsciously affect socionatural behavioral processes. To achieve this goal, the impact of different parameters and parameter combinations on outcome simulacra was investigated (see discussion below and Brouwer 2011). A corollary goal was to analyze the degree to which environmental perturbations affected adaptive strategies and land-use decisions. Prediction of site locations was not an initial goal of the model, although some of the model outputs serve to reinforce "expert knowledge" about where to expect Mesolithic sites. This is a difficult task at best, as much of the assemblage of hunter-gatherer remains are ephemeral and poorly preserved in the archaeological record; nevertheless, constructing theories of subsistence–settlement patterns from existing (albeit scant) empirical evidence can help to fill in explanatory gaps and inform future policy, planning, and land-management decisions.

4.3 Weaknesses and Strengths of GMAD

4.3.1 Weaknesses

While it may seem counterintuitive to begin by discussing the weaknesses of GMAD, this approach serves to underscore the importance of understanding where model pitfalls lie prior to investing the time to execute it. Such consideration of model weaknesses and strengths receives woefully little attention in the literature on archaeological computational modeling, prompting some nonmodelers to question the motivations and goal feasibility of such modeling. Indeed, as discussed by Lovis (Chap. 2) and Peeters and Romeijn (Chap. 3), models that cannot confront uncertainty and error propagation run the risk of returning "just so" stories about behavioral processes in the past. However, if sufficient attention and time is accorded to these unavoidable modeling obstacles, modelers stand to gain not only a more nuanced understanding of the past, but also potential information about humanity that could be useful in present and future decision making. Furthermore, modelers are advised to incorporate the error/uncertainty identification process (a part of model verification), at the outset of model development (ideally within a design of experiment [DOE] framework) and throughout the modeling life cycle.

At the outset, the HGLUM model is static and additive. Any errors in the initial input data (e.g., the geophysical and environmental variables) become compounded with the introduction of vegetation zones and faunal distributions (i.e., error propagation). Each successive step in the landscape modeling introduces new data and therefore uncertainty, although additional verification procedures can be easily implemented to alleviate some of this uncertainty (e.g., quantitative DOE testing for parameter sensitivity as well as qualitative cross-checking simulated vegetation distributions with empirical data such as palynological and macrobotanical records). Given the scope and flexibility of HGLUM, and precluding further field research, error and uncertainty that cropped up were recognized and accepted as part of the process. All of the paleoecological maps must therefore be regarded as a best approximation of the past landscape based on contemporary available data and techniques.

In addition to the above areas of uncertainty production, the job of GMAD modelers is often compounded by the fact that behavioral models are built upon physical models of past reality; these modeling suites involve different boundary conditions, model properties, and possibilities for ground-truthing. For example, assumptions can be made about the physical realm that cannot be made about the human behavioral realm, most specifically that processes in the physical world abide by constant rates of change that are the same today as they were in the past (Comte du Buffon's *Principle of Uniformitarianism* [1749–1804]). Conversely, human behavior—the product of human choice—may be rational or irrational given the context of the choice, and can only be predicted in a generalized sense, based on known sets of recorded behaviors. In the fields of psychology and economics, human decision-making has traditionally been regarded numerically as the nonlinear probability of choosing one possible outcome over others (i.e., von Neumann and Morgenstern's (1947) theory of expected utility and Savage's (1954) theory of subjective expected utility; cf. Camerer and Weber 1992). We must therefore contend with the knowledge that our present day ontologies likely do not adequately approximate the ontologies of people living in the past and that this mismatch will also be a source of great uncertainty in our models.

4.3.1.1 Boundary Conditions

In GMAD, paleogeographic and paleoecological simulations often serve as backdrops for modeling resource distribution and land-use decision-making (Krist 2001; Peeters 2007; Whitley 2000, 2005; Whitley et al. 2009). These backdrops are themselves complex to create (see Brouwer Burg 2013), involving their own inherent uncertainties (see Lovis, Chap. 2). In the case of the model described here, paleogeographic reconstructions were based on geomorphologic–geologic surfaces and digital elevation models (DEMs) using core profiles of the subsurface. In addition, groundwater levels were interpolated from the location of carbon dated peat deposits. Both of these sources of data contributed uncertainty related to error in field collection, dating, expert analysis and classification, and the application of interpolative algorithms. Most of this uncertainty was conceptual in nature (i.e., assumed but not quantified), although the uncertainty contributed by groundwater interpolation was quantified using probability distribution and found to fall within the range of acceptable error (e.g., 2 sigma). Paleoecological models were created as extensions of the paleogeographic reconstructions, involving the overlay of vegetation zones (based on knowledge of established biotic communities with particular growing conditions) and faunal suitability distributions (estimated from observed habitat and ethological preferences). The drawback of this extrapolative procedure is that error and uncertainty present in the initial paleogeographic simulations are carried into subsequent paleoecological simulations, which also entail specific uncertainties and error propagation.

4.3.1.2 Model Properties

The structure and execution of a model can sometimes lead to uncertainty, as can the selection of parameters chosen to represent reality. Model verification procedures, which determine if the model is running as it should, are critical to execute in the early phases of model development and can best be examined with SA and DOE procedures (see Sect. 4.3.1). Since the model described here was tested in previous studies (see Eastman 1999; Krist 2001), the parameters of the model and their values were thus identified as the more likely location of uncertainty production. Saisana et al. (2005, p. 309) note that the uncertainty of a particular parameter can arise during the selection of parameters, the selection of data, the editing of data, the normalization of data, the weighting of the overall scheme, the weighting of values, and the running of a composite parameter (or indicator) formula. SA is perhaps the best way to uncover some of this uncertainty; as a method of model verification, SAs can reveal which parameters require special attention and which can be eliminated wholesale to increase modeling efficiency and decrease overall levels of error.

4.3.1.3 Ground-Truthing

The archaeological record must also be considered, as it supplies empirical data on past physical landscapes and material correlates of past human behaviors. This record is often used as comparison for simulated outcomes, a useful posttest evaluation of initial modeling assumptions about the physical world and behavioral processes. There are many constraints on the archaeological record: it is a biased and partial record of past events and therefore, if some portion of archaeological data is withheld for post hoc testing of simulation models, special consideration must be given to the representative nature of the existing record as well as the persistent underlying threat of tautological argumentation. Furthermore, while ground-truthing may be a viable option for post hoc testing in the natural and behavioral sciences, it is often not a feasible option for archaeologists given the vagaries of the archaeological record; land zoning and property ownership concerns; and time, finance, and labor costs.

4.3.2 *Strengths*

While the drawbacks of multi-tiered GMAD appear numerous, its utilization also yields important benefits. First, the incorporation of detailed and accurate paleoecological models, based upon the more predictable laws and behaviors displayed by physical and nonhuman biotic agents, can provide a firm foundation for modeling the more unpredictable and sometimes irrational behavior or human agents. This is one potential drawback of more abstract ABM simulations, where the goal of illustrating patterns based on specific behavioral principles may outweigh considerations of environment or spatial context (e.g., Brantingham 2003; Premo 2006; Wobst 1974). In this way, ABM is much more a heuristic, exploratory device that can in some cases—when the model is verified and validated—be used to predict other areas in the landscape where similar behavioral processes occurred.

Second, GMAD can also serve heuristic and exploratory purposes, although it is not currently suited to high-volume recursive modeling of behavioral processes and thus, obtaining a robust bandwidth of possible behavioral outcomes (and identifying those that are most probable) is not an easy task, as it involves coupling ABM and GMAD tools, both of which are detailed and nuanced research specialties (see Gilbert 2008, p. 68). Nevertheless, the inclusion of detailed and accurate paleoecological surfaces can provide other advantages to the modeling process. For example, when the location of water-logged versus dry areas for the time period between 6500 and 6000 years BP is established with multiple lines of empirical evidence, then better-informed approximations of settlement placement can be obtained (especially residential settlements). In a sense, incorporation of detailed paleogeographic and ecological data can provide a firm and relatively accurate foundation upon which to model the more nuanced, nonlinear behavioral processes of hunter-gatherers.

Third, while iterative simulation modeling is not easy to implement into GMAD programs, there are new GIS techniques and add-on software programs that can be incorporated to add dynamism to such modeling. In the two-tiered architecture of HGLUM, the paleoecological base was generated from empirical data using ESRI Arc-GIS software. The result of this modeling produced raster-based land-cover maps for specified time slices (from 11,000 to 6000 years BP), which were then exported to the open-source environmental modeling software package known as PCRaster (http://pcraster.geo.uu.nl). The PCRaster platform can facilitate GIS-produced maps and has the ability to allow multiple iterations of socionatural algorithms on static landscapes. In addition, landscape evolution itself can be modeled with this software.

4.4 Assessing the Utility of Sensitivity Analysis for GMAD

To approximate the utility of SA for GMAD, statistical procedures derived from corollary SA methodology described in the earth sciences (Lenhart et al. 2002; van Griensven et al. 2006) and behavioral ecology (Happe et al. 2006; Vonk Noordegraaf et al. 2003) were applied to HGLUM. For further background on SA and a description of types, see Sect. 1.4 in Chap. 1.

4.4.1 Applying SA to GMAD

4.4.1.1 Methodology

To identify where uncertainty and error were introduced to HGLUM, SA was applied to (a) the weighting of parameter values and (b) the running of a composite parameter formula. To determine the overall impact of input factors, model outputs were compared both qualitatively and quantitatively.

HGLUM consists of a cascading set of factors or parameters considered important to hunter-gatherers when making decisions about land use (Fig. 4.1; for further details on the model, please see Brouwer 2011, pp. 212–268). The first phase of the modeling uses food resource distribution surfaces as input and evaluates which parts of the landscape would be viable for specific resource extraction activities based on the type of subsistence/settlement strategy being practiced. The second phase of the modeling employs some of the spatial surfaces generated in phase one, as well as additional surfaces related more directly to nonfood resource landscape criteria (e.g., proximity to land resources, shelter, view, ground dryness).

For the purpose of this SA, four parameter orders are present, reflecting the cascading nature of the multi-criteria decision model (Fig. 4.2). First order parameters include the most basic model inputs affecting resource acquisition (e.g., suitability distributions of fauna, themselves based on the parameters of food distribution and cover/shelter). Second order parameters are those that draw upon first order parameters and partially underpin fourth order parameters (i.e., decision-making criteria for resource acquisition choices), along with third order parameters that are based more concretely on the presence/absence of landscape features. Fourth order parameters comprise decision-making criteria for settlement choices given a selected strategy for resource acquisition and mobility.

To evaluate overall confidence in the decision model, areas of uncertainty, error propagation, and sensitivity are investigated using a corner-test SA and DOEs, a SA technique used to explore model robusticity as well as the range of variation parameters have on outputs. To demonstrate the process involved, the corner-test SA is first described for first order faunal parameters (i.e., red deer, wild boar, beaver, and small terrestrial animals) analyzed using the design rubric of residentially oriented foragers who want to maximize resources (Fig. 4.2). Then, the DOE is applied and results are discussed. For this demonstration one 25 × 25 km area in the central river

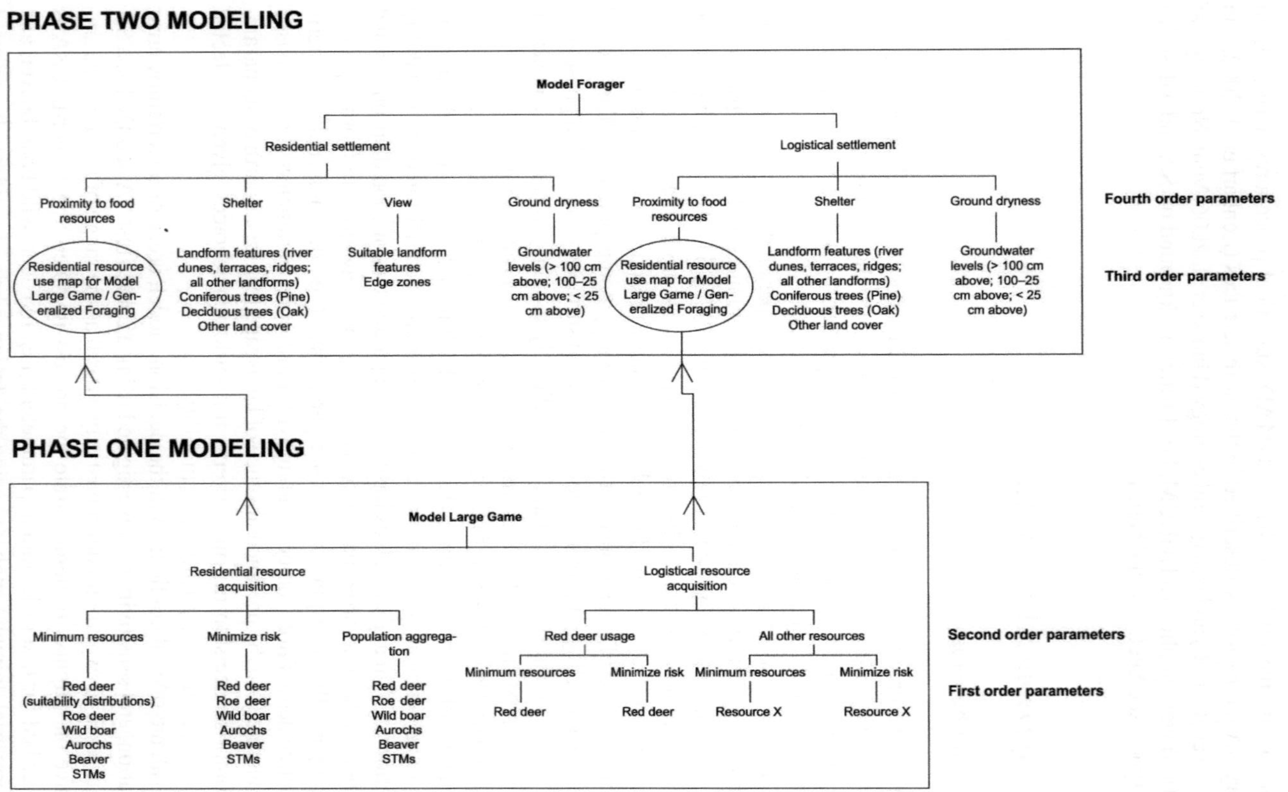

Fig. 4.2 Schematic representation of parameter orders in the decision-making model for a foraging strategy. *NB:* This represents only one modeled scheme for foragers

valley of the Netherlands is focused on, with SA and DOE applied to output displays for early and late time periods (11,000–10,000 and 7000–6500 years BP). The impact of parameter value variation is evaluated quantitatively through basic exploratory data analysis (EDA) and simple statistical measures (*t*-tests and linear regression analysis), as well as qualitatively through visual comparison of output spatial displays. As will be argued below, both approaches to the data supply insightful information.

4.4.1.2 Corner-Test SA

This phase of model verification and testing departs from "initial" parameter rankings that represent emically informed weighting of faunal resources derived from ethnographic data on boreal/temperate forest hunter-gatherer decision-making (see Brouwer 2011, pp. 212–268), with a specific focus on residential resource provisioning carried out with the objective of obtaining a minimum number of resources (Table 4.1). Two executions of the corner-test SA are run on paleo-landscape surfaces from the beginning and end of the Mesolithic period (e.g., 11,000–10,000 and 7000–6000 years BP) and are referred to as Series 1 and Series 2.

An extreme multiway or corner-test SA is next applied to the ensemble of faunal parameters for this decision, in which each faunal parameter is set to the highest weight in the pairwise comparison matrix (9) and all other parameters are set to the lowest weight (1/9). Table 4.2 illustrates a single iteration of the corner-test applied to red deer, where red deer is set as very strongly more important than all other parameters (principle eigenvector value: PEV = 0.64). This same scenario was executed for all other species, in which each succeeding species was set as strongly more important than the rest.

When qualitatively compared, this corner-test procedure demonstrates that changes in the weight of the resource parameter beaver have greatest impact on the suitability of the landscape for the decision of attaining minimum resources (Fig. 4.3). The beaver parameter is marked as highly sensitive, acting to skew the rest of the landscape to appear much less suitable for the outset decision criteria and therefore, extra precaution must be taken when factoring how much weight to

Table 4.2 Parameter rankings for attainment of minimum resources with a residential resource use strategy

Series 1	Red deer	Wild boar	Aurochs	Beaver	STMs	PEV
Red deer	1	9	9	9	9	0.64
Roe deer	1/9	1	1	1	1	0.07
Wild boar	1/9	1	1	1	1	0.07
Aurochs	1/9	1	1	1	1	0.07
Beaver	1/9	1	1	1	1	0.07
STMs	1/9	1	1	1	1	0.07

*STM = small terrestrial mammal

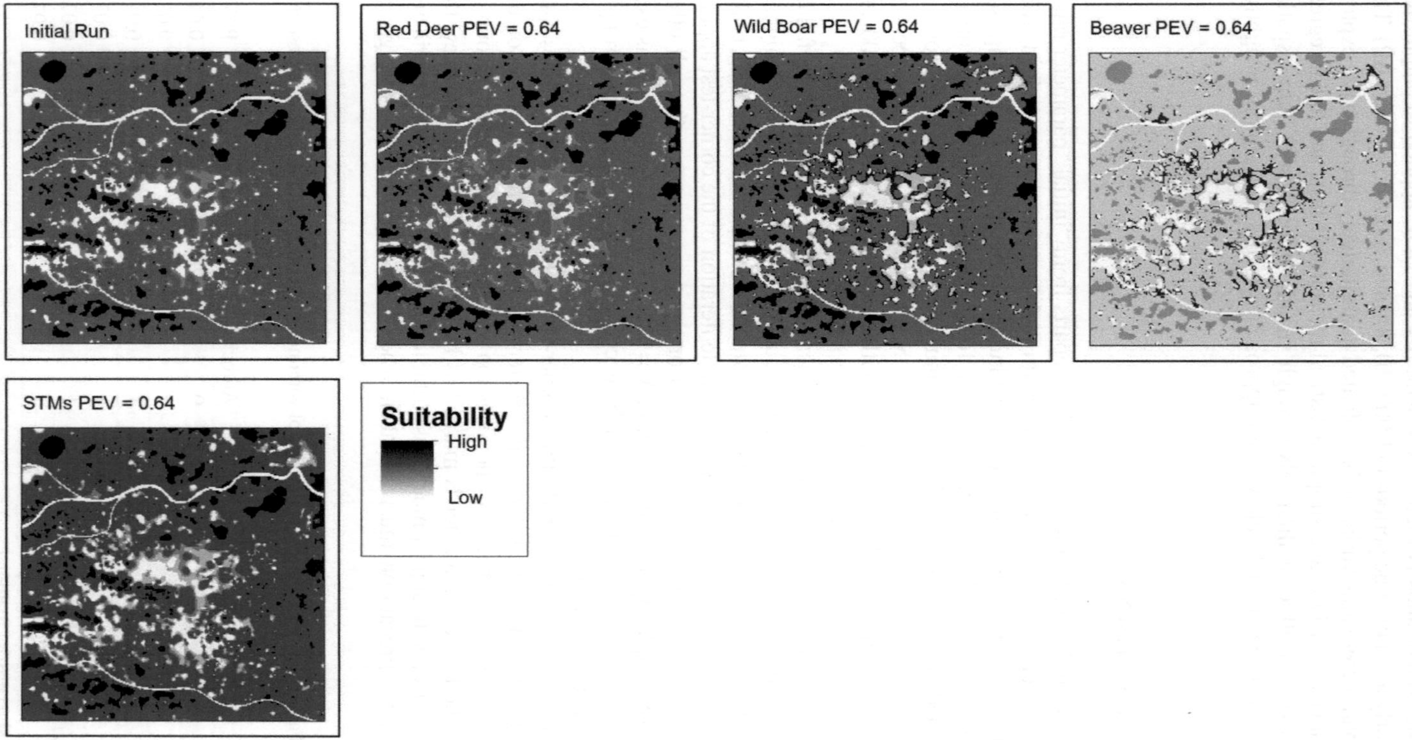

Fig. 4.3 Results of Series 1, with each species set as most important (Polderweg area 11,000–10,000 years BP). *NB:* Faunal categories "roe deer" and "aurochs" not shown because their surfaces were indistinguishable from red deer. Initial run values: red deer = 0.47, roe deer = 0.47, wild boar = 0.20, aurochs = 0.12, beaver = 0.06, small terrestrial mammals (STMs) = 0.03

Table 4.3 Means analysis of Series 1

Series 1: Polderweg 11–10,000 years BP	Mean suitability value	*N*	Standard deviation	Variance	Skewness
Initial Run	46.28	62,500	18.74	351.11	0.26
Red Deer	46.29	62,500	18.61	346.16	0.18
Roe Deer	46.29	62,500	18.61	346.16	0.18
Wild Boar	47.24	62,500	21.28	452.94	0.01
Aurochs	46.29	62,500	18.61	346.16	0.18
Beaver	22.90	62,500	15.04	226.20	2.98
STMs	55.38	62,500	21.58	465.59	−1.13

accord this parameter. The sensitivity of the beaver parameter is likely due to its specific habitat preferences, which are more constrained than the other faunal habitats. It is assumed that Mesolithic hunter-gatherers did not schedule their seasonal rounds around the presence/absence of beaver alone, although the presence of beaver may have negatively impacted resource extraction decisions for hunter-gatherers geared toward large game, as beaver dam building can break up the landscape and create obstacles for tracking prey. However, it is also known that for hunter-gatherers following a general foraging strategy within a catchment area, the rich aquatic and wetland habitat created by beavers and their dams would most likely be viewed as a beneficial quality.

Summary mean statistics can be compared to quantitatively investigate the impact of differential resource weighting. Table 4.3 shows that, for the given study area and time period, the parameters beaver and STMs return model output that is most different from the model output generated by varying the other parameters.

One important outcome of this phase of the SA involves the removal of unnecessary parameters. As seen in Table 4.3, red deer, roe deer, and aurochs all yield the same mean suitability values, standard deviation, variance, and skewness, likely due to their assumed identical habitat requirements. Thus, roe deer and aurochs can be collapsed into the red deer parameter in order to improve modeling efficiency and decrease the risk of error introduced through over-parameterization.

4.4.1.3 DOE

Another verification technique can be applied in which first order parameters are varied systematically according to a DOE framework (using the open-source statistical discovery software JMP; available at http://www.jmp.com), such that more sophisticated statistical analyses can be applied to the resulting data set. For this stage of the analysis, 16 model runs[2] are executed in which each faunal parameter is assigned a suitability value between 0 and 3 (Table 4.4). Each run of the DOE is

[2] This number was chosen because it represents the least number of combinations that are still mathematically distinct for parameters scaled between four suitability values, 0–3.

Table 4.4 DOE for Polderweg faunal suitability from 11,000 to 10,000 years BP (Series 1)

Series 1	Red deer (RD)	Wild boar (WB)	Beaver (BV)	Small terrestrial mammals (STMs)	Average suitability values
1	1	0	0	1	50.33
2	1	1	2	0	28.69
3	2	0	3	0	26.26
4	2	1	1	1	44.92
5	0	1	0	2	53.50
6	3	3	0	0	47.65
7	1	2	3	2	30.60
8	1	3	1	3	52.53
9	0	2	1	0	40.67
10	3	1	3	3	40.26
11	2	2	0	3	54.52
12	3	2	2	1	41.82
13	3	0	1	2	47.74
14	0	0	2	3	45.72
15	0	3	3	1	33.64
16	2	3	2	2	45.47

	Less important					More important		
1/9	1/7	1/5	1/3	1	3	5	7	9
Extremely	--	Strongly	--	Equally	--	Moderately	--	Very strongly

Fig. 4.4 Nine-point ranking scale (adapted from Krist, 2001, p. 148 and Eastman, 1999)

translated into a pairwise comparison matrix to derive PEVs that sum to one for each run. This weighting strategy follows that outlined by Eastman (1999) and entails a nine-point ordinal scale for ranking parameters in order of importance (Fig. 4.4; see Brouwer 2011, pp. 204–211; Eastman 1999 for a full description of this weighting procedure).

A *t*-test is used to determine which parameters have the greatest overall impact on the model output. Both beaver and small terrestrial mammals (STMs) returned statistically significant *p* values (<0.05; Table 4.5).

The JMP prediction profiler (a useful visual tool that can reveal parameter interactions) is employed to determine which combinations of parameters and weights will yield the most suitable conditions (in this case, for obtaining minimum resources while following a large-game foraging strategy). When desirability is set to maximum (0.995), the tool indicates that heavily weighting red deer, wild boar, and STMs, while lightly weighting beaver, will yield the outputs with the highest suitability (Fig. 4.5). The figure also indicates how individual parameters impact overall suitability outputs. For example, as beaver suitability increases, the desirability of the overall output

Table 4.5 Parameter significance for faunal suitabilities from 11,000 to 10,000 years BP BP

Term	Estimate	Standard error	*t* ratio	Prob>|*t*|
Intercept	44.465135	2.038133	21.82	<0.0001*
RD	0.5199283	0.636606	0.82	0.4314
WB	0.6990823	0.636606	1.10	0.2956
BV	−6.246922	0.636606	−9.81	**<0.0001***
STMs	3.8977846	0.636606	6.12	**<0.0001***

(Bold values denote statistically significant p values).

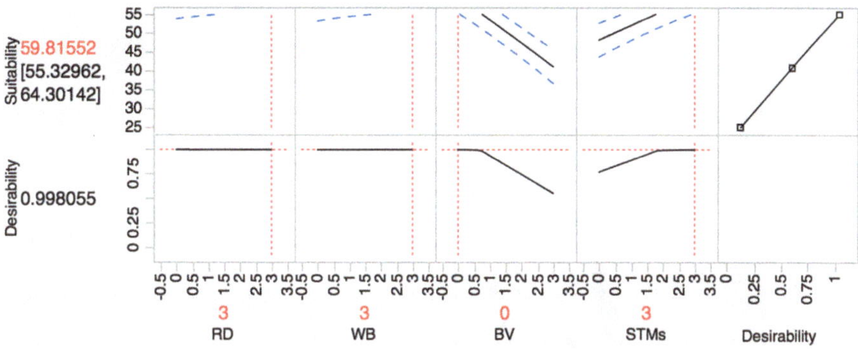

Fig. 4.5 Prediction profiler for faunal suitabilities from 11,000 to 10,000 years BP

decreases and thus, the heavier beaver is weighted, the greater the negative affect it will have on output. Conversely, as STM suitability increases, the desirability of the overall output increases. Red deer and wild boar have negligible impact on output, likely indicating that the habitat requirements of these species are met widely throughout the area, while STMs and beaver have more restricted habitats.

When considered more broadly, this finding makes sense as the landscape during the stipulated time period (11–10,000 years BP) was dry and understandably unfavorable to beaver. What happens if the same input parameter changes are run on a landscape more favorable to beaver and less favorable to red deer, wild boar, and STMs (e.g., peaty wetlands and tidal influenced channels from ca. 6500 to 6000 years BP—Series 2)? Fig. 4.6 and Table 4.6 indicate that the situation stays the same: the parameter beaver remains the most important in terms of affecting model output, despite the change in landforms and vegetation.

The same DOE framework described above is applied to Series 2 of the model (Table 4.7). The results indicate that the same pattern seen in the qualitative output obtains.

Oftentimes in geospatial modeling, an index of parameter sensitivity (*I*) is calculated by approximating "the ratio between the relative change of model output and the relative change of a parameter" (Lenhart et al. 2002, p. 646). Transcribed for this archaeological example, a sensitivity index can be derived by taking the difference of each priority run (e.g., red deer most important, all other parameters least important) from the initial run. For clarity, sensitivity classes can be applied (Tables 4.8 and 4.9).

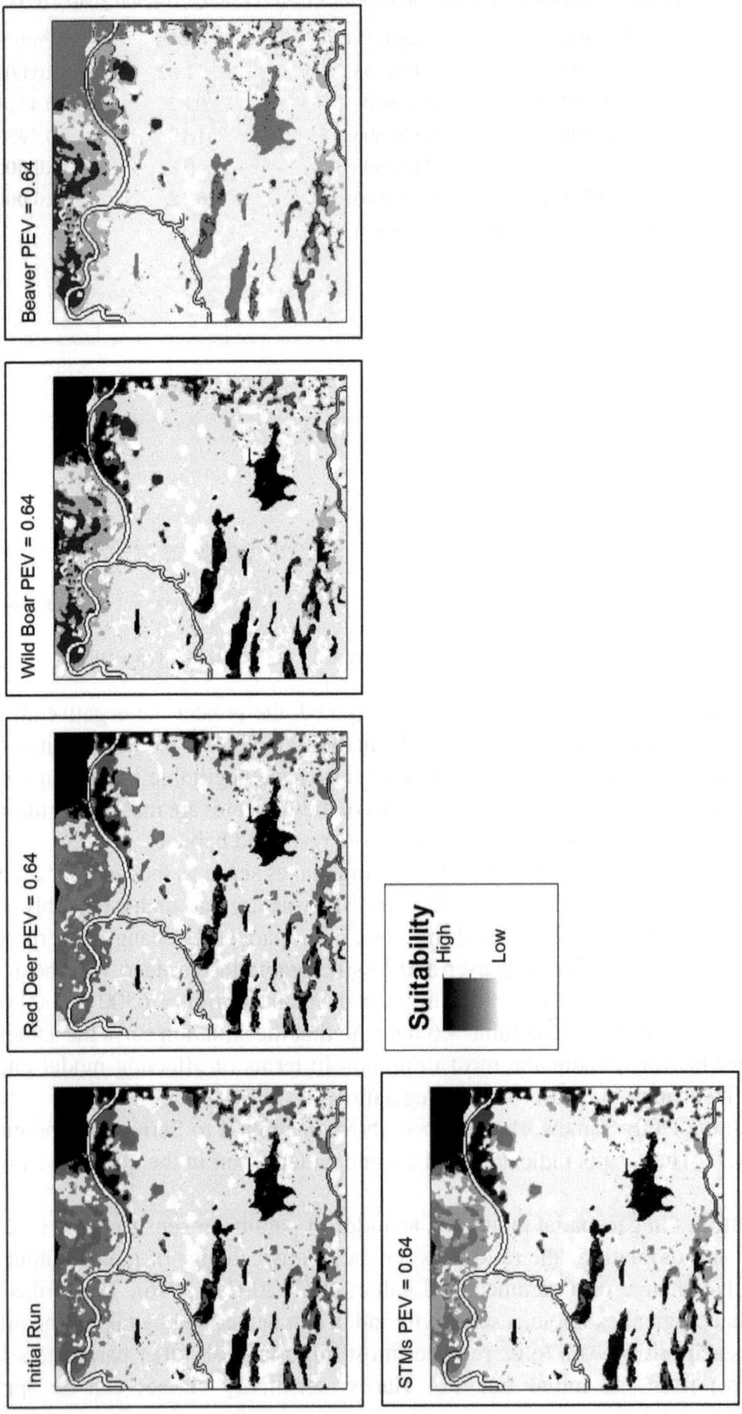

Fig. 4.6 Results of Series 2, with each parameter set in turn as most important (Polderweg area 7000–6000 years BP)

Table 4.6 Means analysis of Series 2

Series 2: Polderweg 7000–6000 years BP	Mean	N	Standard deviation	Variance	Skewness
Initial	22.32	62,500	31.57	996.8	1.48
Red deer	24.13	62,500	34.27	1174.10	1.50
Wild boar	24.29	62,500	36.25	1314.10	1.45
Beaver	20.41	62,500	22.92	525.55	2.16
STMs	21.92	62,500	34.62	1198.78	1.62
Total	22.61	312,500	32.31	1043.96	1.63

Table 4.7 DOE for Polderweg faunal suitability from 6500 to 6000 years BP (Series 2)

Series 2	Average suitability values	Run	Average suitability values	Run	Average suitability values
Initial	14.70	7	15.00	13	14.17
1	14.13	8	13.57	14	13.58
2	15.34	9	14.75	15	15.04
3	15.48	10	14.21	16	14.57
4	14.64	11	13.14		
5	13.27	12	14.79		
6	14.56				

Table 4.8 Sensitivity classes (adapted from Lenhart et al. 2002, p. 647)

Class	Index	Sensitivity
I	$0.00<\|I\|>0.05$	Negligible to small
II	$0.05<\|I\|>0.20$	Medium
III	$0.20<\|I\|>1.00$	High
IV	$\|I\|>1.00$	Very high

Table 4.9 First order parameter sensitivity classes

Parameter importance	Mean suitability value	Difference in means[a]	Sensitivity class
Initial run	46.28	–	–
Red deer	46.29	0.01	I
Wild boar	47.24	0.96	III
Beaver	22.90	23.4	**IV**
STMs	55.38	1.13	**IV**

[a]Taken by subtracting mean of priority runs for each parameter from the mean of the initial run (bold values denote high sensitivity).

Once again, the parameters beaver and STMs are revealed to be the most sensitive. It should also be noted that under this classification system, the parameter "wild boar" also has high sensitivity. For this reason, all three of these parameters should be accorded special attention during the weighting process.

These first order model iterations reveal that the parameter with the most restricted distribution (here beaver) will have the greatest impact on model output, that is, it is the most sensitive in the collection of first order parameters.

For this reason, researchers should take extra precautions when considering how much weight to assign this parameter, and the degree to which it would have affected past resource allocation choices.

The combined strategy of using corner-test SA and range of variation DOE for exploring parameter behavior was developed specifically for the HGLUM model but could be applied to any GMAD model. This approach represents a robust method for calibrating and verifying models that incorporate both natural and social data. The above results have hopefully made clear that SAs incorporated throughout the modeling process are incredibly important tools for highlighting the nuances of parameter behavior and model functionality. Additionally, SAs encourage investigation of outset modeling assumptions concerning parameter selection and weighting.

4.5 Discussion and Conclusion

The SA demonstration above reveals that uncertainty has been introduced in each stage of the multi-tier, multi-criteria decision model, and error is successively compounded during each modeling phase. Thus, if the research goal is to recreate reality by developing facsimiles of past socionatural systems, the GMAD model has failed. However, the intended research goal is focused instead upon understanding pushes and pulls of socionatural dynamics in the past through the stated use of iterative simulacra, and in this vein the model has succeeded. While in the geosciences, SA implementation focuses strictly on uncertainty quantification, the procedure has been used here to reveal parameter utility and impact. Thus, if the goal of GMAD is to learn about the archaeological record (and thus the human behavior recorded within it), then something of value has been learned: the intricacies of model assumptions, input parameters, and weighting decisions have been explored in greater detail, all of which are reflective of the array of different choices and choice-making patterns that were available to hunter-gatherers living in the postglacial Netherlands. In this sense, the heuristic aim of HGLUM has been satisfied.

The SA demonstration above also helps to answer some important meta-modeling questions for GMAD. First, although the SA described above does not have the capacity to systematically quantify the amount of error and uncertainty generated in the construction and execution of the model, this verification technique can determine where uncertainty is introduced and the relative influence of this uncertainty on model output. The modeler then must decide if the model output falls within a reasonable range of error and uncertainty and can be accepted as is, or if the output is significantly different from expected results and demands revisiting and reconfiguring model properties, boundary conditions, assumptions, and included parameters and their weights. This situation leads to a second concern regarding the biased and incomplete nature of the archaeological record, which will continue to hamper modeling output by preventing error or uncertainty-free reconstructions of past dynamics. In fact, such models will always contain some fuzzy assumptions about the real world in the past. Archaeological computational modelers must continue to acknowledge this fact as a prima facie assumption to the entire modeling endeavor. Rather than render all archaeological modeling moot, such acknowledgment and critical evaluation of outset assumptions can serve as a silver lining: by actively investigating the nature of uncertainty and error in archaeological computational models, the modeling community only stands to improve overall understandings of model functionality and in the long run, of socionatural dynamics in the past. SA has a unique role to play in this regard, as a key that can unlock the nuances of models by identifying the range of variation and sensitivity present.

A third question facing GMAD modelers specifically involves the use of qualitative versus quantitative verification procedures. GIS technologies readily produce spatially oriented graphical output in the form of maps, and it often appears easier to qualitatively evaluate model output via visual comparison. The question that arises is whether these qualitative comparisons reveal significant differences when analyzed quantitatively. As the DOE procedure described above illustrates, there is indeed agreement between qualitative and quantitative evaluations of model outputs. Nonetheless, this chapter also strives to underscore the importance of utilizing multiple types of verification techniques as a way of improving model robusticity and meta-level understandings of model intricacies. Thus, it is strongly advised that both qualitative and quantitative evaluations be carried out as part of this process.

In sum, while GMAD models are non-recursive in nature, they still stand to contribute much to explorations of past socionatural dynamics. A primary benefit of using such models involves the coupling of detailed geographic surfaces drawn from empirical, real-world data, with more fuzzy assumptions of human decision-making and behavioral processes drawn from ethnographic and ethnohistoric accounts. This GMAD coupling is often complicated as it draws upon disparate data sets, of varying quality and quantity. Additionally, the coupling of social and natural models demands different SAs for verification and validation. Here, both corner-test SAs and DOE analyses are carried out to underscore the importance of such verification procedures. It is recommended that other GMAD models as well as other spatially based models of human–landscape interactions (e.g., ABM) also be incorporated throughout the life cycle of a model, from development and execution to post hoc validation. This method represents a parsimonious way for archaeological computational modelers to systematically confront, cope, and compensate for error and uncertainty.

References

Barton, C. M., Ullah, I. I. T., Bergin, S. M., Mitasova, H., & Sarjoughian, H. (2012). Looking for the future in the past: Long-term change in socioecological systems. *Ecological Modelling, 214*, 42–53.

Binford, L. R. (1980). Willow smoke and dog's tails: Hunter-gatherer settlement systems and archaeological site formation. *American Antiquity, 45*, 4–20.

Brantingham, P. J. (2003). A neutral model of stone raw material procurement. *American Antiquity, 68*(3), 587–509.

Brouwer, M. E. (2011). *Modeling Mesolithic hunter-gatherer land use and post-glacial landscape dynamics in the Central Netherlands*. Ph.D. Thesis, Department of Anthropology, Michigan State University.

Brouwer Burg, M. E. (2013). Reconstructing "total" paleo-landscapes for archaeological investigation: An example from the central Netherlands. *Journal of Archaeological Science, 40*, 2308–2320.

Buffon, G.-L. Leclerc, Comte de (1749–1804). *Histoire naturelle, générale et particulière*. Paris: l' Imprimerie Royale.

Camerer, C., & Weber, M. (1992). Recent development in modeling preferences: Uncertainty and ambiguity. *Journal of Risk and Uncertainty, 5*, 325–370.

Danielisová, A., & Pokorný, P. (2011). Pollen and archaeology in GIS. Theoretical considerations and modified approach testing. In P. Verhagen, A. G. Posluschny, & A. Danielisová (Eds.), *Go your own least cost path: Spatial technology and archaeological interpretation* (Proceedings of the GIS session at EAA 2009, Riva del Garda, September 2009. BAR International Series 2284. Riva del Garda, Italy). Oxford, UK: Archaeopress.

Doran, J. (2008). Review of "the model-based archaeology of socionatural systems". *Journal of Artificial Societies and Social Simulation, 11*, 1–4.

Eastman, J. R. (1999). *IDRISI 32: Guide to GIS and image processing* (Software manual, Vol. 2). Worcester, England: Clark Labs, Clark University.

Gilbert, N. (2008). *Agent based models*. Thousand Oaks, CA: Sage Research Methods.

Happe, K., Kellerman, K., & Balmann, A. (2006). Agent-based analysis of agricultural policies: An illustration of the agricultural policy simulator AgriPoliS, its adaptation, and behavior. *Ecology and Society, 11*(1), 49.

Jankowski, P., Andrienko, N., & Andrienko, G. (2001). Map-centered exploratory approach to multiple criteria spatial decision making. *International Journal of Geographical Information Science, 15*(2), 101–127.

Kelly, R. L. (1995). *The foraging spectrum: Diversity in hunter-gatherer lifeways*. Washington, DC: Smithsonian Institution Press.

Krist, F. J. J. (2001). *A predictive model of Paleo-Indian subsistence and settlement*. Ph.D. Thesis, Department of Anthropology, Michigan State University.

Lake, M. W. (2000). MAGICAL computer simulation of Mesolithic foraging. In T. A. Kohler & G. J. Gumerman (Eds.), *Dynamics in human and primate societies: Agent-based modelling of social and spatial processes* (pp. 107–143). New York: Oxford University Press.

Laughlin, W. S. (1980). *Aleuts: Survivors of the Bering Land Bridge*. New York: Holt, Rinehart and Winston.

Leclerc, G.-L. (1749–1804). *Histoire naturelle, générale et partiulière*. Paris: Imprimerie Royale.

Lenhart, T., Eckhart, K., Fohrer, N., & Frede, H.-G. (2002). Comparison of two different approaches of sensitivity analysis. *Physics and Chemistry of the Earth, 27*, 645–654.

Peeters, J. H. M. (2007). *Hoge Vaart-A27 in context: Towards a model of Mesolithic–Neolithic land use dynamics as a framework for archaeological heritage management*. Ph.D. Thesis, Department of Archaeology, University of Amsterdam, Amsterdam.

Premo, L. S. (2006). *Patchiness and prosociality modeling: The evolution and archaeology of plio-Pleistocene Hominin food sharing*. Ph.D. Thesis, University of Arizona, Tuscon, Arizona.

Rogers, E. (1967). Subsistence areas of the Cree-Ojibwa of the Eastern Subarctic: A preliminary study. *National Museum of Canada Bulletin, 204*, 59–90.

Rogers, E. (1969). Natural environment—Social organization—Witchcraft: Cree versus Ojibway—A test case. In D. Damas (Ed.), *Contributions to anthropology: Ecological essays* (National Museum of Canada Bulletin 230, pp. 24–39). Ottawa, ON: National Museum of Canada.

Rogers, J. D., Nichols, T., Emmerich, T., Latek, M., & Cioffi-Revilla, C. (2012). Modeling scale and variability in human–environmental interactions in Inner Asia. *Ecological Modelling, 241*, 5–14.

Saisana, M., Saltelli, S., & Tarantola, S. (2005). Uncertainty and sensitivity analysis techniques as tools for the quality assessment of composite indicators. *Journal of Royal Statistical Society, Series A, 168*(2), 307–323.

Savage, L. J. (1954). *The foundations of statistics*. New York: Wiley.
van den Biggelaar, D., Kluiving, S., Kasse, K., & Kolen, J. (2014). Why would we need archaeological remains? Modelling Late Glacial land use without archaeological traces, a case study from Flevoland (central Netherlands). Poster presented at the 3rd International Landscape Conference, Rome, Italy. 17th–20th September, 2014.
van Griensven, A., Meixner, T., Grunwald, S., Bishop, T., Diluzio, M., & Srinivasan, R. (2006). A global sensitivity analysis tool for the parameters of multi-variable catchment models. *Journal of Hydrology, 324*, 10–23.
von Neumann, J., & Morgenstern, O. (1947). *Theory of games and economic behavior* (2nd ed.). Princeton, NJ: Princeton University Press.
Vonk Noordegraaf, A., Nielen, M., & Kleijnen, J. P. C. (2003). Sensitivity analysis by experimental design. *European Journal of Operational Research, 146*, 433–443.
Whitley, T. G. (2000). *Dynamical systems modeling in archaeology: A GIS approach to site selection processes in the greater Yellowstone region*. Ph.D. Thesis, Department of Anthropology, University of Pittsburg, Pittsburg.
Whitley, T. G. (2005). A brief outline of causality-based cognitive archaeological probabilistic modeling. In M. van Leusen & H. Kamermans (Eds.), *predictive modeling for archaeological heritage management: A research agenda*, Vol. 29 (pp. 123-138). Rijksdienst voor het Oudheidkundig Bodemonderzoek (ROB), Amersfoort.
Whitley, T. G., Moore, G., Goel, G., & Jackson, D. (2009). Beyond the marsh: Settlement choice, perception and spatial decision-making on the Georgia coastal plain. In B. Frischer, J. Crawford, & D. Kollers (Eds.), *Making history interactive: Proceedings of the 37th computer applications and quantitative methods in archaeology (CAA) Conference, Williamsburg, VA* (pp. 380–390). Oxford, UK: Archaeopress.
Wobst, H. M. (1974). Boundary conditions for Paleolithic social systems: A simulation approach. *American Antiquity, 39*(2), 147–178.

Chapter 5
Assessing Nonlinear Behaviors in an Agent-Based Model

Jon W. Carroll

5.1 Introduction

This chapter discusses the role of sensitivity analysis in the development of an Agent-Based Model (ABM) created to explore cultural transmission processes in small-scale social networks during the Springwells phase (ca. A.D. 1160–1420) of the Late Prehistoric period in the Great Lakes region of North America. ABM is a computational method that allows us to simulate how the interactions of individual components within a system produce emergent phenomena that eventually become hallmark characteristics of a system (Epstein 2006; Gilbert and Troitzsch 2005; Gilbert 2008; Kohler and Gumerman 2000; Kohler and van der Leeuw 2007; Railsback and Grimm 2012; Wurzer et al. 2015). ABM is noted for its ability to employ "anthropologically plausible" (Dean et al. 1999, p. 180) rules that set the conditions for how agents might interact. Moreover, simulation as a method "can be seen as a species of model capable of investigating complex, multifaceted systems, and most importantly, as a means of constructing experimental scenarios that could never normally be observed" (McGlade 2005, p. 558).

With ABM, "Agents" are a specific component of the computer program used to embody social actors (Gilbert 2008, p. 5), and they may collect information about their environment while making decisions about behaviors to engage in as dictated by specific model programming rules (Kohler 2000). One of the main benefits of ABM is that researchers can observe dynamic relationships manifesting between agents at multiple social and spatial (sociospatial) scales (Kohler 2000). Assuming proper model conceptualization and implementation, interaction between individual agents produces emergent phenomena that scale-up to the system

J.W. Carroll (✉)
Department of Sociology, Anthropology, Social Work and Criminal Justice, Oakland University, Rochester, MI, USA
e-mail: jwcarroll@oakland.edu

M. Brouwer Burg et al. (eds.), *Uncertainty and Sensitivity Analysis in Archaeological Computational Modeling*, Interdisciplinary Contributions to Archaeology, DOI 10.1007/978-3-319-27833-9_5

(the largest, or global) level from behaviors of individual agents (Graham 2006). Just a few examples of how ABM modeling has augmented traditional archaeological interpretation include studies relating to Anasazi culture change in the Southwest (Dean et al. 1999), Roman social interaction in Europe (Graham 2006), and the distribution of Late Prehistoric ceramic styles in the Great Lakes region of North America (Carroll 2013).

A separate but related area of interest here is the study of cultural transmission (CT) (O'Brien 2008; O'Brien and Shennan 2010; Stark et al. 2008), where CT variation has been used to explain how changes in material culture are tied to the social context of interactions (Bentley and Shennan 2003; Carroll 2013; Eerkens and Lipo 2007; Premo and Scholnick 2011; White 2013). ABM and CT studies may be synergistically combined to simulate the differential flow of information among ethnographically derived scenarios relating to group interactions. Such models can generate expectations relating to changes in CT and material culture, which may be useful to archaeologists investigating cultural processes in the past.

5.1.1 Model Overview

This investigation uses the open source ABM package NetLogo 4.1.2 (Wilensky 1999) to explore changes in CT relative to changes in sociospatial interaction patterns. NetLogo is specifically designed to model complex systems and their emergent properties. Complex systems are self-organized, path dependent, and historically contingent systems that exhibit emergent properties as agents within the system interact (Crawford et al. 2005; Messina 2001; O'Sullivan et al. 2006). Identifying the individual parts within a system is essential for establishing model components, but the emergent properties of that system may only be observed through *interactions* of those components (Holland 1998).

The terms "complexity" and "complex systems" refer here to a particular scientific framework and not to social complexity in the traditional anthropological sense. Complexity does not inherently refer to degrees of integration or social organization (e.g., band, tribe, chiefdom, state) but instead refers to an alternate way to think about science in that it does not follow a reductive model (Wolfram 2002). A complex systems framework works well computationally because it allows the researcher to pose questions that can only be explored through simulation.

The *Intercommunity Cultural Transmission Model (ICTM)* (Carroll 2013) discussed here simulates the exchange of packets of information between communities interacting within a small-scale social network that lacks communication pathways in any form other than person-to-person interaction (White 2013). The primary goal is to explore interactional scenarios that should result in differential rates of CT between communities. The ICTM simulates randomized, nearest neighbor, and aggregated CT scenarios thus elucidating how packets of information propagate through social networks operating under different sociospatial conditions. In other words, the purpose of the ICTM is to identify how ideas spread through societies differently depending on the social context.

Persons, communities, and aggregation points are the three basic entities that exist within the model or *world*. The spatial location for each community is randomly assigned. Each community then spawns a resident population of people using a random normal distribution averaging five persons per community with a standard deviation of three. This figure may seem low; however, everyone is potentially eligible for exchange depending on the value of a person's randomly assigned potential. In an abstract model such as the ICTM, persons spawned might represent a single gender in a community, which places community population in line with many estimates of small-scale society demographics. Every person has a randomly assigned influence value that represents both the ability to influence others and an individual's susceptibility to outside influence (Mahajan and Peterson 1985; Rogers 2003).

Once a visitor from an outside community arrives at a new location, the opportunity for cultural transmission begins. Residents of the target community interact with the new arrivals and assess newcomer levels of influence in relation to themselves. If a new arrival interacts with a local person who has a lower influence threshold, then the local person adopts the nonlocal cultural packet. This process repeats until all agents at the target location have interacted with the newcomers. The number of agents adopting new packets of information are summed and scored after each iteration.

It is important to emphasize that the intentionally abstract design of the model does not reflect real-world space or time. While it is possible to integrate geospatial data into NetLogo, this simulation does not attempt to recreate actual geographic space using topologically accurate spatial data. The geography influencing the agents occurs in default NetLogo model space. Model time is measured through increments referred to as "ticks" and governed by interactions between agents, not as calculations representing weeks, months, or years. The clock advances one tick when all persons exchanged have an opportunity to influence all susceptible persons at all destinations in the world.

Gilbert and Troitzsch (2005) note that research design and degrees of model abstraction greatly affect programming and what questions a model can explore. The fewer variables a model contains, the more abstract the model. Every time a variable is added to a model, there is the potential for complicating the assessment of relationships between input parameters and output data. The ICTM is constructed with a design that broadly applies to research questions relating to CT while simultaneously minimizing operational assumptions (Gilbert and Troitzsch 2005, p. 19). The formal ICTM assessment processes include verification, sensitivity analysis (DeVisser 2010; Santner et al. 2003), and validation and are described below.

5.2 Model Assessment: Verification, Sensitivity, and Validation

5.2.1 Code Verification

The first step in the development process was code verification. Verification is an assessment process where a simulation is evaluated to ensure that functions are working as designed (Gilbert and Troitzsch 2005, p. 19; Oreskes et al. 1994).

This can be a time-consuming process because each procedure in the programming code has to be inspected and its product observed. Many programmers regardless of the software platform refer to this process as "debugging." The verification phase for the ICTM is represented by the creation, verification, and subsequent replacement of 39 versions of code before arriving at the version used for the experiments discussed below. Early versions of the ICTM code contained simple flaws like improper syntax resulting in the simulation freezing at different points during the first trial runs. Adjustments were made to the code as programming flaws were observed. Later versions of the code included refining the model's initial setup conditions to reflect population sizes that align with demographic expectations associated with small-scale societies. Once these modifications were made then verification focused on how agents responded as parametric adjustments were introduced.

5.2.2 Sensitivity Analysis

Sensitivity analysis is the process of evaluating "the extent to which the behavior of the simulation is sensitive to the assumptions which have been made" (Gilbert and Troitzsch 2005, p. 24). During this process, a modeler is concerned with assessing the degree to which inputs in the model affect outputs. Sensitivity analysis is crucial to understanding whether or not the operating assumptions of the model are reasonable by revealing potential discrepancies in variable relationships (DeVisser 2010; Railsback and Grimm 2012, pp. 291–297). Arguably, sensitivity analysis is underutilized as a standard practice in computational archaeological modeling when compared to its systematic application across other disciplines.

One way to explore a model's sensitivity is to systematically vary parameters by a specified amount and then observe variations in output. Disproportionate or nonlinear relationships between these variables may indicate underlying problems within the model. However, the researcher must also keep in mind that nonlinear sensitivity may also indicate an unforeseen legitimate interaction between input and output values. Sensitivity analysis for the ICTM assessed the effect of varying exchange percentages on the total number of persons influenced through CT during a model run. A sensitivity index (SI) was constructed and applied to ICTM assessment as outlined by Lenhart et al. (2002).

$$\frac{\Delta Y_{\pm i} / Y_D}{2\Delta P_{D\&\#x0026;i} / P_D} \tag{5.1}$$

The SI above is calculated where *Y* represents the dependent variable output, *P* represents the threshold of the parameter of interest, *i* represents the value of the parameter as it is adjusted above and below the default model, and *D* represents the baseline model value (DeVisser 2010, p. 3; Lenhart et al. 2002, pp. 646–647). Table 5.1 outlines the classes of sensitivity used to interpret sensitivity analysis results.

Table 5.1 Categorical classifications for sensitivity (DeVisser 2010; Lenhart et al. 2002)

Sensitivity index	Class	Sensitivity
<0.05	I	Insensitive
0.05 to <0.20	II	Moderate
0.20 to <1.00	III	Highly
≥1.00	IV	Extremely

A baseline for these experiments consisted of 50 communities with a 50 % exchange rate for varying interactional scenarios discussed below. Exchange percentages varied at intervals ranging between 5 and 100 % to test the sensitivity specifically associated with exchange parameter changes. Each interval was run 100 times and then the mean for persons influenced through cultural transmission was calculated. The *mean for all persons influenced* was selected as an appropriate measure for model sensitivity both within and across exchange scenarios because of the stochasticity built into NetLogo, which uses a random number generator to provide randomization based on the system clock. Every run of the model will differ slightly from other iterations. However, even in spite of the embedded randomization of the ABM, patterns will emerge after a model runs hundreds or thousands of times, and this allows us to arrive at probabilistic generalizations regarding model parameters, behaviors, and output.

The SI results indicate moderate or high sensitivity (Table 5.2) to adjustments in the exchange parameter when the destination for travelers is randomized. This sensitivity manifests in a *nonlinear* pattern as indicated in Fig. 5.1. The *random destination* CT (influence) fall-off rate is not as rapid as in the *nearest neighbor* scenario discussed below, but there is still a nonlinear transmission signature associated with this form of sociospatial interaction.

Adjustments in exchange percentages in *nearest neighbor* scenarios result initially in highly sensitive (Table 5.2) *nonlinear* (Fig. 5.1) outcomes at low exchange rates, but trend toward moderate sensitivity, and ultimately become insensitive at higher exchange rates. This is attributed to the distributed nature of the social network, where opportunities for individuals to interact with others holding lower influence thresholds are limited because of small-scale interactions manifesting at a local level. Such a scenario effectively acts as a "bottleneck" for influence threshold diversity, thus limiting influence propagation within the network to a localized spatial scale between participants. All influential interactions take place very early in nearest neighbor exchange scenarios and then CT levels-off very quickly.

Sensitivity for exchanges with *one aggregation point* as a destination was classified as high (Table 5.2) regardless of the amount of variation implemented in the exchange parameter, but sensitivity manifests in a more *linear* manner (Fig. 5.1). As more people aggregate, each interpersonal interaction builds upon another and leads toward cultural transmission and propagation through the entire social network. Potential influencers arrive earlier or later depending on the distance required to travel from their home communities (thus resulting in a linear transmission pattern), but any change in exchange rates is highly sensitive because all influencers are aggregating at a central point where everyone has an opportunity to interact with everyone else.

Table 5.2 Sensitivity analysis for changes in CT relative to exchange percentages

Exchange scenario	Exchange percentage	Sensitivity index
Random destination	5	0.433
	10	0.317
	20	0.251
	30	0.257
	40	0.257
	50	0.000
	60	0.441
	70	0.211
	80	0.227
	90	0.216
	100	0.162
Nearest neighbor	5	0.396
	10	0.250
	20	0.271
	30	0.188
	40	0.188
	50	0.000
	60	0.094
	70	0.031
	80	0.063
	90	0.055
	100	0.019
One aggregation point	5	0.494
	10	0.464
	20	0.451
	30	0.287
	40	0.344
	50	0.000
	60	0.619
	70	0.550
	80	0.627
	90	0.682
	100	0.555

5.2.3 Validation

Validation consists of evaluating that the components within the model operate in a way that approximates a realistic target behavior (Gilbert and Troitzsch 2005, p. 19; Oreskes et al. 1994). It is out of necessity that this simulation is designed with a high

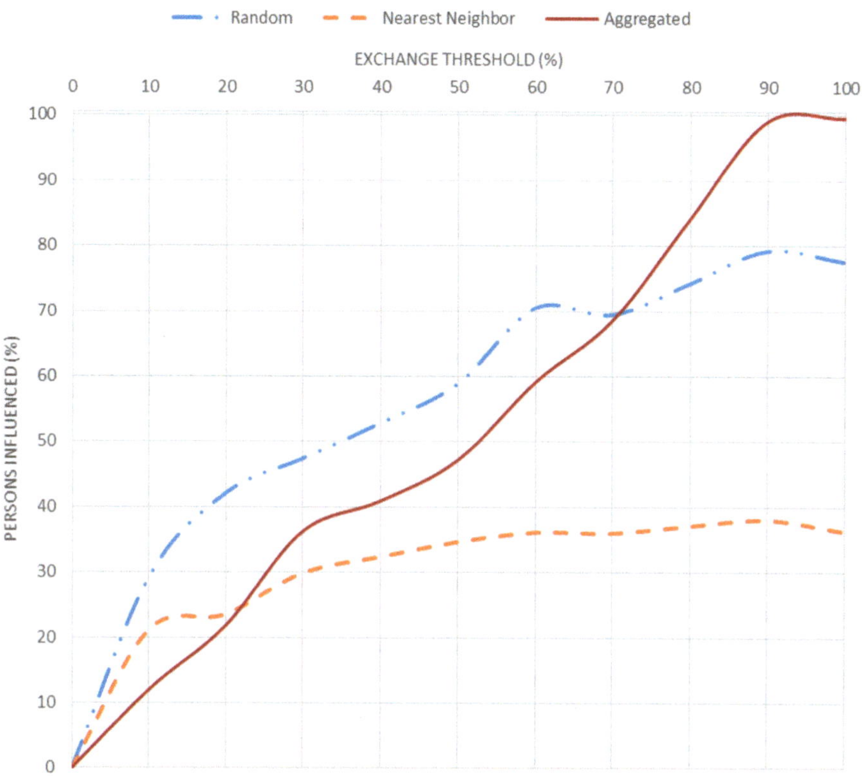

Fig. 5.1 Relative percentages of persons influenced by differing CT exchange scenarios

level of abstraction because as Oreskes et al. (1994) note, validation is difficult if not impossible to achieve in open systems (such as social networks) because not every contingency can be accounted for. Many archaeologists recognize that uncertainty is pervasive in archaeology. It permeates all aspects of what we do from the field to the lab. It is argued here that this is precisely why archaeological modelers should lean toward the abstract in model design. It is a best practice when modeling human behaviors riddled with so many unknowns (see Premo 2010 for more regarding levels of abstraction and ABM model design).

It is with these caveats in mind that CT rates produced by the ICTM serve to validate the model because its output data conform to established theory as presented by the diffusion of innovations literature (Mahajan and Peterson 1985; Rogers 2003). This research predicts accelerated diffusion patterns will generate *nonlinear* CT rates, and that standard diffusion patterns will generate *linear* CT rates. The relationship of these adoption patterns to model behaviors, model space, and ultimately their relevance to archaeological modeling, is discussed below.

5.3 Interpretations

The ICTM model assessment indicates that different interactional scenarios result in different rates of CT at different sociospatial scales within the ABM. These variances in CT are dependent on the social context of how people propagate packets of information through social networks. ICTM model outputs produce adoption curves that fit with general expectations relating to the spatial proximity of participants exchanging ideas in a network. That is, the closer participants are to each other, the faster ideas will spread between communities.

The *nearest neighbor* exchange scenario is analogous to what archaeologists might characterize as localized communication between neighboring communities. Nonlinear adoption curves are produced under these conditions. The model illustrates that opportunities for CT to occur are far more limited in this exchange scenario with influence propagating and diminishing quickly. Regional interaction among communities is modeled through the *random destination* exchange scenario. Nonlinear adoption curves are also produced under these conditions. The model demonstrates that under these conditions there is a greater potential for influence to travel through the network resulting in a higher (but not highest) percentage of persons influenced by others. A *one aggregation point* exchange scenario where all members interact and exchange ideas at a specific point within the region is the scenario that results in the highest percentage of persons influenced overall, even if this is achieved at a relatively slower (linear) rate of transmission. This scenario is analogous to regional, corporate gatherings that might occur for a variety of purposes.

5.4 Conclusion

The role that sensitivity analysis played in the assessment of ABM design was crucial for understanding model behaviors. This phase of the ICTM assessment process allowed for a systematic exploration of variable parameters and their effects on model outputs. Sensitivity analysis also served as a bridge for model validation by relating model behaviors to expectations generated by the diffusion of innovations literature. The insights provided by the assessment process revealed that the "people" living in this digital world were indeed capable of engaging in multiscalar social interactions, just like those living in Springwells phase indigenous communities on the Midcontinent.

Computational methodologies provide rigorous approaches to exploring hypothetical scenarios in which people might interact. These capabilities are especially useful in the absence of robust archaeological datasets. The need for employing archaeological computer modeling became apparent during pilot research intended to readdress what was known about Springwells phase sociopolitical interaction and integration. Late Prehistoric Springwells archaeological sites are relatively rare and some have argued that this may be attributed to the wholesale destruction of the physical environments where these sites were located throughout the Great Lakes region

(Fitting and Zurel 1976). This combined with fragmentary survey and excavation data, and a lack of synthetic research, are just a few reasons why this period of North American prehistory remains enigmatic.

Computational simulation provides an additional line of evidence for interpreting small archaeological datasets like those associated with the Springwells phase. The ABM results presented here indicate that the single dominant factor determining the propagation of influence through a distributed social network is aggregation. These experiments indicate that both space and social contexts have pronounced effects on the rate at which CT propagates through small-scale social networks. This may seem intuitive, but in the age of Facebook and Twitter, it is easy to lose sight of what it once took for ideas to "trend" in small-scale, indigenous social networks, where participants relied primarily on direct social interaction to perpetuate information about themselves and the world around them.

Finally, sensitivity analysis included as part of the ICTM development process provided an enhanced understanding of model behaviors that might otherwise go unnoticed, and this has resulted in greater understanding of the explanatory capabilities of computational methods such as ABM. It is advocated here that sensitivity analysis should be a standard component of the archaeological computer modeling process. In doing so, researchers may find themselves appreciating important and unanticipated insights that systematic model assessment can reveal.

References

Bentley, R. A., & Shennan, S. J. (2003). Cultural transmission and stochastic network growth. *American Antiquity, 68*(3), 459–486.

Carroll, J. W. (2013). *Simulating Springwells: A complex systems approach toward understanding late prehistoric social interaction in the Great Lakes Region of North America*. Ph.D. dissertation, Department of Anthropology, Michigan State University. University Microfilms, Ann Arbor.

Crawford, T. W., Messina, J. P., Manson, S. M., & O'Sullivan, D. (2005). Complexity science, complex systems, and land-use research. *Environment and Planning B: Planning and Design, 32*, 792–798.

Dean, J. S., Gumerman, G. J., Epstein, J. M., Axtell, R. L., Swedlund, A. C., Parker, M. T., et al. (1999). Understanding Anasazi culture change through agent based modeling. In T. A. Kohler & G. J. Gumerman (Eds.), *Dynamics in human and primate societies: Agent-based modeling of social and spatial processes* (pp. 179–205). Oxford, England: Oxford University Press.

DeVisser, M. H. (2010). Identifying sensitivity thresholds in environmental models: When does a model become insensitive to change? In *Paper presented at the American Society for Photogrammetry and Remote Sensing 2010 Annual Conference, San Diego, CA*.

Eerkens, J. W., & Lipo, C. P. (2007). Cultural transmission theory and the archaeological record: Providing context to understanding variation and temporal changes in material culture. *Journal of Archaeological Research, 15*, 239–274.

Epstein, J. M. (2006). *Generative social science: Studies in agent-based computational modeling. Princeton studies in complexity*. Princeton, NJ: Princeton University Press.

Fitting, J. E., & Zurel, R. L. (1976). The Detroit and St. Clair River area. In D. S. Brose (Ed.), *The late prehistory of the Lake Erie drainage basin: A 1972 symposium revisited* (pp. 214–250). Cleveland, OH: The Cleveland Museum of Natural History.

Gilbert, N. (2008). *Agent-based models. Quantitative applications in the social sciences.* Los Angeles, CA: Sage.

Gilbert, G. N., & Troitzsch, K. G. (2005). *Simulation for the social scientist* (2nd ed.). Maidenhead, England: Open University Press.

Graham, S. (2006). Networks, agent-based models and the Antonine itineraries: Implications for Roman archaeology. *Journal of Mediterranean Archaeology, 19*(1), 45–64.

Holland, J. H. (1998). *Emergence: From chaos to order*. Reading, MA: Addison-Wesley.

Kohler, T. A. (2000). Putting the social sciences together again: An introduction to the volume. In T. A. Kohler & G. J. Gumerman (Eds.), *Dynamics in human and primate societies: Agent-based modeling of social and spatial processes* (pp. 1–18). Oxford, England: Oxford University Press.

Kohler, T. A., & Gumerman, G. J. (2000). *Dynamics in human and primate societies: Agent-based modeling of social and spatial processes*. Oxford, England: Oxford University Press.

Kohler, T. A., & van der Leeuw, S. E. (2007). *The model-based archaeology of socionatural systems* (1st ed.). Santa Fe, NM: School for Advanced Research Press.

Lenhart, T., Eckhardt, K., Fohrer, N., & Frede, H. (2002). Comparison of two different approaches of sensitivity analysis. *Physics and Chemistry of the Earth, 27*, 645–654.

Mahajan, V., & Peterson, R. A. (1985). *Models for innovation diffusion* (Sage University papers series quantitative applications in the social sciences). Beverly Hills, CA: Sage.

McGlade, J. (2005). Systems and simulacra: Modeling, simulation and archaeological interpretation. In H. D. G. Maschner & C. Chippindale (Eds.), *Handbook of archaeological methods* (pp. 554–602). Lanham, MD: AltaMira Press.

Messina, J. P. (2001). A complex systems approach to dynamic spatial simulation modeling: LandUse and LandCover change in the Ecuadorian Amazon. Ph.D. Dissertation, Department of Geography, The University of North Carolina at Chapel Hill. University Microfilms, Ann Arbor.

O'Brien, M. J. (Ed.). (2008). *Cultural transmission and archaeology: Issues and case studies*. Washington, DC: Society for American Archaeology.

O'Brien, M. J., & Shennan, S. (Eds.). (2010). *Innovation in cultural systems: Contributions from evolutionary anthropology*. Cambridge, MA: MIT Press.

Oreskes, N., Shrader-Frechette, K. and Belitz, K. (1994). Verification, validation, and confirmation of numerical models in the earth sciences. *Science 263(5147)*, 641–646.

O'Sullivan, D., Manson, S. M., Messina, J. P., and Crawford, T. W. (2006). Space, place, and complexity science. *Environment and Planning A, 38*, 611–617.

Premo, L. S. (2010). On the role of agent-based modeling in post-positivist archaeology. In A. Costopoulos & M. Lake (Eds.), *Simulating change: Archaeology into the 21st century* (pp. 28–37). Salt Lake City, UT: University of Utah Press.

Premo, L. S., & Scholnick, J. B. (2011). The spatial scale of social learning affects cultural diversity. *American Antiquity, 76*, 163–176.

Railsback, S. F., & Grimm, V. (2012). *Agent-based and individual-based modeling: A practical introduction*. Princeton, NJ: Princeton University Press.

Rogers, E. M. (2003). *Diffusion of innovations* (5th ed.). New York: Free Press.

Santner, T. J., Williams, B. J., & Notz, W. (2003). *The design and analysis of computer experiments* (Springer series in statistics). New York: Springer.

Stark, M. T., Bowser, B. J., & Horne, L. (Eds.). (2008). *Cultural transmission and material culture: Breaking down boundaries*. Tucson, AZ: University of Arizona Press.

White, A. (2013). An abstract model showing that the spatial structure of social networks affects the outcomes of cultural transmission processes. *Journal of Artificial Societies and Social Simulation, 16*(3).

Wilensky, U. (1999). *NetLogo. Center for connected learning and computer-based modeling*. Evanston, IL: Northwestern University.

Wolfram, S. (2002). *A new kind of science*. Champaign, IL: Wolram Media.

Wurzer, G., Kowarik, K., & Reschreiter, H. (2015). *Agent-based modeling and simulation in archaeology*. Cham, Switzerland: Springer International.

Chapter 6
Scale Dependency in Agent-Based Modeling: How Many Time Steps? How Many Simulations? How Many Agents?

Joshua Watts

6.1 Introduction

Depending on the degree of abstraction intended by the modeler, a valid agent-based model (ABM) should be structurally analogous to the real-world system of interest and should be able to generate patterns similar to the real system across multiple spatial and temporal scales. If the scale-sensitive parameters have been poorly calibrated or the researcher has informed the model with empirical data of questionable resolution or accuracy—common situations in computational archaeological ABM—even agents with phenomenal logic processes will not generate interesting or useful system-scale patterns.

The case argued in this chapter is that some effort should be made in archaeological ABM to pursue and formalize a process of exploring the sensitivity of models to scale dependency. While the approach advocated here is broadly consistent with other approaches to sensitivity analysis in ABM, I argue that model verification and validation tests should include scale-dependent structural features and parameters. While increasingly common in geography, particularly land-use modeling, such tests have not been widely adopted by archaeological ABM researchers (e.g. Evans and Kelley 2004; Goodchild 2001; Jantz and Goetz 2005; Kim 2013).

My research on the organization of the Hohokam economy, particularly focused on the trade networks that distributed pottery from specialist producers to far-flung consumers in prehistoric central Arizona, has relied heavily on ABM methods (Watts 2013; Watts and Ossa in press). The process of implementing and testing a set of simple models related to that research provides an example of the systematic approach to testing scale-dependent features of models advocated in this chapter. What follows is not a cautionary tale; instead the case study is intended to illustrate

J. Watts (✉)
Center for Social Dynamics and Complexity, Arizona State University, Tempe, AZ, USA
e-mail: jswatts@asu.edu

M. Brouwer Burg et al. (eds.), *Uncertainty and Sensitivity Analysis in Archaeological Computational Modeling*, Interdisciplinary Contributions to Archaeology, DOI 10.1007/978-3-319-27833-9_6

the potential of testing scale dependency to economize the process of validating and collecting data from large simulation models. Careful testing of scale-dependent features of my Hohokam trade models has contributed to new insights into the organization of a nascent market-based economy.

As hinted at above, these topics are discussed in the context of my background in computational modeling and simulation, which in recent years has focused on a pattern-oriented modeling approach (Grimm et al. 2005; Railsback and Grimm 2012). In that tradition, different models and model configurations are treated as hypotheses about the organization of a real-world system. Patterns in simulated data are then compared to those in empirical data at different scales to evaluate the fit of the data to the various hypotheses. Those models that cannot reproduce patterns like those observed in the real system are discarded. While concerns for sensitivity to scale in some model features and parameters should be widely relevant across most ABM traditions, the discussion below is oriented toward economizing the testing and data collection of semi-realistic simulation models in the context of an eventual comparison to empirical archaeological data.

6.2 General Strategy

During the development and testing of a model, researchers should frequently revisit the real-world system they are modeling and question what they hope to learn by collecting data from running their simulations. Assumptions about the resolution and scale of temporal, spatial, and agent population features of the model are fundamental structural features, whether explicitly specified or implicit (Stanilov 2011). As with other parameters typically tested in a sensitivity analysis, scale-sensitive features should also be systematically explored. Testing scale-dependent features and parameters is an important part of the calibration of a model. But because those are often fundamental assumptions built into the model, it is important (and occasionally difficult) to identify, isolate, and test those features. It is worth reiterating that for models of complex social systems there are almost always ways to implement those models to run more economically, but importantly, testing scale dependency can encourage better decisions about which compromises are less likely to affect the interpretations stemming from the ABM research.

Whether focused on the numbers of agents in a simulation or length in time steps to run a simulation, the analysis should begin with running a relatively large number of simulations across a relatively wide range of parameter values. If the model is stochastic, then some effort should be made to identify an adequate sample size to run for each configuration of the model (see also Kim 2013).

Depending on the structure of the data saved from each simulation, and whether those data are collected at the end of a simulation or throughout the run, it is important to identify statistical methods to compare the behavior of one model configuration to another (and preferably compare the output of those simulations to empirical data from the real-world system). I have found that storing simulation output data in a matrix (often a similarity matrix comparing the agents or aggregates of agents at different scales) and calculating correlations between the matrices with Mantel tests (Rosenberg and Anderson 2011) is a useful way to summarize similarities between simulations that have a large amount of output from many different agents or over long simulations. Also, data in these matrices can be collapsed at different spatio-temporal scales, which is very useful in a pattern-oriented modeling approach.

Plotting what has been learned by running many simulations across different values for a scaled feature or parameter (such as length of the simulation) will generate a marginal returns curve. If a simulation run to 1000 time steps develops patterns that are interesting and relevant to the research, it may be that those patterns are identifiable in a much shorter run. At 10 time steps, the simulation output probably looks nothing like 1000 time steps, but at 100 time steps the patterns may be indistinguishable from the longer run. In that context, so little may be learned by running another 900 time steps that it is preferable to recalibrate and run shorter simulations. As in the described case, many scale-sensitive parameters will have decreasing returns to scale. For those parameters with decreasing returns to scale, the sensitivity analysis should be oriented toward identifying the calibration point(s) where diminishing or even negative returns set in.

Alternately, there may be some scale-dependent parameters that have constant or increasing returns to scale, or where value thresholds correspond to interesting aggregate behaviors in the model. Some emergent patterns will only occur with a large enough population, or a model may not settle down, regardless of how long the simulation is run. It is important to identify these sensitive scale-dependent parameters as they should not be calibrated to a set value and forgotten, particularly if the modeler intends to compare the simulation output to empirical data from the real system. Instead, different configurations of these features or parameters should probably be considered as distinct hypotheses to be compared with archaeological data.

To summarize, identify those parameters with decreasing returns to scale and calibrate the model accordingly. Also, identify those parameters with constant, increasing, or unpredictable returns to scale and allocate resources to ensure that data are collected from different configurations that may function as discrete hypotheses. There is nothing new in the process described here; instead, I am simply reiterating that the approach should be applied to scale-dependent structural features and parameters of the model. The following subsections briefly outline approaches to the problems of how long to run a simulation, exploring how grid resolution and absolute size of agent population may affect the model, and finally I introduce the related problem of how many simulations are needed to adequately capture the behavior of a stochastic model.

6.2.1 How Long?

There are several aspects related to time that are important to consider when implementing a computational ABM. While many approaches to ABM are abstract enough that time is measured in ticks that represent generations of agents, most archaeological uses of ABM tend to be semi-realistic in their treatment of time: they rely on modeling platforms that, at least in their intention, are primarily discrete time with various agent and landscape processes triggered each time step. Event-based models or hybrids treat time differently; but for discrete time or hybrid models it is important to be explicit about what is represented by a time step. The resolution of that time step—whether it models a second, a season, a year, a generation, or even if it represents any real unit of time at all—is an important structural feature of the model and one that provides opportunities and constraints for calibration and sensitivity testing (Kim 2013).

For example, if a time step represents a year, and the archaeological phase being modeled lasts 200 years, then it may be worth exploring what happens when running simulations for much longer or much shorter than the target length. But generally, in that case the modeler has locked him- or herself into a particular approach to managing time. If, on the other hand, the modeler is interested in testing, for example, more general social science concepts, then the testing of different temporal resolutions and simulation durations becomes a potentially important part of the verification and validation of the model.

In those cases where time-related features are somewhat flexible, there is an opportunity to both explore the behavior of the model across a range of values and, importantly, economize the process of collecting data from many simulations (if running a stochastic model). Adjustments to the resolution of time steps or the duration of a simulation will in many cases have diminishing returns to scale. Documenting the payoff for running a simulation at finer or coarser time steps and for running longer or shorter simulations should encourage better calibration of the model. That calibration should also negate the need to run subsequent testing or data collection simulations for an excessively and unnecessarily long time, economizing CPU time (and money, depending on the machines being used).

6.2.2 Agent Populations and Landscape Resolution

Similar to the considerations of time resolution and duration, a modeler must also make a series of compromises related to abstracting their model implementation from the real-world system of interest (e.g. the spatial extent of the world occupied by the agents, the resolution of the landscape, and numbers of agents populating that landscape). In many cases, any empirical data informing the model may constrain some of these decisions. For example, if raster GIS data are used to define the world of the model, it may make sense to default to the resolution of that data when developing the rest of the model (Batty 2005; Fossett and Dietrich 2009; Liu and Yang 2012). Importantly, though, in that case it is often worth investigating whether patterns that emerge in a simulation are different if the data underlying the world are aggregated at larger scales (or interpolated to smaller scales). Spatial resolution has been shown to be an important concern in a recent ABM research on land use (Chen and Mynett 2003; Evans and Kelley 2004; Jantz and Goetz 2005; Kok et al. 2001; Menard and Marceau 2005; Veldkamp et al. 2001). In cases where the landscape itself functions as a cellular automata, and each cell is potentially updated every time step, resolution may factor heavily on the initialization time and performance of a simulation.

Of particular relevance in archaeological approaches is the problem that much of the data informing our modeling are themselves estimates of questionable accuracy. Population estimates, for example, may inform the numbers of agents initialized in a simulation. But often our confidence in those numbers is quite low (Craig et al. 2012; Doelle 2000; Nelson et al. 2010; Watts 2013). In the case of agent populations, it is important to know how the model responds across a range of possible values, and likewise it is good to know if there are diminishing returns to scale. If patterns generated are similar with smaller populations, then there is an opportunity to economize subsequent data collection runs.

Regarding both agents and grid cells, it is important to revisit the question of what they represent. Are the agents individuals? Households? Are there different kinds of agents in the model? For some systems, defining agents as individuals is both inefficient and unnecessary. At least in most current computational ABM platforms, agents are each allocated RAM and the necessary CPU time, and large numbers of agents can tax even high-performance computers. A coarser resolution of households or village segments as agents may make sense. But there are also topics where the resolution of agents and grid cells is integral to the model and less flexible. Still, it is important to document the model's sensitivity to those assumptions.

6.2.3 How Many Simulations?

While the problem of how many simulations to run of a particular stochastic model configuration is more about experimental design and sampling than it is strictly about sensitivity to scale in a model, it nonetheless is a pet peeve of mine. They are not totally unrelated, though. Scale-related decisions about implementing and calibrating the model will, more than anything else in the ABM code, contribute to the time required to run a simulation. If the model is implemented at such a fine resolution (or grand scale) as to prohibit an appropriate sample size from being collected, then in many cases revisiting the original model design and calibration would be warranted.

As with much archaeological research, pragmatic concerns often dominate decisions regarding sample sizes in ABM; and researchers habitually strain to rationalize whatever sample size was available to them given their resources. There is no compelling reason as to why this tendency from observational archaeology should extend to experimental contexts, particularly in the case of ABM.

Two extremes of a sampling tradition in archaeological ABM could be summarized as a "Monte Carlo" approach or a "CPU time-limited" approach. The Monte Carlo approach tends to be favored when models are simple and simulations fast; an arbitrary large number of simulations is run and generally considered a reasonable sample of the range of behaviors that might be generated by the model. Alternately, the CPU time-limited approach comes into play for large, slow, and usually relatively realistic models.

I prefer that sampling decisions be data driven, focused on identifying where diminishing returns sets in. If adding one more case provides effectively no new information, why collect, process, and analyze that data? That point may occur at 10 simulations or 10,000, but regardless of the speed of simulations it is more responsible to base that decision on model behavior rather than an arbitrary cutoff. If the model has already been simulated enough times to have a sense of the distribution of summary statistics, it may make sense to defer to sampling strategies common in more experimental sciences. Sokal and Rohlf (1995) provide a few options (one is described in detail in an example below). Given a sense of the distribution of outcomes, a minimal adequate sample size can be calculated.

Lastly, it may be worth considering an iterative approach when determining the number of simulations to run. Determining a reasonable number of simulations to run before calibrating and testing the model is important, and revisiting that estimate before running any experiments is recommended.

6.3 Sensitivity, Scale, and the Hohokam Economy

The following subsections describe part of the verification and validation of a computational ABM focused on the organization of pottery trade for the prehistoric Hohokam culture of central Arizona. The focus is on two analyses done to better understand the sensitivity of the model to time (how long to run the simulations?), and to better estimate an adequate sample size (how many simulations?). Other questions of scale, such as how many agents, were considered but are not reported here (see Watts 2013). Briefly, though, I provide an explanation of the questions motivating the research, and try to describe and contextualize the ABM that was implemented for the project.

The objective of the research was to first identify a variety of conceptual economic models that may explain spatial patterns of pottery distribution observed in the Hohokam archaeological record. Those models were abstract and theoretically drawn from different sources, including microeconomics, mathematics (network/graph theory), and economic anthropology. ABM methods were adopted to refine expectations generated from those conceptual models for the messy, complicated, real-world system that was the prehistoric Hohokam economy. Those conceptual models were treated as competing working hypotheses about the organization of Hohokam pottery trade networks and implemented as relatively simple ABMs set in the Phoenix Basin of central Arizona. Finally, comparisons of the simulated data to empirical data provided an opportunity to assess whether or not any of the ABM configurations were consistent with Hohokam ceramic datasets. Considerable effort was taken to explore these ABM configurations, including systematically testing the code internal logic and behavior, investigating scale dependency issues (reported here), exploring sensitivity to startup conditions and critical simulation setup assumptions, and running parameter sweeps.

The project's pattern-oriented modeling methodology led to the discard of several hypotheses, narrowing the range of plausible models of the organization of the Hohokam economy. The results suggest that for much of the Hohokam sequence, a market-based system, perhaps structured around workshop procurement and/or shopkeeper merchandise, provided the means of distributing pottery from specialist producers to widespread consumers. Perhaps unsurprisingly, the results of this project were broadly consistent with earlier researchers' interpretations that the structure of the Hohokam economy evolved through time, growing more complex throughout the Preclassic, and undergoing a major reorganization resulting in a less complex system at the transition to the Classic Period.

6.3.1 The Hohokam

Archaeologically, the Hohokam of the lower Salt River Valley and the middle Gila River Valley (collectively called the Phoenix Basin) are relatively well known thanks to over a century of field and laboratory work (Fig. 6.1). The culture history and settlement patterns are reasonably well documented, and recent years have seen a florescence of research oriented toward understanding the economy of the Hohokam (Abbott 2000, 2009; Abbott et al. 2007; Bayman 2001; Doyel 1991; Kelly 2013; Watts 2013; Woodson 2011). I briefly summarize some of that work here to provide a context for the ABM that was implemented for the current project. Fig. 6.2 outlines the Hohokam chronology for the Phoenix Basin.

The Phoenix Basin is at an elevation of around 335–365 m above sea level at the basin floor and encompasses some 9300 km^2. The region is set in basin and range topography in the heart of the Sonoran Desert (nearby summits approach 1200 m), with annual rainfall near 18–20 cm. Rainfall varies widely every year, and often occurs in short, locally intense storms during the summer. Warm temperatures (annual averages near 21 °C), intense summer heat with 3 months of average highs over 38 °C, and rare frosts/freezes are typical. Vegetation is dominated by scrub trees, shrubs, and cacti, with narrow riparian areas adjacent to the rivers and major side drainages. Prehistorically, stream flow in the rivers (particularly the Salt) was substantial and generally reliable thanks to large catchment areas.

Though small groups of earlier peoples had settled and probably farmed in the Phoenix Basin much earlier, the first clearly Hohokam settlements in the Basin date to shortly before AD 450, sharing much in common with contemporary groups in northern Mexico and the southwestern United States. During the earliest phases of the Hohokam sequence, evidence of production (primarily based on ceramics) indicates that most manufacture, exchange, and consumption was local to settlements. Populations were generally small, but showed slow, steady growth from very early on (all statements regarding Hohokam demography here and hereafter were derived

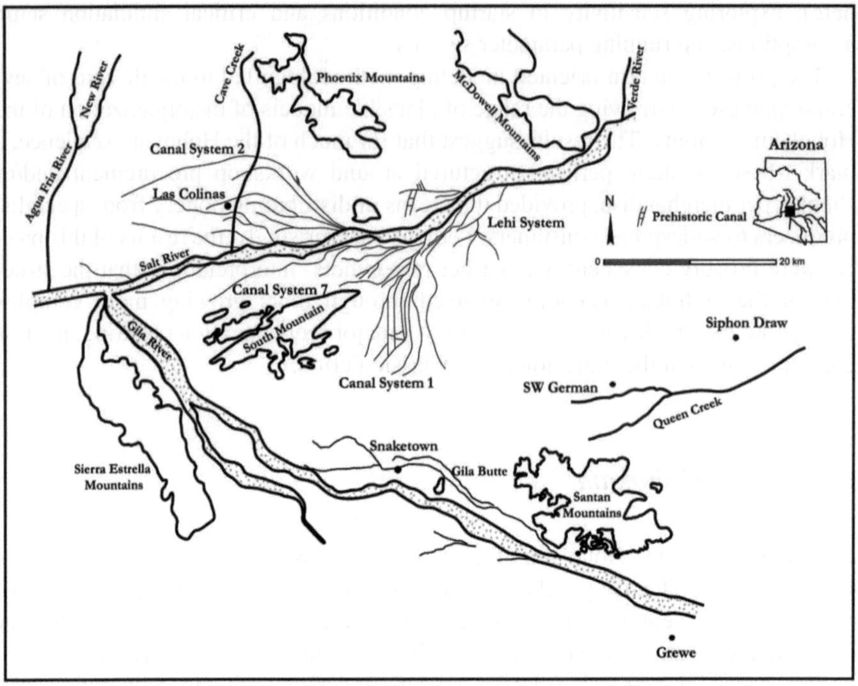

Fig. 6.1 The Phoenix Basin in central Arizona (Watts 2013)

from Doelle 1995, 2000; Nelson et al. 2010; see also Hill et al. 2004; Craig et al. 2012; Woodson in press).[1]

The Hohokam were not long settled, though, before a small number of communities began to produce pottery for trade. Specifically, by the Vahki and Estrella phases (ca. AD 500) there is evidence that two communities, one in the vicinity of South Mountain and the other along the middle Gila River (probably near Gila Butte), were producing a majority of the ceramics consumed around the Phoenix Basin (see Fig. 6.1). Specialized production in subsequent Preclassic phases has also been proposed for several other types of goods, including projectile points (Hoffman 1997), shell jewelry (Howard 1993), ground stone tools (Hoffman and Doyel 1985; Doyel 1991), and tabular knives (Bernard-Shaw 1983). A program of large-scale irrigated agriculture was initiated at this time, with communities north

[1] Estimating populations for the Hohokam, particularly during the Preclassic, is notoriously difficult and attempts have generated widely varying results. Site sizes, room counts, and the use-life of pit houses in the Hohokam culture area are exceedingly difficult to assess with any accuracy. In my opinion, the work of Doelle (1995, 2000), Craig et al. (2012), and others working from similar room or house count data probably underestimates the actual population of the greater Phoenix Basin. But regardless of the real numbers, the general trends drawn from Doelle (1995, 2000) and updated by Matthew Peeples and the Arizona State University Biocomplexity Project (Nelson et al. 2010) likely capture the general trajectory of Hohokam population growth through time.

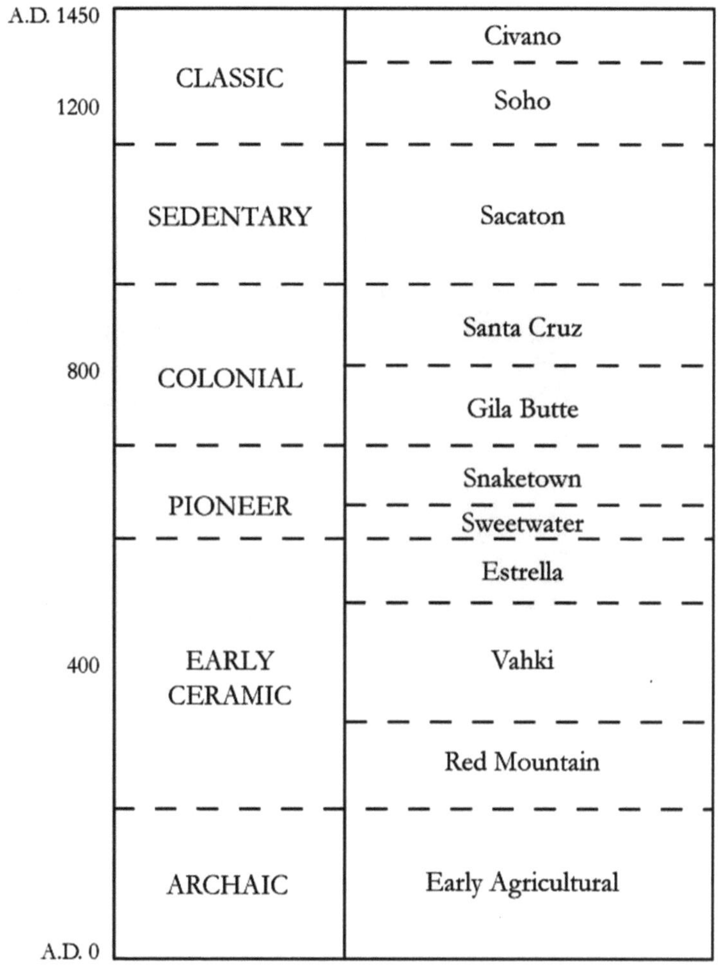

Fig. 6.2 The Hohokam chronology (Watts 2013)

of the Salt River leading the way. A variety of domesticates, including edibles and other crops, were farmed in these systems. Truly impressive canals (some exceeding 32 km in length, 4–5 m depth, and 15 m across) were established well before AD 800 (Howard 1993; Woodson 2010).

Settlements in the Phoenix Basin persisted through circa AD 1450, though evidence from various artifact classes, particularly ceramics, suggests that the pattern of specialized production and trade may have been disrupted and perhaps reorganized at different times. In particular, an important shift in Hohokam material culture began sometime around AD 1150–1175, corresponding to poorly understood shifts in the organization of the Hohokam economy. The model discussed here was implemented to better understand the organization of that economy, focused particularly on the mechanisms that moved pottery from producers to consumers.

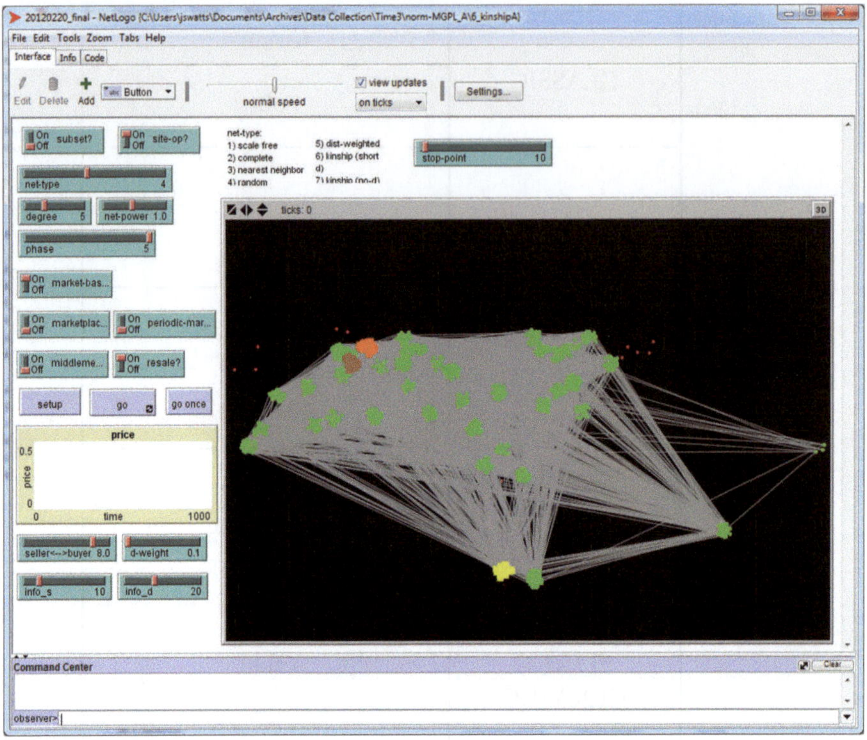

Fig. 6.3 NetLogo screen shot showing agent networks. Clusters of farmers in the Phoenix Basin are shown as *green circles*, the multi-color patches are the producers, and the links show the connections between the various agents. Model parameter settings are shown as sliders and switches to the *left* of the display window (Watts 2013)

6.3.1.1 Model Background

The following provides a brief description of the Hohokam trade and exchange model—and its various configurations—that was created for this research project. Most of the work to implement the model was completed in 2011. NetLogo, a Java-based software package for writing and running simulations of agent-based models, was used throughout the project (Wilensky 1999). Screen shots of an example simulation are shown in Figs. 6.3 and 6.4. Note that the source code and full documentation for a variant of this model has been peer reviewed, certified, and is posted to OpenABM.org at the persistent URL https://www.openabm.org/model/4385/version/1/view.

The purpose of the model was to understand how structural and processual changes in exchange systems effected patterns of pottery distribution for the prehistoric Hohokam of the Phoenix Basin. Fundamentally, this model was intended to encourage better interpretations of the archaeological record more so than it was

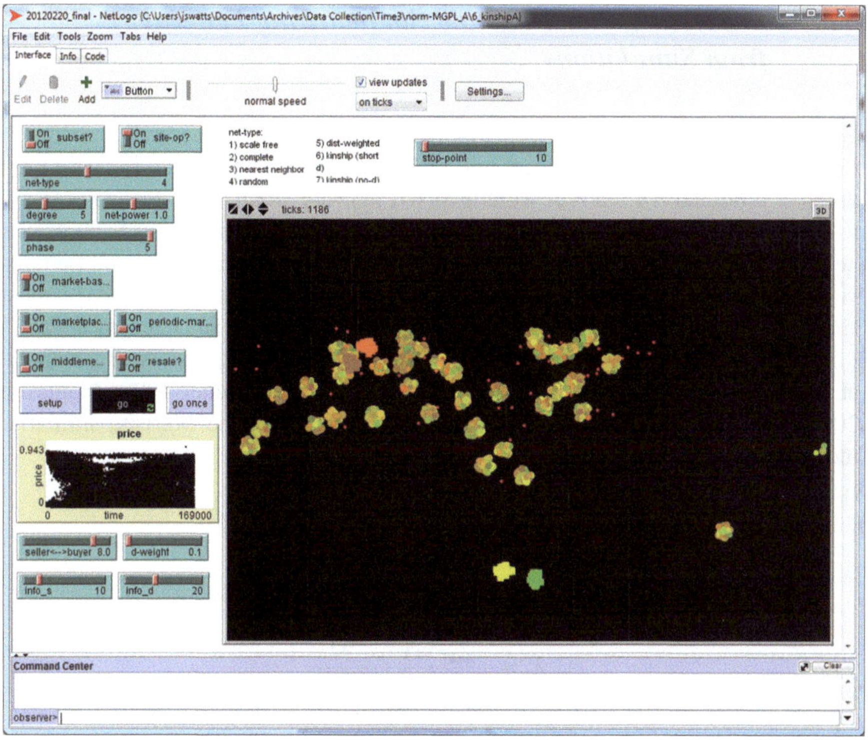

Fig. 6.4 NetLogo screen shot showing an in-progress simulation. Farmers are shown as *circles* with the color and size updated according to the size and mixture of pottery in their household midden (Watts 2013)

about bringing a new perspective to a particular complex social process through modeling and simulation. For the most part, it was a relatively simple, abstract model; but it was an ABM informed by (and compared to) empirical real-world data. It was not a highly parameterized, highly realistic model of the Hohokam occupation or the broader Hohokam agricultural economy. Each simulation transferred pottery from producers to consumer households through differently structured trade networks and according to different rules for exchange. The networks and rules were generalized from various theoretical and ethnographic sources. Eventually the households would discard the pottery from different producers, creating a virtual archaeological record. The resulting output from each simulation was a list of hundreds or thousands of "houses" with associated counts of the different pottery types that were discarded by that household. A sample of the simulated data could be compared to the empirical ceramic data from the archaeological record, and also be easily compared to other simulations run with the same or different parameter settings.

6.3.2 *Processing Raw Data and Summarizing Patterns from Simulations*

Each of the raw data files generated by the simulations was structurally analogous to a list of archaeological features and related ceramic ware counts. Because hundreds or thousands of features were involved in every simulation, it was necessary to summarize that data. Extracting a structurally comparable sample of features was necessary for the statistics used to assess the similarity of the simulated patterns versus the real data patterns. To get at patterns at different spatial scales, the sample simulated data were then collapsed at two higher levels: sites and canal systems.

Once the right sample was extracted, Morisita similarity matrices were generated at the three different spatial scales (Chao et al. 2006; Hammer 1999; Magurran 2004; Morisita 1959; Wolda 1981). Per Hammer (1999), the Morisita similarity index is calculated:

$$\lambda_1 = \frac{\sum_i x_{ji}\left(x_{ji} - 1\right)}{\sum_i x_{ji}\left(\sum_i x_{ji} - 1\right)} \tag{6.1}$$

$$\lambda_2 = \frac{\sum_i x_{ki}\left(x_{ki} - 1\right)}{\sum_i x_{ki}\left(\sum_i x_{ki} - 1\right)} \tag{6.2}$$

$$d_{jk} = \frac{2\sum_i x_{ji} x_{ki}}{\left(\lambda_1 + \lambda_2\right)\sum_i x_{ji} \sum_i x_{ki}} \tag{6.3}$$

where x_j and x_k are the ceramic assemblages of the two features being compared. Once calculated, the Morisita similarity index is a value between zero and 1, with results closer to 1 indicating greater similarity. When comparing the pottery counts of many features to many other features, it was useful to bundle the many Morisita indices into a half-matrix. The half-matrix, for each of the feature, site, and canal system scales, became a highly compact summary of the output of a simulation. The first half-matrix shown in Table 6.1 is a 5 by 5 example of the summary described here.

After the raw simulation data were converted to similarity matrices, the next step in the analysis was to run a series of Mantel tests. Mantel tests assess the correlation between two similarity matrices and provide a good summary of how well a particular simulated data set compares to other simulations or the actual archaeological data. Per Rosenberg and Anderson (2011), the basic Mantel statistic is calculated:

$$Z = \sum_{ij} X_{ij} Y_{ij} \tag{6.4}$$

Table 6.1 Example showing the calculation of the Mantel statistic

Item					
Matrix I					
Features	A	B	C	D	E
A					
B	0.49				
C	0.80	0.93			
D	0.27	0.65	0.45		
E	0.09	0.32	0.83	0.34	
Matrix II					
Features	A	B	C	D	E
A					
B	0.85				
C	0.22	0.30			
D	0.53	0.88	0.60		
E	0.13	0.75	0.25	0.11	
Calculated Mantel statistic	4.71				
Correlation coefficient *r*	–0.05				

where X and Y are the two similarity matrices being compared. Typically, though, a normalized version of the statistic is used, calculated as the correlation between pair-wise elements in the two matrices. As with any product-moment correlation coefficient, the r value ranges between -1 and 1, with higher positive values suggestive of greater structural similarity of the two compared matrices. Table 6.1 provides an example of how the Mantel statistic and related correlation coefficient are calculated, using two 5 by 5 half-matrices populated with Morisita similarity indices.

For the model testing examples described below, a series of Mantel tests was used to compare a large set of the simulations, and the correlation coefficient provided a concise summary of just how similar or different the output of the simulations were to one another.

6.3.3 *Scale Dependency Tests*

The scale dependency tests described here were conducted to assess how many simulations should be run and how long each simulation should be run in order to capture the range of behavior shown by a particular model configuration. As seen above, the term "model configuration" refers to the specific setup conditions of the model when initialized to run as one of the conceptual model hypotheses. Testing was completed on ten model configurations, which group into three broader categories: three naïve network models, two from anthropological theory, and five from economic theory (see Watts 2013 for the justification and full explanation of these model configurations).

6.3.3.1 Test: Simulation Duration

This test was designed to determine how long to run each simulation for subsequent testing and data collection phases of the project. Each model configuration was run 24 times, and the pottery distribution data were saved at 25, 50, 100, 200, 400, and 800 time steps. The maximum range that was tested, 800 time steps, was selected based on my familiarity with the model from the programming and code verification stages of the project; 800 time steps was a very long time to run this ABM. Multiple simulations were run to document whether the model output varied significantly run-to-run, but the specific number of simulations for each configuration (24 runs) was somewhat arbitrary. Subsequent tests were conducted to determine an appropriate sample size when running experiments, but those had not been completed when this test was conducted. Many of the behaviors in the model were event based rather than triggered by discrete time instructions, so even 20–40 time steps may represent tens of thousands of transactions. Output data were then compared at the feature, site, and canal system scales (using the Morisita similarity index and Mantel tests defined above) at the six different duration lengths to determine if there was an inflection point where adding more time steps did not significantly change the simulation output.

6.3.3.2 Results: Simulation Duration

The results of the test suggested that most of the model configurations settled rather quickly into consistent patterns. Some simulations were more variable, but in no cases was it necessary to run the simulation out the full 800 time steps to capture the distribution pattern associated with a particular configuration. As shown in the following analysis, 200 time steps was more than adequate in most cases to ensure that the simulations had every opportunity to settle into a pattern generally representative of the model configuration. These results, and a preference to overrun the simulations rather than risk running them too short, led me to settle on 400 time steps as the duration for simulations for the rest of the testing and data collection phases of the project.

For each of the ten model configurations, the 24 simulations each generated six output data files—one saved for each pause at 25, 50, 100, 200, 400, and 800 time steps. A total of 1440 data files were collected for this test. Each of those data files was summarized at the three spatial scales important to this project (feature, site, and canal system scales), resulting in 4320 total processed data files contributing to this assessment. Morisita similarity matrices were used to summarize patterns within a single simulation. Mantel tests were used to measure correlations between the different data collection pauses in the time series for a single simulation.

Specifically, the analysis procedure was to compare the final output (800 time steps) from each simulation to each earlier pause in that run (25, 50, 100, 200, and 400 time steps) using Mantel tests. The mean and standard deviation were calculated for the Mantel correlation coefficients at each pause for the 24 identically

Table 6.2 Average time series Mantel correlation coefficients for all configurations. *Note*: Std. Dev. = standard deviation

Time series	All model configurations					
	Feature		Site		Canal system	
	Mean	Std. Dev.	Mean	Std. Dev.	Mean	Std. Dev.
25 vs. 800	0.071	0.038	0.471	0.208	0.467	0.328
50 vs. 800	0.126	0.050	0.530	0.199	0.494	0.345
100 vs. 800	0.220	0.058	0.572	0.185	0.553	0.312
200 vs. 800	0.321	0.066	0.576	0.186	0.532	0.314
400 vs. 800	0.417	0.072	0.616	0.187	0.539	0.309

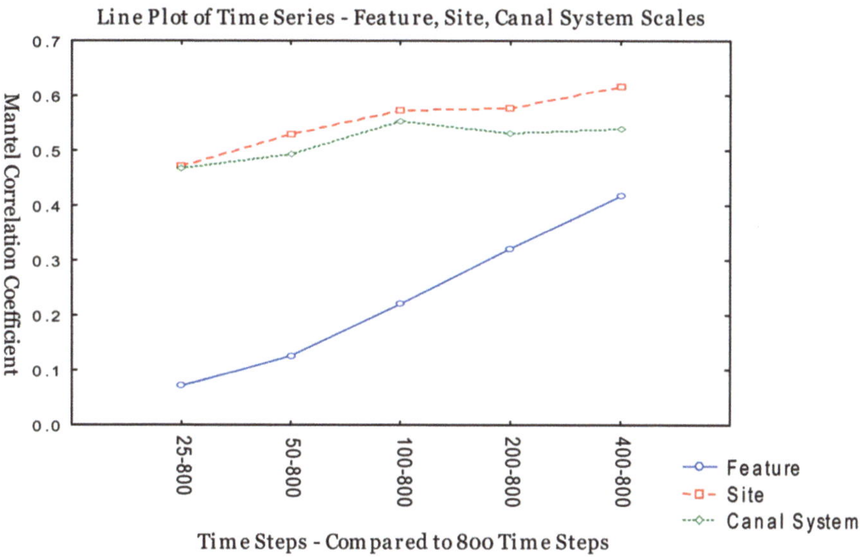

Fig. 6.5 Plot of time series Mantel correlation coefficients from Table 6.2 (Watts 2013)

configured simulations. These calculations were repeated for the three spatial scales and all model configurations. Finally, to establish a reasonable length to run simulations, summary statistics for the set of model configurations were calculated. Those results are shown in Table 6.2 and Fig. 6.5, and suggest that both the site and canal system scales stabilize into long-run patterns relatively quickly. For those scales, no improvement was typically seen beyond 100 time steps. Alternately, the feature scale was much more erratic at the start, with very low Mantel scores comparing early time steps with the final output, but that scale gradually settled into relatively consistent patterns by the 200 or 400 time step marks. To allow the feature scale some opportunity to settle into more interpretable patterns, and with confidence that the site and canal system patterns were robust, the decision was made to run the remaining simulations out to 400 time steps.

6.3.3.3 Test: Sample Size (Number of Simulations)

The second test reported here was designed to determine how many simulations were necessary to capture the range of behaviors that may affect the output data. While in theory it was possible to run each model configuration thousands of times, due to limited time and computing power it was worth assessing when the marginal returns of running one more simulation added nothing (or almost nothing) to what was learned about the behavior of the model. The test was to run each model configuration 100 times, creating a "population" set, and to determine what size of smaller sample (if any) would provide summary statistics representative of the larger set. Every simulation was run out 400 time steps, per the results of the previous test. Each model configuration had some randomized behavior during the initialization and execution of the simulation, and this test was designed to help understand just how much that stochasticity affected the output of the run, and how much one run varied from another run. The result of this test was an assessment of the appropriate sample size of simulations needed to represent the population of all possible outputs from any particular model configuration. Preliminary informal tests conducted during the implementation phase suggested that for some settings, a relatively small sample of simulations (e.g. 15–20 runs) had summary statistics very close to those taken from a much larger population (100 runs). If, instead, 100 simulations had proved inadequate for capturing the behavior of a given model configuration, more would have been added. Fortunately, given the considerable length of time required to run these simulations, a sample larger than 100 runs proved unnecessary.

6.3.3.4 Results: Sample Size (Number of Simulations)

The sample size test indicated that for most configurations relatively few simulations (5–20) were adequate to summarize the range of output data from any particular model configuration. The results of this test did vary depending on the configuration, though. For example, the centralized redistribution configuration was quite consistent in its output, and very few simulations were required to capture the full range of behaviors. Alternately, model configurations whose distribution networks were widely variable every simulation, such as the shopkeeper merchandise hypothesis, required many more simulations to summarize the range of possible outputs. Still, in only a few cases was it necessary to run more than 20 simulations (see details below); but in an effort to be appropriately cautious, I settled on a sample of 40 simulations for most of the remaining tests and data collection simulations.

For each of the ten model configurations, 100 simulations were run, and each configuration generated a unique output data file. A total of 1000 data files were collected for this test. Each of those data files was summarized at the three spatial scales important to this project (feature, site, and canal system scales), resulting in 3000 total data files contributing to this assessment. The analysis proceeded as follows:

1. Saved output data from a simulation (pottery counts from house features) were collapsed to three Morisita similarity matrices (one each for the three spatial scales).
2. A series of large Mantel test matrices were generated comparing each of the matrices to the other 99. This effort for each of the ten model configurations was captured in a 100 by 100 half-matrix. Each of the ten half-matrices represented 4900 comparisons of models initialized in the same way, creating the "population" from which a sample or subset of comparisons should have been adequate for capturing the patterns of interest.
3. A sample size test (Sokal and Rohlf 1995) was used to determine a reasonable number of simulations per model configuration. The set of Mantel scores from (2) informed a conservative estimation of an adequate sample size for a given margin of error and confidence. The adequate sample size (taken from the population of 100 simulations) was calculated using the method described in Sokal and Rohlf (1995), defined below. Table 6.3 shows the outcome of this process for the tested configurations at the three spatial scales. The results vary depending on the spatial scale, but generally a total of 40 simulations per configuration was a good compromise across most configurations and scales. Due to relatively large standard deviations, the fine-grained and noisy feature scale would have required much larger sample sizes to reach the same confidence levels as the site and canal system scales. The sample size estimates were calculated as follows:

$$n \geq 2\left(\frac{\sigma}{\delta}\right)^2 \left\{t_{a[v]} + t_{2(1-P)[v]}\right\}^2 \tag{6.5}$$

where:

n = number of needed samples
σ = true standard deviation (use a coefficient of variation for convenience)
δ = smallest true difference to detect (a percentage of means)
v = degrees of freedom of the sample deviation
α = significance level (such as 0.05)
P = desired probability that a difference will be significant (power of test)
$t_{a[v]}$ and $t_{2(1-P)[v]}$ = values from a two-tailed t-table with v degrees of freedom, corresponding to probabilities of α and $2(1-P)$, respectively

For example, to have 80 % certainty of detecting a 10 % difference between two means at the 5 % significance level (and for very high value degrees of freedom), given Cv coefficient of variation taken from the 100 runs of a particular model configuration:

$$n = 2\left(\frac{Cv}{0.1}\right)^2 (1.96 + 0.841)^2 \tag{6.6}$$

Table 6.3 Calculated sample size—all spatial scales

Model configuration	Spatial scale		
	Canal system	Site	Feature
Random	34	29	4842
Complete	33	31	10,404
Scale Free	37	28	10,957
Centralized	39	31	5823
Kinship A	60	12	10
Marketplace	32	25	6984
Shopkeeper	67	23	49
Workshop	31	26	8421
Peddler	39	37	1857
Individual	38	28	5845
Mean	41.0	27.0	5519.2
Standard deviation	11.7	6.2	3719.4

Finally, to calculate the number of simulations needed for the appropriate sample size N (see Table 6.3):

$$N_{(\text{simulations})} = \sqrt{2n} \tag{6.7}$$

Overall, this assessment of just how many simulations the model needs to run to summarize its behavior allowed me to economize CPU time for the rest of the project—as reported in Watts (2013).

6.4 Conclusion

Understanding the response of a simulation model to scale-sensitive structural features and parameters is an important aspect of calibrating and testing that model leading up to other sensitivity analyses and data collection experiments. The approach advocated in this chapter is to encourage researchers to identify and explore scale-sensitive aspects of their models (such as the resolution or absolute size of the models) with particular focus on the concern that in many ABM studies there are diminishing returns to scale. Given that it is quite difficult to design ABMs to be valid models of real-world processes across a very wide range of spatiotemporal scales, it is important to calibrate models to perform well within a reasonable range of scales. Too fine a resolution or too many agents may give highly granular results offering no new insights into the processes operating on the real system. Alternately, too coarse a resolution or too few agents may limit important patterns from emerging during a simulation. The examples discussed in this chapter, drawn from my research on the organization of the Hohokam economy, illustrate how a modeler may approach the problem of calibrating a model and related analyses for more productive and efficient ABM research.

Acknowledgments Parts of this chapter were adapted from my dissertation, and I appreciate the input on that document from my committee, including David Abbott (chair), Michael Barton, Marco Janssen, and Sander van der Leeuw. Michael Barton, Sean Bergin, and Wendy Cegielski helped with the initial brainstorming of the topic, and Kristin Gade had to suffer through my attempts to render the main argument. Note that the testing and experiments described here were conducted on computers purchased with the aid of an award from the Society for American Archaeology (2012 Fred Plog Memorial Fellowship).

References

Abbott, D. R. (2000). *Ceramics and community organization among the Hohokam*. Tucson, AZ: University of Arizona Press.

Abbott, D. R. (2009). Extensive and long-term specialization: Hohokam ceramic production in the Phoenix Basin, Arizona. *American Antiquity, 74*(3), 531–557.

Abbott, D. R., Gallaga, E., & Smith, A. M. (2007). Ballcourts and ceramics: The case for Hohokam marketplaces in the Arizona desert. *American Antiquity, 72*(3), 461–484.

Batty, M. (2005). Agents, cells, and cities: New representational models for simulating multiscale urban dynamics. *Environment and Planning A, 37*, 1373–1394.

Bayman, J. M. (2001). The Hohokam of Southwest North America. *Journal of World Prehistory, 15*(3), 257–311.

Bernard-Shaw, M. (1983). The stone tool assemblage of the Salt-Gila Aqueduct Project site. In L. S. Teague & P. L. Crown (Eds.), *Hohokam archaeology along the Salt-Gila Aqueduct Central Arizona Project* (Material culture, Vol. 8, pp. 373–443). Tempe, AZ: Arizona State Museum Archaeological Series 150, Arizona State Museum.

Chao, A., Chazdon, R. L., Colwell, R. K., & Shen, T.-J. (2006). Abundance-based similarity indices and their estimation when there are unseen species in samples. *Biometrics, 62*, 361–371.

Chen, Q., & Mynett, A. E. (2003). Effects of cell size and configuration in cellular automata based prey/predator modeling. *Simulation Modelling Practice and Theory, 11*, 609–625.

Craig, D. B., Wallace, H. D., & Lindeman, M. W. (2012). Village growth and ritual transformation in the southern southwest. In S. A. Herr & L. C. Young (Eds.), *Southwestern Pithouse Communities, AD 200–900* (pp. 45–60). Tucson, AZ: University of Arizona Press.

Doelle, W. H. (1995). Appendix D: A method for estimating regional population. In M. D. Elson, M. T. Stark, & D. A. Gregory (Eds.), *The Roosevelt Community Development Study: New perspectives on Tonto Basin prehistory* (Anthropological Papers, Vol. 15). Tucson, AZ: Center for Desert Archaeology.

Doelle, W. H. (2000). Tonto Basin demography in a regional perspective. In J. S. Dean (Ed.), *Salado* (Amerind Foundation New World Studies, Vol. 4, pp. 81–105). Albuquerque, NM: University of New Mexico Press.

Doyel, D. E. (1991). Hohokam cultural evolution in the Phoenix Basin. In G. J. Gumerman (Ed.), *Exploring the Hohokam: Prehistoric desert peoples of the American Southwest* (pp. 231–278). Albuquerque, NM: University of New Mexico Press.

Evans, T. P., & Kelley, H. (2004). Multi-scale analysis of a household level agent-based model of land cover change. *Journal of Environmental Management, 72*, 57–72.

Fossett, M., & Dietrich, D. R. (2009). Effects of city size, shape, and form, and neighborhood size and shape in agent-based models of residential segregation: Are Schelling-style preference effects robust? *Environment and Planning B: Planning and Design, 36*, 149–169.

Goodchild, M. (2001). Issues in spatially explicit modeling. In D. Parker, T. Berger, & S. M. Manson (Eds.), *Agent-based models of land-use and land-cover change* (pp. 13–17). LUCC Report Series No. 6. LUCC Focus 1. Irvine.

Grimm, V., Revilla, E., Berger, U., et al. (2005). Pattern-oriented modeling of agent-based complex systems: Lessons from ecology. *Science, 310*, 987–991.

Hammer, O. (1999). PAST: PAleontological STatistics. 2.17 ed. Natural History Museum, University of Oslo.

Hill, J. B., Clark, J. J., Doelle, W. H., & Lyons, P. D. (2004). Prehistoric demography in the southwest: Migration, coalescence, and Hohokam population decline. *American Antiquity, 69*(4), 689–716.

Hoffman, C. M. (1997). *Alliance Formation and Social Interaction During the Sedentary Period: A Stylistic Analysis of Hohokam Arrowpoints*. Unpublished Ph.D. Dissertation, Arizona State University.

Hoffman, T. L., & Doyel, D. E. (1985). Ground stone tool production in the New River Basin. In D. E. Doyel & M. D. Elson (Eds.), *Hohokam settlement and economic systems in the Central New River Drainage, Arizona* (Vol. 2, pp. 521–564). Phoenix, AZ: Soil Systems Publications in Archaeology 4.

Howard, A. V. (1993a). Marine shell artifacts and production processes at Shelltown and the Hind site. In W. S. Marmaduke & R. J. Martynec (Eds.), *Shelltown and the Hind site: A study of two Hohokam craftsman communities in Southwestern Arizona* (pp. 321–423). Flagstaff, AZ: Northland Research.

Howard, J. B. (1993b). A paleohydraulic approach to examining agricultural intensification in Hohokam irrigation systems. *Research in Economic Anthropology, 7*, 263–332.

Jantz, C. A., & Goetz, S. J. (2005). Analysis of scale dependencies in an urban land-use-change model. *International Journal of Geographical Information Science, 19*(2), 217–241.

Kelly, S. (2013). *A Multi-factor Analysis of the Emergence of a Specialist-based Economy among the Phoenix Basin Hohokam*. Unpublished Ph.D. Dissertation, Arizona State University.

Kim, J. H. (2013). Spatiotemporal scale dependency and other sensitivities in dynamic land-use change simulations. *International Journal of Geographical Information Science, 27*(9), 1782–1803.

Kok, K., Farrow, A., Veldkamp, A., & Verburg, P. H. (2001). A method and application of multi-scale validation in spatial land use models. *Agriculture, Ecosystems and Environment, 85*(1–3), 223–238.

Liu, T., & Yang, X. (2012). Geospatial modeling of urban landscape changes through an agent-based approach. In *Proceedings—AutoCarto 2012—Columbus, Ohio, USA*.

Magurran, A. E. (2004). *Measuring biological diversity*. Oxford, England: Blackwell.

Menard, A., & Marceau, D. J. (2005). Exploration of spatial scale sensitivity in geographic cellular automata. *Environment and Planning B: Planning and Design, 32*, 693–714.

Morisita, M. (1959). Measuring of the dispersion and analysis of distribution patterns. *Memoires of the Faculty of Science. Kyushu University, Series E. Biology, 2*, 215–235.

Nelson, M. C., Kintigh, K. W., Abbott, D. R., & Anderies, J. M. (2010). The cross-scale interplay between social and biophysical context and the vulnerability of irrigation-dependent societies: Archaeology's long-term perspective. *Ecology and Society, 15*(3), 31.

Railsback, S. F., & Grimm, V. (2012). *Agent-based and individual-based modeling: A practical introduction*. Princeton, NJ: Princeton University Press.

Rosenberg, M. S., & Anderson, C. D. (2011). PASSaGE: Pattern analysis, spatial statistics and geographic exegesis, version 2. *Methods in Ecology & Evolution, 2*(3), 229–232.

Sokal, R. R., & Rohlf, J. (1995). *Biometry: The principles and practice of statistics in biological research* (3rd ed.). New York, NY: W.H. Freeman.

Stanilov, K. (2011). Space in agent-based models. In A. J. Heppenstall, A. T. Crooks, L. M. See, & M. Batty (Eds.), *Agent-based models of geographical systems* (pp. 253–270). Dordrecht, The Netherlands: Springer.

Veldkamp, A., Verburg, P. H., Kok, K., de Koning, G. H. J., Priess, J., & Bergsma, A. R. (2001). The need for scale sensitive approaches in spatially explicit land use change modeling. *Environmental Modeling and Assessment, 6*(2), 111–121.

Watts, J. (2013). *The organization and evolution of the Hohokam economy: Agent-based modeling of exchange in the Phoenix Basin, AD 200–1450*. Unpublished Ph.D. Dissertation, Arizona State University.

Watts, J., & Ossa, A. (in press). Trade network topologies and agent-based modeling: Economies of the Sedentary period Hohokam. *American Antiquity*.

Wilensky, U. (1999). *NetLogo. Center for connected learning and computer-based modeling*. Evanston, IL: Northwestern University. http://ccl.northwestern.edu/netlogo/.

Wolda, H. (1981). Similarity indices, sample size and diversity. *Oecologia, 50*, 296–302.

Woodson, M. K. (2010). *The Social Organization of Hohokam irrigation in the Middle Gila River Valley, Arizona*. PhD Dissertation, Arizona State University, Tempe, AZ.

Woodson, M. K. (2011). Hohokam pottery production areas and the organization of ceramic production and exchange in the Phoenix Basin. *Journal of Arizona Archaeology, 1*(2), 128–147.

Woodson, M. K. (in press). Building and cleaning the Snaketown Canal: Hohokam labor requirements and work force sizes in the Middle Gila River Valley. *Journal of Arizona Archaeology*.

Chapter 7
The Sensitivity of Demographic Characteristics to the Strength of the Population Stabilizing Mechanism in a Model Hunter-Gatherer System

Andrew A. White

7.1 Introduction

An understanding of the demography of prehistoric hunter-gatherer systems is relevant to numerous questions of anthropological and archaeological significance: human colonization of empty landscapes; patterns of gene flow on evolutionary timescales; factors affecting intensification, population growth, and the emergence of food producing economies; and the basic structure and organization of populations throughout the vast majority of human prehistory.

Agent-based models (ABMs) have the potential to be powerful tools for understanding the demography of prehistoric hunter-gatherer populations for two main reasons (see White 2014). First, they allow us to dispense with some of the principal assumptions (e.g., infinite populations that remain stable in size, fixed/homogenous birth/death rates, and random mating) that limit the usefulness of equation-based models for exploring demography in populations where human-level interactions and stochastic processes are important factors. Second, they allow one to investigate model systems with demographic characteristics that are unlike those of the small number of ethnographic cases for which we have data.

In any demographic model where birth and death are represented, changes in population size are the result of the combined effects of mortality and fertility. If fertility exceeds mortality, population size will increase over time. If mortality exceeds fertility, population size will decrease over time. If stability of population size is desired in a model, the combined effects of mortality and fertility must somehow be balanced to prevent sustained population growth or decline. In equation-based demographic models, the existence of a "balance point" between mortality

A.A. White (✉)
South Carolina Institute of Archaeology and Anthropology, University of South Carolina, Columbia, SC, USA
e-mail: aawhite@mailbox.sc.edu

M. Brouwer Burg et al. (eds.), *Uncertainty and Sensitivity Analysis in Archaeological Computational Modeling*, Interdisciplinary Contributions to Archaeology, DOI 10.1007/978-3-319-27833-9_7

and fertility can be imposed simply by setting birth rates and death rates equal to one another in the equation. The situation can be quite different in an ABM, however, where the exact mortality and fertility rates experienced by a population can be affected both by the values of global parameters (e.g., the probability of an individual's death at any given step) and by the micro-level behaviors of individuals and families interacting within a system affected by those parameters (e.g., family-level decisions about reproduction based on the current size and composition of the family). Because mortality and fertility outcomes emerge dynamically from both the "top down" and "bottom up" in this kind of model, balance between the two cannot be simply imposed with a static equation that sets the sum of global birth and death rates to zero. Feedbacks between population size and behaviors or parameters related to birth or death are required to regulate population size.

This paper uses Version 3 of the ForagerNet3_Demography model (FN3D_V3) to investigate how the strength of a mortality-based feedback mechanism for stabilizing population size affects demographic outcomes in the model. Baseline probabilities of death in the FN3D_V3 model are set by an age-specific "mortality schedule." In previous work with this model (e.g., White 2014), these probabilities were adjusted (increased or decreased) each step in response to the current population size during a model run. If the population at a given step exceeded a particular size threshold (set by a parameter), for example, the probability of death was raised proportionally by the amount the population size exceeded the threshold. If the population size was less than the threshold size, the probability of death was reduced proportionally. This feedback between population size and mortality provided a simple means to stabilize the size of the population. The mortality-based feedback was designed as a homeostatic mechanism necessary to the operation of the model rather than a representation of any particular ethnographically demonstrated cause–effect relationship between population size and morality rates. Because it adjusts the values of global parameters that affect the behaviors of systems of individuals and families in the FN3D_V3 model, however, the design and operation of the mortality-based feedback mechanism embedded in the model has potential effects on other demographic outcomes: behaviors related to household size and composition, marriage, and fertility articulate with one another and are potentially affected by the way in which global changes in death probabilities are instituted.

In this paper, I analyze the sensitivity of these nonmortality demographic outcomes to the strength of the mortality-based feedback mechanism that is embedded in the model. I add a parameter (*popMortAdjustMult* which stands for "population mortality adjustment multiplier" and is abbreviated here as *pMAM*) to the model that can be used to vary the "strength" of the population size-based adjustment to the probability of death. Holding the values of all other parameters constant, I perform an experiment that uses 1000 separate runs to sweep through a wide range of values for *pMAM*. Results suggest that the strength of the mortality-based feedback is positively associated with the range of variability in outcomes such as mean household size, mean male age at marriage, mean percentage and intensity of polygynous marriage, mean total fertility, and mean inter-birth interval (because polygynous marriage was permitted in these experiments, mean female age at marriage was always

15—the earliest age at which marriage was possible). The smaller population sizes produced by stronger feedbacks exhibit a greater degree of variability in behaviors related to marriage, reproduction, and household size. This is potentially significant both in terms of planning and implementing experiments with the FN3D model and for understanding the demographic characteristics of past human systems that existed in the context of strong constraints on population growth.

7.2 The Model

The FN3D_V3 model is a nonspatial ABM designed to serve as a platform for exploring hunter-gatherer demography. It is a development from the ForagerNet2 (White 2012) and FamilyNet2 (White 2013) models. It is a generalized model that is not intended to exhaustively represent all details of any given hunter-gatherer system. The exclusion of extraneous detail is a purposeful strategy to aid in constructing a model whose structure and behavior are understandable and potentially relevant to many cases. In the terminology of Gilbert (2008), FN3D_V3 is a "middle range" model that aims "to describe the characteristics of a particular social phenomenon, but in a sufficiently general way that their conclusions can be applied" to many examples of the same phenomenon (Gilbert 2008, p. 42).

The FN3D_V3 model was written in the Java programming language and built using Repast J (Recursive Porous Agent Simulation Toolkit, Java version), a free, open-source agent-based modeling and simulation toolkit that was created at the University of Chicago in collaboration with Argonne National Laboratory (North et al. 2006). The raw code for the FN3D_V3 model and detailed descriptions of its classes, variables, parameters, structure, and operation are provided online at www.openabm.org. Documentation of Repast can be found at www.repast.sourceforge.net. This section provides a brief overview of the design and operation of the model augmented by a short description of factors affecting fertility, mortality, and stable population size in the model.

7.3 General Design, Operation, and Model Validity

The FN3D_V3 model has three main "levels": person, household, and system. Each agent in the model represents an individual person that is a discrete entity with a unique identity. Households are coresidential groupings of persons that form through marriage and change in size and composition primarily through marriage, reproduction, and mortality. Social links define relationships between pairs of living persons and are used to enforce marriage prohibitions. The system of the model is composed of all persons and households in existence at a given point in time. Model-level parameters set conditions for all persons or all households in the world and define aspects of the system: all persons become eligible to marry at the same age, for example. There is no spatial component to interaction and behavior, eliminating the potential effects of information flow, mobility, and population density on the analysis performed here.

Methods are named sections or "chunks" of code that perform a sequence of operations when called. Methods representing marriage, reproduction, and death operate at the person and household levels in this model. Individual persons and households make probabilistic decisions about reproduction, marriage, and infanticide based on the current dependency ratio of the household (the ratio of the number of consumers to the number of producers in the household). While the base probabilities affecting reproduction and mortality are set by model-level parameters (i.e., they are the same across the population), the economic circumstances of individual households affect the behavior of individuals in those households on a case-by-case, step-by-step basis (see below).

At the start of each run, the model produces an initial population of a specified number of persons of random sex and random age between 15 (the age at which the potential for reproduction begins) and 20. The initial households in a model run are created through marriages between eligible males and females in this initial population. A model run starts with an initial population of reproductive-age adults rather than a "realistic" population age distribution in order to allow the characteristics of the living population to emerge through person- and household-level interactions and behaviors.

Following the creation of the initial population, time passes in the form of discrete steps. Each step represents 1 week (5200 steps representing 100 years). At each step the model initiates a sequence of operations that includes the methods for marriage, reproduction, and death. This same sequence of operations is repeated in every subsequent step until the model has completed a specified number of steps.

The validity of a model (how well the model represents what it is intended to represent) can be evaluated by comparing the behaviors of the model with the known behaviors of the real world systems it purports to represent (see Gilbert 2008). A summary of ethnographic data on variables related to hunter-gatherer reproduction, marriage, and household size is presented in Table 7.1. Data from the experiments discussed below ($n = 1000$ runs) demonstrate that, at the settings utilized for this paper, the model produces distributions of values for most of these

Table 7.1 Summary of ethnographic data on hunter-gatherer fertility, mortality, and marriage age

Variable	Range	Approximate mean	Reference(s)
Total fertility rate	2.6–8.0 births	5.4 births	Hewlett (1991), Table 2; Pennington (2001), Table 7.2
Inter-birth interval	2.5–4.0 years	–	Kelly (1995), Table 6.7; Pennington (2001), Table 7.4
Intensity of polygyny	0–10 wives	–	Betzig (1986), Keen (2006)
Infant mortality	10–30 %	20 %	Hewlett (1991), Table 3; Kelly (1995), Table 6.9
Female age at marriage	5–22 years	14 years	Binford (2001), Table 8.07
Male age at marriage	12–35 years	21 years	Binford (2001), Table 8.07

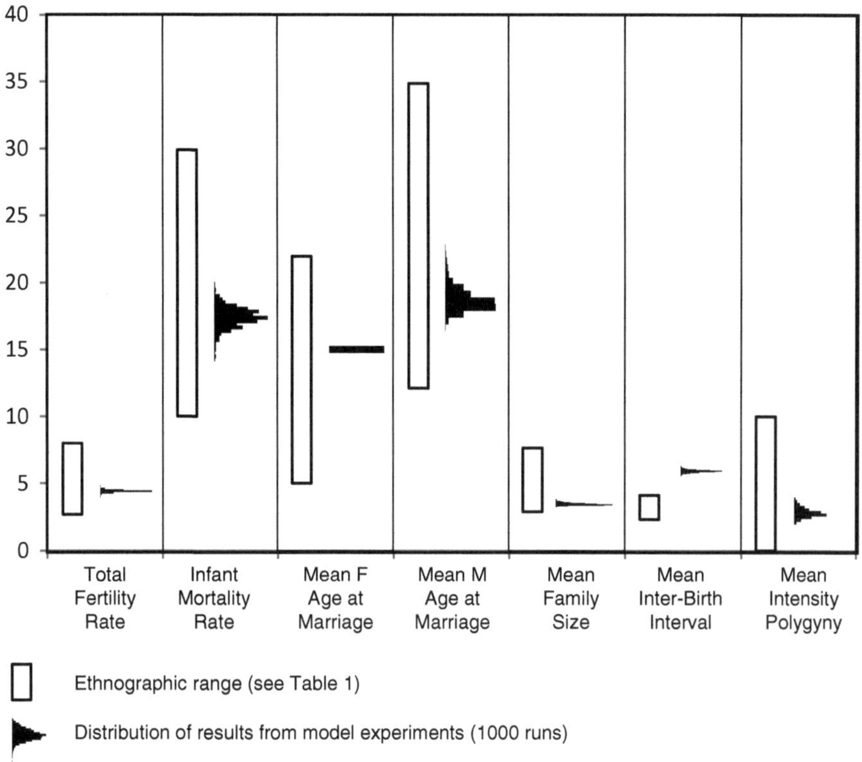

Fig. 7.1 Comparison of distribution of demographic outcomes from model experiments with ranges documented in ethnographic record

variables that overlap the ethnographic ranges (Fig. 7.1). The exception is inter-birth interval, which is greater in the model runs than in observed ethnographic cases (about 6 years in the model vs. an ethnographic range of 2.5–4 years). The high values for inter-birth interval are probably related to the high value (age 14) set for the parameter *ageAtProduction*, which determines when subadults become producers (see below). At the settings utilized in this paper, the populations in the model have relatively low fertility, family size, and mean male age at marriage.

The demographic outcomes compared in Fig. 7.1 are system-level characteristics that are the result of the interplay between person- and household-level interactions and behaviors and the model-level "rules" and constraints that influence marriage, reproduction, and mortality. The households that form within the model systems are verifiably consistent with those documented among ethnographic hunter-gatherers in terms of their size, composition, and developmental cycles (see White 2013, pp. 157–158). These points of consistency suggest that the FN3D_V3 model reasonably captures many basic aspects of hunter-gatherer systems and is therefore a useful tool for investigating the demographic characteristics of hunter-gatherer populations and understanding how the strength of a mortality-based feedback related to population size affects those demographic characteristics.

7.4 Fertility, Mortality, and Stability of Population Size

Fertility, mortality, and population size in the FN3D_V3 model are affected by: (1) the values of model-level parameters that apply to the entire population; (2) person- and household-level behaviors and interactions; and (3) feedbacks among various components of the model. This section describes how fertility and mortality are represented in the model and how population size is regulated.

7.4.1 Fertility and Reproduction

Following the start of a model run, new persons in the population are created through reproduction. Only married females who are neither currently pregnant nor in a period of postpartum amenorrhea are eligible to become pregnant. The maximum period of postpartum amenorrhea (a period of infertility following childbirth) is set by the value of the parameter *maxPPA*. When *maxPPA* = 72 weeks (18 months), the probability that a female will return to a fertile state each week following childbirth is calculated as 1/72 (0.0139). Females who remain infertile during this period automatically regain fertility after 72 weeks.

A female's *potential* fertile period occurs between the ages of 11 and 55. The yearly base probabilities of a married, fertile female becoming pregnant are not constant, but vary with age following a pattern similar to that documented for the !Kung (Howell 1979) and the Ache (Hill and Hurtado 1996) (Table 7.2). The peak reproductive years are between ages 21 and 40. These base probabilities in Table 7.2 are adjusted by multiplication with the value of a model-level parameter (*fertilityMultiplier*). For a 24-year-old female, for example, the base probability of pregnancy each step of her 24th year is 0.00673 if the value of *fertilityMultiplie*r is set to 1.4 ($0.25 \times 1.4/52$). The *fertilityMultiplier* parameter can be used to adjust the model through a continuous range of global low to high fertility conditions while maintaining the shape of the age-specific curve.

The dependency ratio of a household is the ratio of food consumers (the total number of persons in a household) to food producers (the number of persons who are actively procuring and/or preparing food). In the model, the dependency ratio of a household affects the reproductive behavior of the household. The probability of pregnancy is reduced if the addition of another child would raise the household's dependency ratio above 1.75 (1.75 was chosen to represent the dependency ratio of a "typical" hunter-gatherer household based on ethnographic data presented by Binford [2001:230]). This represents the existence of mechanisms for avoiding pregnancy based on household-level economics. The chance of avoiding pregnancy is determined by calculating how much above 1.75 the dependency ratio would rise if another child were to be added and taking this amount as a percentage of 1.75 (e.g., the chance of avoidance is 100 % if another child would raise the dependency ratio of the household to 3.5). Successful reproduction results in the creation of a child of random sex who is then added to the household.

Table 7.2 Age-specific yearly base probabilities of pregnancy and death in the FN3D_V3 model

Age category (years)	Base probability of pregnancy	Base probability of death
0	0	0.07
1	0	0.07
2	0	0.06
3	0	0.05
4	0	0.04
5	0	0.03
6–10	0	0.02
11–15	0.01	0.015
16–20	0.15	0.015
21–25	0.25	0.015
26–30	0.28	0.015
31–35	0.28	0.015
36–40	0.25	0.015
41–45	0.15	0.018
46–50	0.08	0.02
51–55	0.01	0.03
56–60	0	0.04
61–65	0	0.08
66–70	0	0.12
71–75	0	0.20
76–80	0	0.30
81–85	0	0.30
>85	0	1.00

The reproduction methods also include a mechanism for terminating the life of a newborn infant (i.e., committing infanticide). The chance of infanticide is calculated using the dependency ratio in the same way as avoidance of procreation: the difference is that the birth and subsequent death of a child figure into infant mortality rates where avoidance of procreation does not. The sex of a child does not affect the probability of infanticide in the model.

7.4.2 *Mortality*

Each person is exposed to a risk of death at each step. The yearly base probabilities of death are age-specific and follow a pattern similar to that documented for the Ache (Hill and Hurtado 1996) and the Tsimane (Gurven and Kaplan 2007) (see Table 7.2). If a person reaches a certain maximum age (set by the value of the parameter *maxAge*), death is automatic. The base yearly probabilities of death are adjusted by multiplication with the value of a model-level parameter (*mortalityMultiplier*) that can be used to produce a continuous range of low to high mortality conditions while maintaining the shape of the age-specific curve. The value of *mortalityMultiplier* was held constant at one for the experiment in this paper. Infants can experience increased mortality rates through the economically sensitive infanticide mechanism that is represented in the model (see above).

7.4.3 Stability of Population Size

The model uses a feedback mechanism to stabilize the size of the population. A model-level parameter (*popMortAdjustPoint*) specifies the population size above which probabilities of death are increased and below which probabilities of death are decreased. At each step, the model adjusts death probabilities by comparing the current size of the population to the size of the population specified by *popMortAdjustPoint*. The variable *popMortAdjustment*, calculated at each step, is used to make a global adjustment to the age-specific probabilities of individual death. If the current population is 605, for example, and *popMortAdjustPoint*=500, the *popMortAdjustment* is 1.21 (605/500). If the current population is 400 and *popMortAdjustPoint*=500, the *popMortAdjustment* is 0.8 (400/500).

After being calculated based on population size, the value of *popMortAdjustment* is affected by the value of the parameter *popMortAdjustMult* (*pMAM*). The parameter *pMAM*, the main variable in the experiment described below, controls the "strength" of the mortality-based feedback to population size. It is applied by simply multiplying the set value of the parameter (which stays constant during a run and is applied every step, regardless of whether the population is above or below the *popMortAdjustPoint*) by the calculated value of *popMortAdjustment*. If the value of *pMAM* is two, for example, the *popMortAdjustment* calculated in a given step is doubled. Values of *pMAM* less than one reduce the strength of the mortality adjustment, while values greater than one increase it. Because *pMAM* is continuously variable, it can be used to sweep through mortality-based feedbacks that vary in strength from zero (no death) to infinity (certainly of death).

The probability of death at each step for each person is calculated by multiplying that person's age-specific probability of death by the calculated value of the *popMortAdjustment*. In the case of a 25-year-old (with a yearly probability of death of 0.015) in a population of 605 persons with a *popMortAdjustmentPoint* of 500 and a *pMAM* of 1.8, for example, the probability of death each step is 0.000627 ($(0.015/52)\times(605/500\times1.8)$), 0.0326 each year.

Note that a *popMortAdjustPoint* of 500 does not mean that the population will stabilize to a size around 500: it simply means that the base probabilities of death are positively or negatively adjusted based on whether population size is above or below 500. At a given value of *popMortAdjustPoint*, the particular size at which a model population stabilizes is a product of the balance between fertility and mortality. Populations with relatively low rates of fertility and high mortality tend to stabilize at sizes significantly below *popMortAdjustPoint*, while populations with high fertility rates and low mortality tend to stabilize at sizes well above *popMortAdjustPoint*.

7.5 Experiment and Results

Experimental data were generated to explore the relationships between the strength of the mortality-based feedback mechanism (the value of *pMAM*) and a variety of demographic outcomes: mean population size, mean household size, mean male age at marriage, mean percentage and intensity of polygynous marriage, mean total fertility, and mean inter-birth interval (defined in Table 7.3). A total of 1000 runs were performed, varying the value of *pMAM* randomly between 0.10 and 4.00 while holding the values of all other parameters constant (Table 7.4). A random rather

Table 7.3 Definition of demographic outcomes in experiment (data collected over last 500 years of experiment)

Demographic outcome	Definition
Mean population size	The mean size (number of persons) of the total population
Mean household size	The mean size (number of persons) of households. For purposes of data collection, a "household" is defined as a family unit containing an adult male and at least one other person
Mean male age at marriage	The mean age (years) of males at that time of their first marriages
Mean percentage of polygyny	The mean percentage of marriages that are polygynous (one male, multiple females) at each step
Mean intensity of polygyny	The mean number of wives per married male
Mean total fertility	The mean number of children born per female that survives to age 45
Mean inter-birth interval	The mean number of years between births

Table 7.4 Values of key parameters in experiments

Parameter	Description	Value
popMortAdjustPoint	Population threshold for adjusting death probabilities	300 (constant)
popMortAdjustMult (pMAM)	Strength of mortality-based feedback mechanism for stabilizing population size	0.1–4.0 (random)
ageAtMaturity	Age (in years) at which a person is eligible to marry (and therefore eligible to reproduce)	15 (constant)
agetAtProduction	Age (in years) at which a person is counted as a "producer" for purposes of calculating the dependency ratio of a household	14 (constant)
maxAge	Maximum age (in years) a person may attain	86 (constant)
popMortAdjustPoint	Population size above which base probabilities of mortality are increased and below which base probabilities of mortality are decreased	500 (constant)
maxPPA	Maximum duration (in weeks) of postpartum amenorrhea	72 (constant)
sustainableCP	Value of dependency ratio considered "normal"; a dependency ratio > *sustainableCP* has positive effect on probabilities of avoiding reproduction or committing infanticide	1.75 (constant)
fertilityMultiplier	Adjusts the base age-specific probabilities of pregnancy by a set factor	1 (constant)
mortalityMultiplier	Adjusts the base age-specific probabilities of death by a set factor	1 (constant)

than systematic sampling strategy was employed for the sake of the rapid production of data that would allow basic patterns to be recognized. The value of *pMAP* was arbitrarily set at 300.

Each model run was 1000 years (52,000 steps) in duration (Fig. 7.2). The first 500 years of each run are a stabilization period during which the size and structure of the population emerge. Figure 7.3 shows change in population size during an

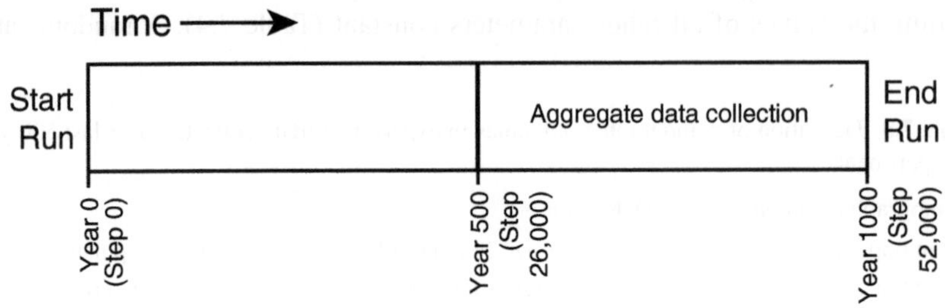

Fig. 7.2 Structure of 1000-year experiment run with data collection during second 500-year period

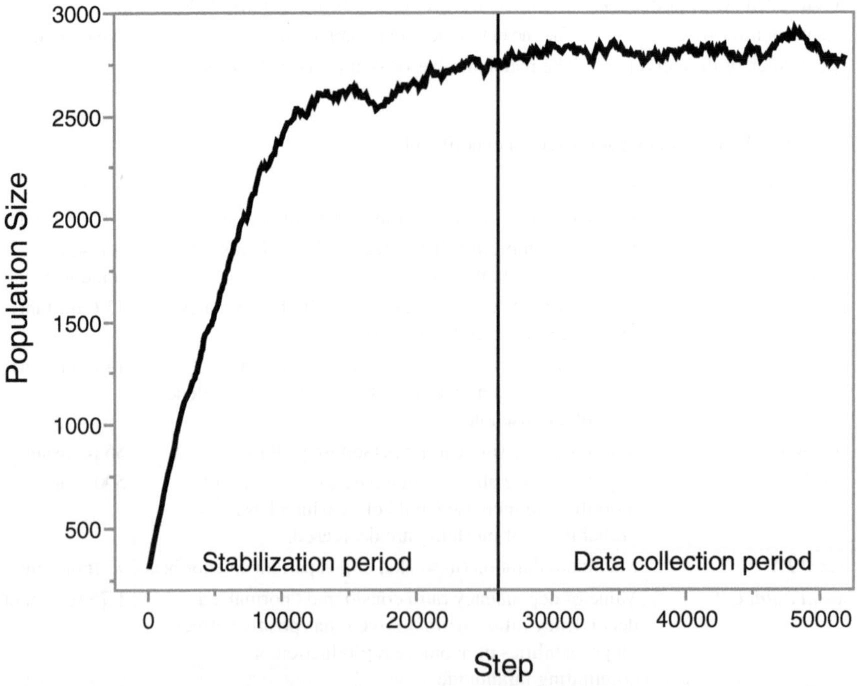

Fig. 7.3 Change in population size during a single experiment run with a low setting of *pMAM* (0.1). The 500-year stabilization period allows fertility and mortality to balance

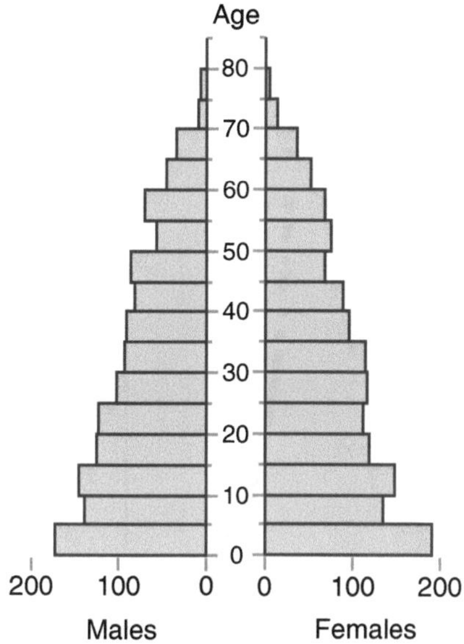

Fig. 7.4 Age structure pyramid from example run shown in Fig. 7.3. Data from 2817 individuals collected at step 39,001

example run with a low setting of *pMAM*: the population requires hundreds of years to stabilize in size. Figure 7.4 shows the age–structure pyramid of the population from that example run at step 39,001 (midway through the data collection period). Data required for calculating relevant demographic variables are collected over the course of the second 500 years of the run. Summary data are produced at the end of a run and appended to a data file for analysis.

Results from this experiment suggest a number of relationships between the value of *pMAM* and the demographic outcomes. The value of *pMAM* is closely related to population size, with smaller populations exhibiting a greater degree of variability in behaviors related to marriage, reproduction, and household size.

7.5.1 Mean Population Size

The value of *pMAM* is clearly related to the mean size of the population during a model run (Fig. 7.5). As shown by the reference lines in Fig. 7.5a, the point at which population size "balances" is maintained slightly below the set threshold (i.e., the value of *pMAP*, in this case 300) when *pMAM* is set to one. Mean population size increases rapidly as the value of *pMAM* is decreased below one: the mortality "penalty" is not sufficiently strong to offset fertility and constrain the population size to anywhere near the set threshold of 300. Mean population sizes smaller than 300 are produced when the value of *pMAM* is greater than one, but the effect is weaker than when *pMAM* is below one. The relationship between *pMAM* and mean population size is linear when both axes are logarithmic (Fig. 7.5b).

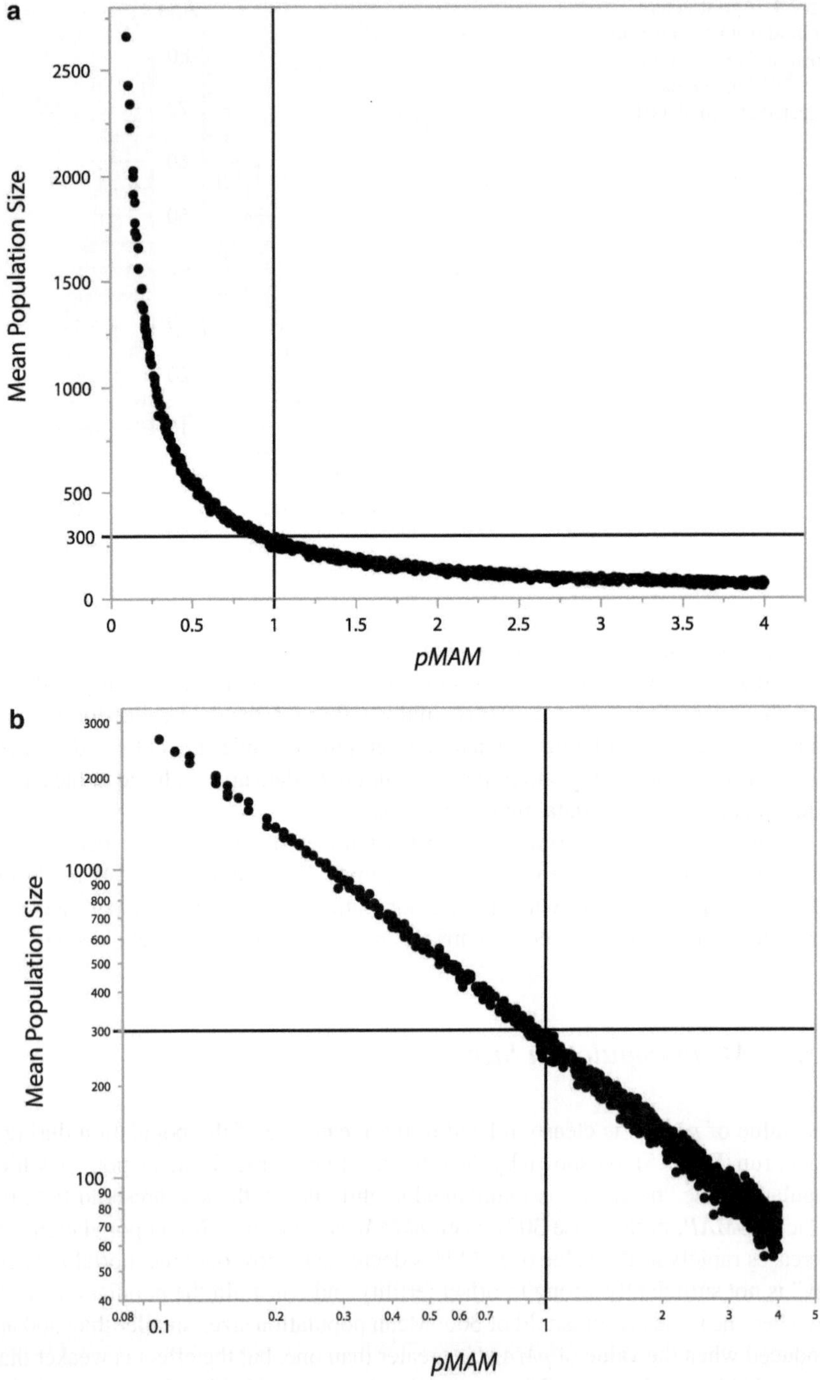

Fig. 7.5 Relationship between value of *pMAM* and mean population size

7.5.2 Other Demographic Outcomes

Relationships between the value of *pMAM* and the six other demographic characteristics defined in Table 7.2 are shown in Fig. 7.6. In each case, higher values of *pMAM* are associated with greater variability of demographic outcomes. This is shown clearly in Fig. 7.7a, which graphs the coefficient of variation (CV) of each demographic outcome by the value of *pMAM* with observations grouped into increments of 0.25. The CV is a dimensionless measure of variation that is calculated by dividing the standard deviation by the mean of a group of observations.

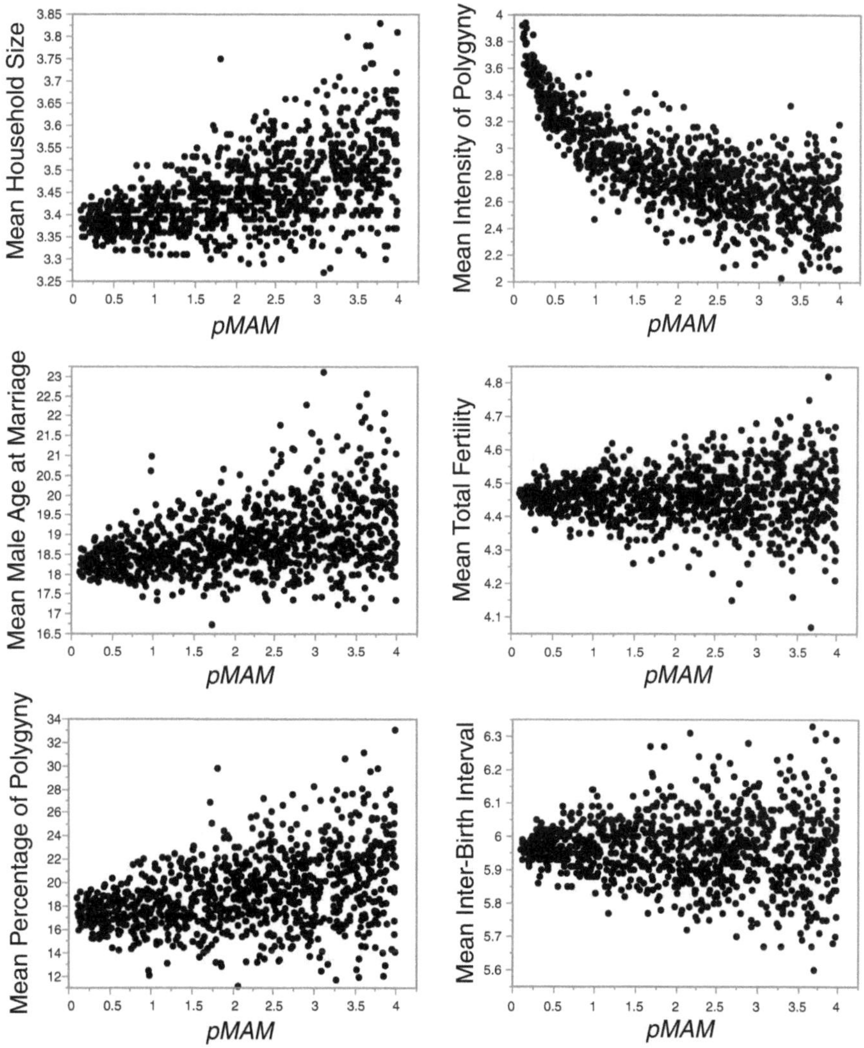

Fig. 7.6 Relationships between value of *pMAM* and demographic outcomes

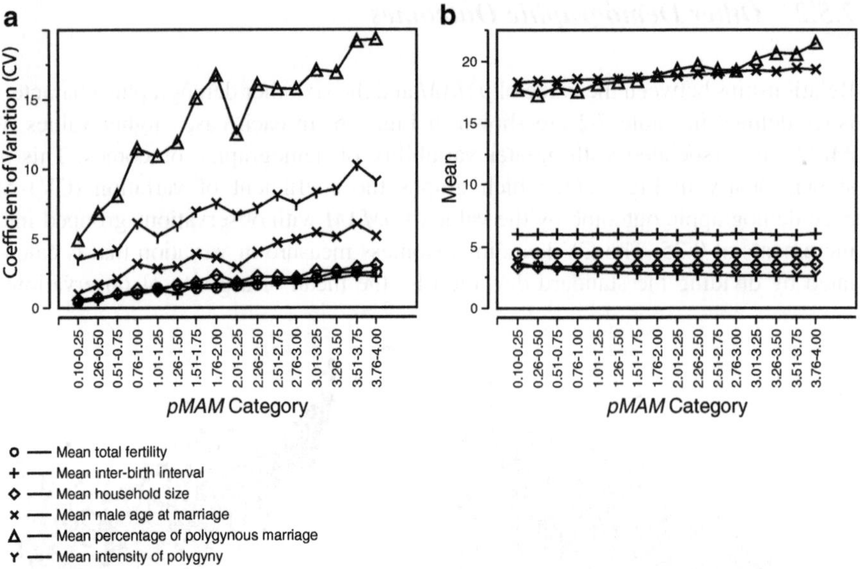

Fig. 7.7 Coefficients of variation (a) and means (b) of demographic outcomes by categories of *pMAM*

Demographic outcomes most closely related to marriage (percentage of polygynous marriage, intensity of polygyny, and male age at marriage) have the highest CVs and show the most pronounced positive relationships between CV and *pMAM*. These three characteristics also exhibit the greatest change in the mean as *pMAM* is varied from 0.1 to 4.0 (Fig. 7.7b).

7.6 Analysis and Discussion

The results from the experiment indicate that the strength of the mortality-based feedback to population size (the value of *pMAM*) is related to both (1) the population size at which the model finds a "balance point" between mortality and fertility and (2) several demographic characteristics that are indirectly affected by mortality. In the first case, the relationship is strong and nonlinear, with the value of *pMAM* being a relatively good predictor of the mean population size. The second case is quite different: it is the amount of variation among runs with identical settings that changes significantly as the value of *pMAM* is adjusted between 0.1 and 4.0.

It is not immediately obvious how a stronger mortality-based feedback to population size produces more variable outcomes in the demographic characteristics of the model populations. Plots of the value of *pMAM* versus infant mortality (yearly probability of death before age 1), child mortality (yearly probability of death between the ages of 2 and 11), and adult mortality (yearly probability of death between the ages of 16 and 51) show a pattern of increasing variation in mortality outcomes as *pMAM* increases in value (Fig. 7.8), very similar to the demographic

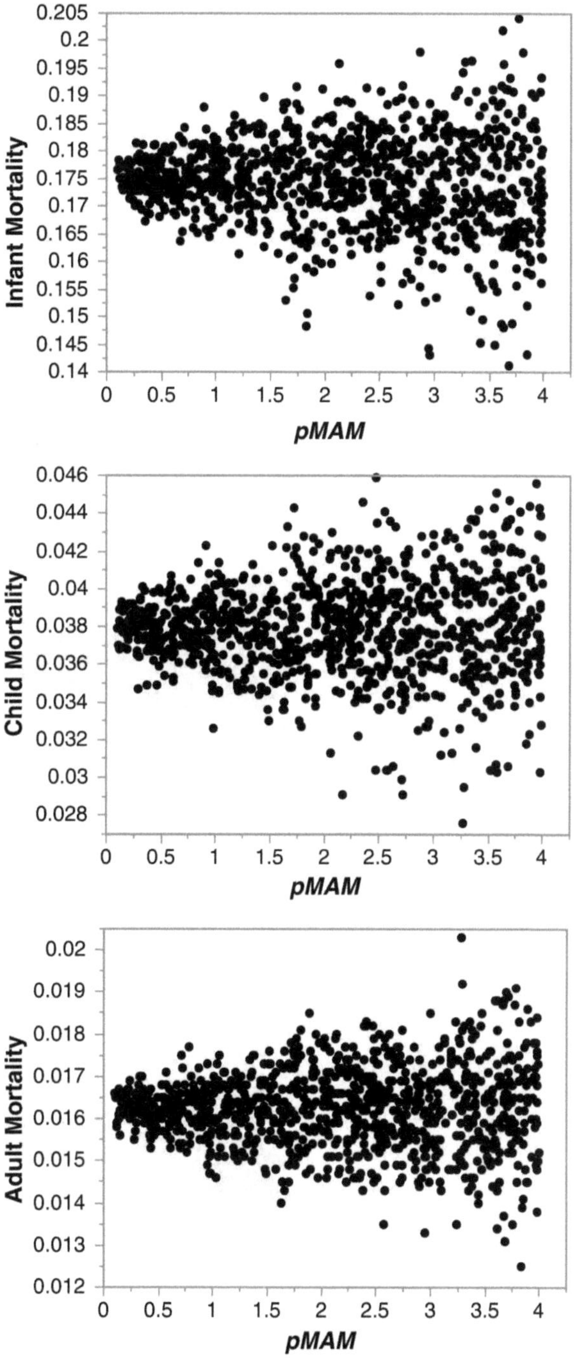

Fig. 7.8 Relationships between *pMAM* and infant, child, and adult mortality rates experienced by model populations

outcomes already discussed. This may seem somewhat counterintuitive, as one might logically expect that a more severe mortality-based constraint on population size would result in uniformly higher rates of mortality. Remember, however, that the actual mortality and fertility rates experienced by a population in a model such as this emerge as the result of numerous factors: a higher value of *pMAM* does not necessarily result in higher mortality rates.

The strongest relationship observed in the experiments was between the value of *pMAM* and the mean size of a population (see Fig. 7.5). In most runs where the value of *pMAM* was greater than two, mean population size was less than 100. In general, the experiments show that variability in demographic outcomes increases as *pMAM* increases and mean population size drops (see Figs. 7.6 and 7.7). These smaller populations do not necessarily experience higher overall rates of mortality and fertility—both of these metrics become progressively less variable as population size increases (Fig. 7.9).

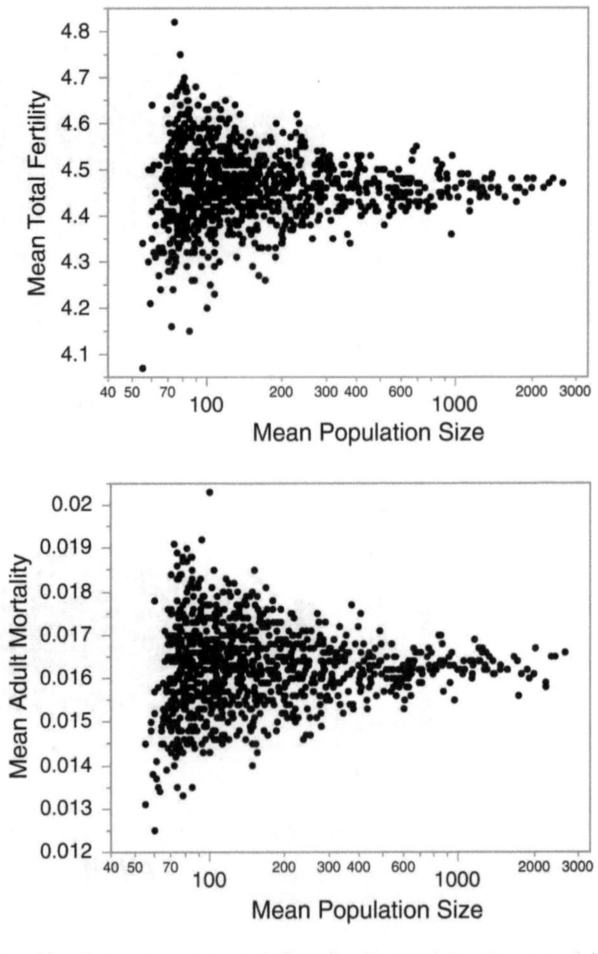

Fig. 7.9 Relationships between mean population size (log scale) and mean adult mortality and mean total fertility experienced by model populations

Overall, it appears that small populations in the model that are exposed to a strong negative feedback on population size can exist in a wider variety of forms than larger populations in terms of patterns and behaviors related to marriage and family size. At least some of this variability is attributable to the relatively large impact that demographic stochasticity can have in small populations: the smaller the population, the greater the proportion of the population is represented by each individual, and the greater the potential impact of each birth and death on the characteristics of the entire population (Moore 2001, p. 403; Shaffer 1981; Wobst 1975). The outcome of a random dice roll affecting reproduction or marriage has a much greater potential effect in a population of 60 than in a population of 2600.

The summary results from the experiments do not allow extensive investigation of how the various demographic outcomes are related in small populations. There are weak/moderate correlations among mean household size, adult mortality, male age at marriage, and the percentage of polygynous marriage. Further work will be required to understand the specific cause–effect relationships that drive these correlations.

The observation of a higher degree of variability in demographic outcomes among populations constrained by a strong mortality-based feedback is noteworthy for two reasons. First, these results suggest care should be taken when choosing population settings for experiments using the FN3D_V3 model. Experiments performed on smaller populations may naturally produce more variable results (in terms of demographic characteristics) than otherwise identical experiments performed on larger populations. That "extra" variability could potentially mask interesting behaviors or differences that are the subject of the experiment.

Second, these results suggest that we might expect significant variability in the demographic characteristics of actual human populations that existed in circumstances similar to those in the model (numerically small populations in environments with strong negative feedbacks to population growth). The results of the simple experiment performed here suggest that multiple "kinds" of marriage/reproductive systems may have been viable at small population sizes. This would be a fruitful area for future modeling work.

7.7 Conclusion

This analysis has shown that the demography of populations in the FN3D_V3 model is sensitive to the strength of the mortality-based feedback that constrains population size. In general, the smaller populations that are exposed to a strong mortality "penalty" have more variable demographic characteristics than larger populations operating under weaker mortality-based feedbacks. These differences could be analytically significant when using the FN3D_V3 model for experimentation and should be kept in mind when planning and implementing experiments. As shown in Fig. 7.1, however, all of the variability produced during the experiment for this analysis (with the exception of inter-birth interval) fall within the range documented among ethnographic hunter-gatherers. This suggests that the feedbacks within the model that allow the system to find a balance between mortality and fertility do not, within the continuum of settings explored here, produce model systems with demographic characteristics that are significantly different from those human hunter-gatherer systems we have observed in the ethnographic present. Even when a harsh mortality penalty is used to constrain populations to one third of the "carrying capacity" of the model environment, the model system that emerges has demographic characteristics that are not unreasonable. This suggests that the model remains a valid representation of a hunter-gatherer system under a wide range of conditions.

References

Betzig, L. L. (1986). *Despotism and differential reproductive success: A Darwinian view of human history*. Chicago: Aldine.

Binford, L. R. (2001). *Constructing frames of reference: An analytical method for archaeological theory building using hunter-gatherer and environmental data sets*. Berkeley: University of California Press.

Gilbert, N. (2008). *Agent-based models. Quantitative applications in the social sciences* (p. 153). Thousand Oaks, CA: Sage.

Gurven, M., & Kaplan, H. (2007). Longevity among hunter-gatherers: A cross-cultural examination. *Population and Development Review, 33*, 321–356.

Hewlett, B. S. (1991). Demography and childcare in preindustrial societies. *Journal of Anthropological Research, 47*, 1–37.

Hill, K., & Hurtado, A. M. (1996). *Ache life history: The ecology and demography of a foraging people*. New York: Aldine de Gruyter.

Howell, N. (1979). *Demography of the Dobe! Kung*. New York: Academic Press.

Keen, I. (2006). Constraints on the development of enduring inequalities in Late Holocene Australia. *Current Anthropology, 47*, 7–38.

Kelly, R. L. (1995). *The foraging spectrum: Diversity in hunter-gatherer lifeways*. Washington, DC: Smithsonian Institution Press.

Moore, J. H. (2001). Five models of human colonization. *American Anthropologist, 103*, 395–408.

North, M., Nicholson, J., Collier, T., & Vos, J. R. (2006). Experiences creating three implementations of the repast agent modeling toolkit. *ACM Transactions on Modeling and Computer Simulation, 16*(1), 1–25.

Pennington, R. (2001). Hunter-gatherer demography. In C. Panter-Brick, R. H. Layton, & P. Rowley-Conwy (Eds.), *Hunter-gatherers: An interdisciplinary perspective* (pp. 170–204). Cambridge: Cambridge University Press.

Shaffer, M. L. (1981). Minimum population sizes for species conservation. *BioScience, 31*(2), 131–134.

White, A. A. (2012). *The social networks of early hunter-gatherers in Midcontinental North America*. Unpublished Doctoral Dissertation, Department of Anthropology, University of Michigan.

White, A. A. (2013). Subsistence economics, family size, and the emergence of social complexity in hunter-gatherer systems in Eastern North America. *Journal of Anthropological Archaeology, 32*(1), 122–163.

White, A. A. (2014). Mortality, fertility, and the OY ratio in a model hunter-gatherer system. *American Journal of Physical Anthropology, 154*(2), 222–231.

Wobst, H. M. (1975). The demography of finite populations and the origins of the incest taboo. In Population studies in archaeology and biological anthropology: A symposium. *Memoirs of the Society for American Archaeology, 30*, 75–81.

Chapter 8
Archaeological Simulation and the Testing Paradigm

Thomas G. Whitley

8.1 Introduction

Simulation in archaeology is not an entirely well-defined field. Broadly speaking, there are many archaeological methods and techniques that could be considered, in some way, *simulating* aspects of the past. This is particularly true where the term "model" is used in the discussion, and even more so when a temporal component of some kind is implied; temporality being a defining characteristic of archaeology. "Model" in this sense refers to a combination of datasets (not always spatial) that may result in an interpretation, but it does not necessarily go beyond the static depiction of that data, despite the invocation of temporality. The classic example is the traditional approach to *archaeological predictive modeling* (e.g., Dalla Bona 1994; Deeben et al. 1997, 2002; Hudak et al. 2002; Judge and Sebastian 1988; Kohler and Parker 1986; Kvamme 1983, 1984, 1985; Parker 1985).

A predictive model may entail many parameters and formulas and can be applied in highly sophisticated ways, but the end result is almost always a dichotomous high/low probability map with little dynamic variability or insight into human behavior. This may in fact stem from the tendency to make predictions about where sites may be found based on where sites are already known, the so-called *inductive* approach (cf. Altschul et al. 2004; Ejstrud 2003; Harris 2006; Kamermans et al. 2009; van Leusen and Kamermans 2005; Verhagen 2005, 2007; Verhagen and Whitley 2012; Whitley 2004a). In other words, we often use the archaeological record to predict where we might find (as yet unknown) archaeological material, but the process has much less to say about how that material got there in the first place

T.G. Whitley (✉)
Department of Anthropology, Sonoma State University, Rohnert Park, CA, USA
e-mail: tgwhitley27@gmail.com

M. Brouwer Burg et al. (eds.), *Uncertainty and Sensitivity Analysis in Archaeological Computational Modeling*, Interdisciplinary Contributions to Archaeology, DOI 10.1007/978-3-319-27833-9_8

than we would like to believe; that is, the *mechanism* is often absent. This may be modeling, but I do not consider this simulation.

I would argue that formal simulations in archaeology, in contrast, are intended to go beyond the *static* display of information. The assumption is that human agency (or cognitive decision-making) is either implicit or explicit in the simulation. Most frequently simulations in economics or the social sciences are distinguished from models by their engagement of a temporal or dynamic *process* (cf. Hartman 1996; Humphreys 2004; Phan and Varenne 2010; Winsberg 2009). This may be thought of as the iterative transformation of input data, or information, into some form of output. Models are also transformations of input data into output representations. They may also include alternative transformations or "feedback" within them, but the output is far more important than understanding or explaining the process itself (Fig. 8.1). In contrast, simulations are not static but both dynamic and mechanistic. Though they need not be inherently dynamical or "self-organizing" (e.g., Axtell et al. 2006; Bonatti et al. 2005; Dean et al. 2006; Kohler and van der Leeuw 2007; Strogatz 2001). Put simply, a simulation is the functional interaction of a set of models, and it produces a typically iterative though not necessarily sequential output, based on different permutations of the input data (Fig. 8.2).

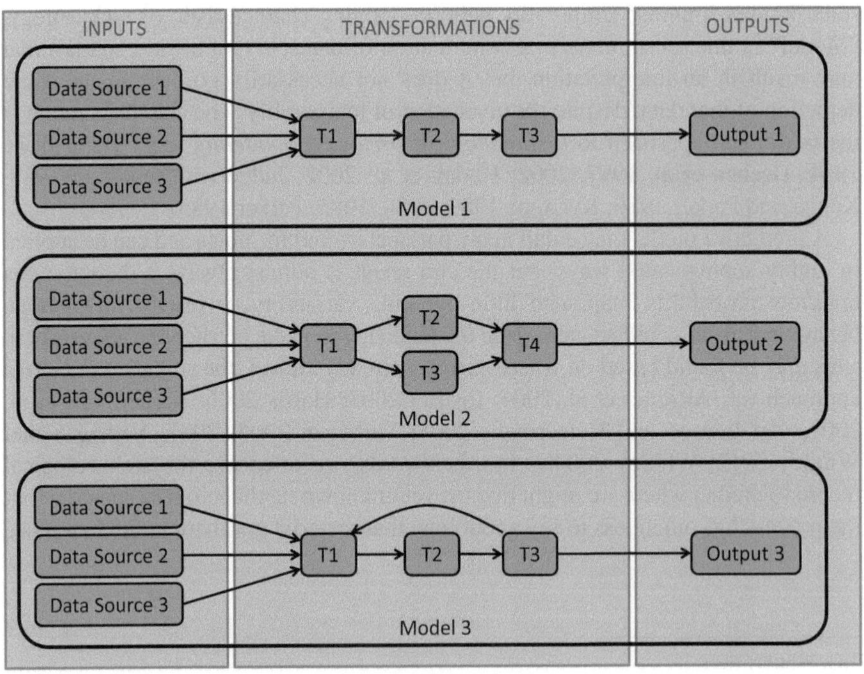

Fig. 8.1 Schematic representation of the structure of "models"

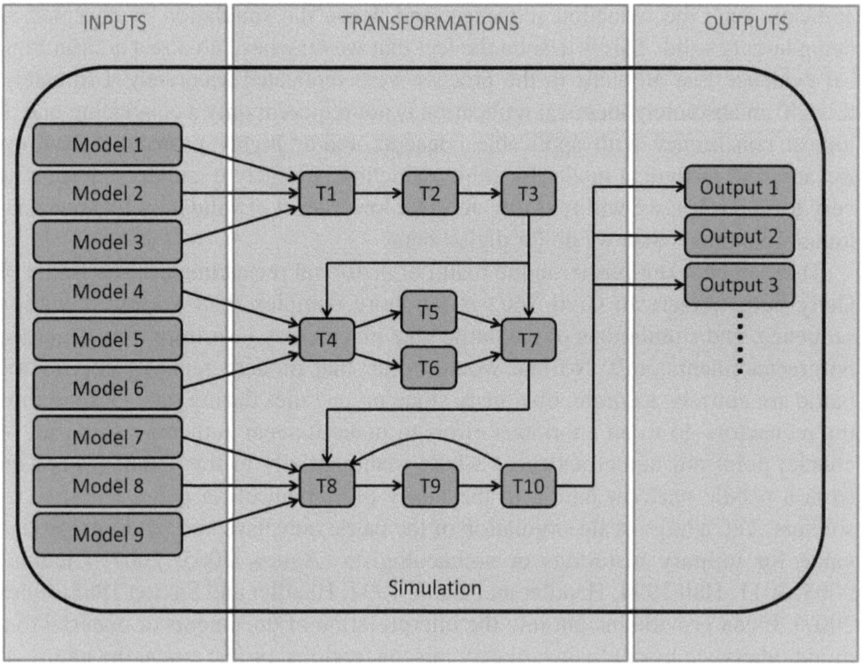

Fig. 8.2 Schematic representation of the structure of a "simulation"

8.2 Analogue Simulations

But archaeological simulations need not imply the use of autonomous computer agents, Geographic Information Systems (GIS), or digital data of any kind. We should remember that specialists in replicating primitive technology are, in essence, creating *analogue* forms of simulation, are acting as "agents" in that process, and they have been doing this for a very long time (e.g., Bordes 1950; Callahan 1994; Crabtree 1972; Crabtree and Butler 1964; Wescott 2011). By reenacting the processes of lithic raw material reduction, for example, and creating functional tools, the lithic specialist is simulating past human choice, decisions, and actions; usually of a single individual, and all in a cause-and-effect framework. If the end result of that simulation is a modern version of a Clovis point, then those actions are the imitation of a learned cognitive process that is theoretically consistent with how the archaeological examples of such tools were created.

The simulation may imply the articulation between physical laws, as a function of the properties of the raw material, and the sequence of actions that produced the chosen outcome. But it does not test or validate those laws or actions in any explicit way. Rather, because the modern simulated point *looks* nearly identical to the authentic one, the reduction sequence, and hence the simulation, is accepted as being largely valid. This is despite the fact that we may have no direct archaeological evidence that all steps in the process were replicated accurately. Ultimately, though, an absolutely identical replication is not required; only a convincing one of logical consistency with applicable concepts and/or highly probable behaviors. Because the analytical model for lithic reduction is largely qualitative, despite its very formal rules, we will typically accept a lower level of validation for such analogue simulations than we do for digital ones.

This can be taken further in the realm of historical reenactments. The Battle of Gettysburg (American Civil War) is far more complex than a lithic reduction sequence, and simulations of the battle take place every year (http://www.gettysburgreenactment.com/). No one would argue that modern reenactments of the battle are entirely accurate, obviously since no one dies during one. Despite this, the reenactors go to an enormous effort to make it seem authentic. One can, of course, point out numerous cases where inauthenticity in the details creeps in: from a plastic uniform button to the faulty placement of an entire battalion of soldiers. Yet, a large-scale simulation of the battle may have very real interpretive value for military historians or archaeologists (Agnew 2005, 2007; Clemons 2008, 2011; Hall 1994; Handler and Gable 1997; Handler and Saxton 1988; Jones 2007). It can provide insight into the interpretation of documents or material that might otherwise be confusing, clarify misconceptions, or just reveal the nature of the human experience.

With reenactments, it may not be the accuracy of the simulation that is enlightening, but the placing of behavior into a sequential and spatial context. Such context may even be seen as testing ideas that have been derived from the historic documents or the archaeological record. This is very different from an inductive archaeological predictive model. Instead of using the fragmentary archaeological record to find more of the same without explanation, the simulation is being used to help *explain* the archaeological record in terms of the mechanisms by which it got there and perhaps why. Or at least it is intended to provide a descriptive context of some kind. This fully engages archaeological simulations of all kinds (digital or analogue) within the realm of explanatory theory. It is also a separation of the *general* processes (i.e., military strategy) from the *specific* details (i.e., the Gettysburg battle narrative itself and its remnant archaeological record).

My point, though, is that the digital application of simulation methods in archaeology, including agent-based modeling (ABM) or multi-agent simulation (MAS) techniques, is part of a long history of experimentation and should not be looked upon as fundamentally, or theoretically, distinct from our approaches to other forms of archaeology. They carry with them the same assumptions regarding our acquisition, manipulation, and interpretation of archaeological or historical knowledge. This is in addition to their independent computational, statistical, or mathematical suppositions. Those may in turn be dependent upon a whole host of methodological or theoretical issues related to advanced mathematics or digital computation.

8.3 Theoretical Assumptions of Archaeological Simulation

It is, in fact, the archaeological assumptions themselves which are perhaps most problematic with respect to our ability to test, refute, or validate digital simulations rather than the absence of, or lack of clarity in, the proper use of the technology or statistical evaluative methods. Developing the techniques of digital simulation is perhaps "…still in its infancy, and computational social scientists are getting on as [if] they were craftsmen of a new method." (Boero and Squazzoni 2005, p. 1.12). But the theoretical basis and the overall approach is nothing particularly new. We are, in fact, applying new methods to an old concept. But the problem is still the same: *How do we know when a simulation actually approximates what really happened in the past?* To get to the heart of that question I would like to begin by breaking down the theoretical assumptions of such simulation.

8.3.1 Systems, Mechanisms, and Iteration

The first assumption that I would make in constructing an archaeological simulation is accepting the notion that human decision-making is a system and not arbitrarily random or a series of unrelated "decision events." By this, I do not imply that there is, or is not, an overarching "systems theory" that is applicable to all of human or social agency (e.g., von Bertalanffy 1970; Luhmann 1975; Parsons 1978; Warren et al. 1998), only that the process of making decisions based on the input of information (spatial or otherwise) is "an assemblage or combination of things or parts forming a complex or unitary whole" (http://dictionary.reference.com/browse/system). In this discussion I am specifically referencing simulations where a choice between multiple outcomes is made by the agent(s). These may be spatial choices, such as the movements of autonomous agents across the digital manifold or things that affect large-scale GIS surface outputs. There may also be other kinds of agent-modeled output, such as tables of numerical data, charts, or graphs.

But this brings up the concept of whether or not we should test human behavior against random occurrences; that is, is "random behavior" the null hypothesis? There is a fair amount of literature on the study of randomness in biological systems, and how much it contributes to social, or other kinds of, behaviors (e.g., Bartumeus 2009; Perony et al. 2012; Schweitzer 2003). This is largely in the sense of how stochastic processes such as Brownian motion, or Levy flights for example, can contribute to human or animal decision-making and by how much. Invoking the effects of stochastic processes on human behavior, though, does not imply that decision-making is at its heart unintentional or that they are distinct episodes of unrelated action. I would argue that we can make an assumption from the outset that some random processes will affect human decision-making, and that some single decisions are, in fact, potentially entirely random. Simulation may be used to examine the amount of randomness in a system, but a decision-making system (i.e., meaning it is intended for repetition) is intentional and thus inherently nonrandom.

Being a system, or system-like, suggests that there is a decision-making *mechanism* to be discovered by the archaeologist. "Mechanism" in this sense is "the agency or means by which an effect is produced or a purpose is accomplished" (http://dictionary.reference.com/browse/mechanism). A somewhat consistent set of criteria *must* have been referenced in making the decision under analysis. If the target decision-making was not a system, it would have been completely *ad hoc* in every instance. This would be regardless of whether the decisions were made by individuals or groups of people in the past. No doubt there are specific instances of decision-making that are *ad hoc*, but being so makes them not particularly iconic or representative of the kinds of things that we as social scientists are likely to study, and they may not be conducive to interpretation through simulation at all since they are not repeatable. It should not be construed that I am in any way arguing that all of the kinds of things that we care about as archaeologists can be digitally simulated. Simulation, whether digital or analogue, is merely a technique to address some kinds of things, not *all* of them.

Another direct implication is that human decision-making is *repetitively* applied. This may seem to be redundant with the notion of systematics, but it also means that the process of decision-making is iterative. It is not just that the same, or similar, processes are carried out each time the decision is being made, but that it is learned behavior and capable of being improved upon or changed. In other words, the process relies on information acquisition, transmission, and retention between and among individuals and groups. But learning specific behaviors may not be active or conscious in all cases. Nonetheless, it is a cultural marker: families, communities, and other spatially or culturally related groups share similar decision-making histories or contexts.

8.3.2 Cognition, Perception, and Decision Topology

Inherent in the desire to understand the system is our generalization from the simulation to a specific target group. But it also implies that there may be other approaches to making the same decisions. Of significant importance is when we consider the influence of Western thought upon how we design those simulations (Boero and Squazzoni 2005, p. 4.50; Janssen and Ostrom 2006: 37). This has been little explored and deserves much more detailed treatment than can be given here. Even when a simulation may replicate very closely the output of a set of archaeological decisions, there may have been other ways in which the same outputs could have been reached with very different transformations. This is the concept of "equifinality" or the idea that there may be multiple causal paths that produce the same outcome (George and Bennett 2005, p. 10). Behavioral systems may evolve under different conditions and with different inputs, yet look very similar.

Importantly, though, such a simulation assumes that a cognitive process is present. ABM and MAS simulations are specifically designed to represent the individual and the group as cognitive decision-makers respectively (Niazi and Hussain 2011, pp. 2–3). Other forms of simulation (large-scale GIS for example) can also imply a cognitive process, but the agents may be less explicit. In a large-scale GIS they may in fact be enacted through the processes of map algebra rather than as distinct computational agents in the manifold. Yet, either situation implies that it is very much *in the heads* of the agents, not external or an outcome imposed upon them. Ignoring the mechanism of cognition, though, and treating it like a "black box" is inherent with inductive predictive models (Whitley 2005, p. 124). By either explicitly applying one or more computer-generated autonomous agents to the process, or assuming the perspective of implicit agents, the archaeologist is making the assumption that the decision is cognitively contextual and has multiple potential outcomes given a broad range of initial and changing conditions. The decision-making process being modeled thus shapes the nature of the simulation.

Multiple variables also must be considered in this decision-making. A decision reliant on only one input variable could not be systematic; it would have to be unilateral. That is not to say that a simulation that looks at only one variable cannot be useful. It may be perfectly appropriate to create a simulation that holds a number of variables to be constant and to manipulate only a single variable through a series of iterations. This can be quite illuminating as to how one variable affects the entire decision-making system. However, the point I make here is that complex *mechanistic* simulations must consider the interaction of multiple variables as the criteria by which a decision is made. In this context, each input variable must have a positive or negative relationship to the decision being simulated. It either facilitates or hinders a specified outcome. This is a direct implication of causality in the process (cf. Pearl 2000; Salmon 1984, 1998). How or why the variable affects the decision is required in order to simulate it, and they must be distinguishable from pseudo-processes that lack a causal/mechanical connection.

Additionally, each variable's positive or negative relationship to the decision is learned from others or developed through personal observation and prediction (e.g., indirect evidence, heuristic mechanisms, past experience, or speculation). This implies a *perception* to the process. It may be manifest as an "egocentric frame of reference" for immediately observable phenomena and a "fixed frame of reference" for stored or predicted information (cf. Hart 1981; Kitchin and Blades 2002). Immersing the digital decision-maker into a spatial, or at least contextual, perception in some way is the very reason why ABM and MAS techniques are frequently chosen for simulations.

But that perception is also dependent upon the nature and quality of the information being perceived. There would be very few instances, for example, where a global frame of reference would be applicable in cognitive agent-based simulations because human beings do not maintain and access spatial data the same way as computers. There is a "fall-off" rate both spatially and temporally to the completeness, accuracy, and quality of information for human decision-makers, and the archaeologist must attempt to recreate this within the simulation. All spatial decisions are, in effect, local and few are based on complete and consistent knowledge across a spatial manifold in the manner in which we often engage GIS, ABM, or MAS simulations (Whitley 2004b).

Therefore, digital simulations that require the concept of cognitive agency may be referred to as being grounded in "decision topology." This relates to the process of making a decision based upon the "shape" or appearance of the input data at the time the decision is being made. It is a concept that is currently widespread in the realm of computational modeling for computer science and engineering applications (e.g., Barber 2007; Kumar and Prabhakar 2010; Pandey et al. 2013). It is employed as a tool to help organize decision-making and maximize information sharing among computerized agents and is intended to simulate the manner in which humans might process information. The idea is that a decision will result from an analysis of the "appearance" of all pertinent data as a whole, and the agent has the flexibility to consider not just the quantitative value of a piece of data, but also its quality and completeness prior to making a decision. In more complex models, there is a conduit of information sharing among agents that enhances the ability to understand the quality of information on hand; that is, agents do not always act in isolation. This is a basic assumption we have to make about human agents in both present and past contexts: they are not isolated and make flexible decisions based on the overall information on hand. But again, simulating a single agent or agents with varying degrees of information sharing may be a useful way to examine the nature of information exchange.

8.3.3 Weighted-Additive Frameworks and Bayesian Probability

The relationship between each variable and the decision outcomes must also be expressed mathematically. Although the decision-makers need not consciously comprehend a mathematical relationship for each influential variable, computerized decision topology simulations are dependent upon defined mathematical *rules, principles, or formulas* to operate because computers are mathematical devices. This means that each variable has to be quantitative. Where a qualitative variable is important, it has to be quantified, or at least ranked, in some manner to be input into a GIS, ABM, or MAS (i.e., categories have to be assigned a positive or negative relative or absolute value). Even the use of fuzzy modeling methods is still a quantification of the variable despite the flexibility in the outcomes.

Fuzzy modeling evolved out of "fuzzy set" theory (also called "fuzzy logic") and is a technique for considering uncertainty by ranking the "truth" or accuracy of information by a degree or percent rather than a binary (true/false) set (Hájek 1998; Halpern 2003; Yager and Filev 1994; Zadeh 1965). It is a form of probabilistic reasoning that can lend a great deal of freedom of choice to a decision-making model. Yet it is still, in effect, a simulation of "qualitative-ness" applied on top of quantitative data (the probability values). Again, though, this may mean that qualitative decision criteria that are not quantifiable (i.e., we do not know or cannot propose a probability value) might not always be subjectable to digital simulation (cf. Pillatt 2012, p. 578).

- ***Bayesian Rule of Total Probability:***

$$P(A) = \sum_i P(A|B_i)$$

Translated:

The probability of any decision is the sum of the probabilities of all exhaustive and mutually exclusive variables that cause that decision.

(i.e. a decision is additive)

- ***Bayesian Rule of Conditional Probability:***

$$P(A|K) = \sum_i P(A|B_i, K)(B_i|K)$$

The probability of any decision is the sum of the probabilities of each causal variable multiplied by the conditional probability of that variable.

(i.e. a decision is weighted)

Fig. 8.3 The Bayesian rules of total and conditional probability (from Pearl 2000: 3–4)

The ultimate decision topology within a fully quantified simulation is theoretically a *weighted-additive* expression of all pertinent variables in the same sense as that described for archaeological predictive models (Kohler and Parker 1986, pp. 422–424) but with the explicit assumption of a causal process. This is because a weighted-additive framework is a covering definition that encompasses all other forms of probability by articulating the overall relationships both within and among variables and all of the decision outcomes. All possible relationships exist in that framework.

Not the only way to illustrate this, but perhaps the best, is with the Bayesian rules of total and conditional probability (Fig. 8.3; Pearl 2000, pp. 3–4). These formulas present a summation of weighted-additive decision-making (i.e., all possible simulation outcomes) specifically in a probabilistic context. A simulation does not necessarily need to invoke *specific* probability in its outputs. However, the idea that an agent is making decisions that are being simulated does imply that there is a *relative* probabilistic nature to the choices being presented. Hence, Bayesian probability and a weighted-additive framework are applicable.

A weighted-additive framework, though, means that all variables have to be *standardized* or placed on the same quantitative scale in relation to each other in order to be comparable. Without comparability, the rules of conditional and total probability are meaningless. But this stands in contrast to saying that the data has to be *normalized*. That would imply the quantification needs to be on a normal (i.e., a sigmoidal probability density function) distribution scale and that may not be the case. Even where a GIS, ABM, or MAS, simulation can consider a variable to have complete neutrality, or where its weight may dramatically fluctuate, it still fits within the framework of comparably weighted probabilities.

But that does not imply that some variables do not have multiplicative, exponential, logarithmic, or fuzzy relationships (with the decision criteria or with each other). It just implies that criteria are evaluated independently as to that mathematical relationship and make up an additive proportion of importance to the decision as a whole, whether they are consciously evaluated or not.

8.3.4 Summary of Theoretical Assumptions

To reiterate the previous points, cognitive agency-based simulations in archaeology entail the following theoretical assumptions:

- Decision-making implies a systematic framework. Ad hoc decisions are not repeatable. Though ad hoc decisions may be simulated, and may be useful for very specific reasons, they are not mechanistic. This does not imply that all criteria are *systemic*, that is, the product of the entire system as a whole. The decision is systemic, but individual components of it, or relationships within it, may not be.
- Arriving at a decision requires an iterative mechanism or step-wise process of some kind. No mechanism means no alternate outcomes are possible.
- Decision-making is subject to repetition, improvement, learning, and alteration. So there must be a direction to the temporality that is implied. A simulation should not function the same backwards as it does forward in time because information is always additive.
- Decision topologies are likely to be increasingly similar among families, communities, and other cultural groups as a function of spatial and kin relationships. So they inherently depend on the ways in which those cultural groupings are defined. But these are open systems and equifinality demands that there could be multiple causal paths to the same or similar outcomes, and we must consider that in our interpretations.
- If a decision is required, then multiple outcomes must be possible. Alternate outputs imply a relative (not necessarily explicit) probability function, while cognitive agency implies choice in those outcomes and some level of control to those probabilities.
- If multiple outcomes are possible, then a systematic process will also require multiple inputs. Decisions are made by evaluating the available criteria. A single criterion alone will not be sufficient to allow agency in a mechanistic decision.
- Input data is always perceived from an agent's perspective and will be both contextual and almost always incomplete or even inaccurate. Our simulations often inappropriately consider only complete information and "top-down" perspectives.
- To be included in a digital simulation, input variables have to be quantified—even when they may originally be considered qualitatively. This does not apply to analogue simulations.
- Decision-making is either explicitly or implicitly a probability function and can be described by the Bayesian rules of conditional and total probability.
- The weighted-additive model of probability functions can cover all varieties of decision-making for digital simulations and is inherently a covering definition for most, if not all, archaeological types of simulations.
- To be incorporated into weighted-additive forms of simulation, input parameters need to be standardized or somehow made comparable with each other. A unit of measure is implied.

These assumptions are completely independent of the mathematical or computational ones associated with the technique or method being used itself. But what do they mean for testing the validity of a simulation? How do these things affect what it is we think we know by creating and using a digital simulation? To answer these questions we need to think about the purposes of why we are using digital simulation in the first place.

8.4 The Goals of Archaeological Simulation

Why should we create a digital simulation? Or an analogue simulation, for that matter? Is the use of GIS, ABM, or MAS intended to *re-create* some aspect of the archaeological past? Is it to explore the data and develop new hypotheses? Or, is the purpose of the simulation to explain previously defined, or hypothesized, archaeological or behavioral spatial patterns? The knowledge that we hope to attain at the end of the process is perhaps the biggest factor in what the simulation will look like and how we will be able to judge its value and effectiveness.

8.4.1 Simulations as Re-creations

If we want to use simulation only as a means to re-create some aspect of the past, then we do not necessarily have any explanatory objectives (cf. Shanks and Tilley 1987). In this sense, no formal explanation is required as an outcome, only the depiction of spatial patterns, context, experience, or some other attribute of the archaeological past. The viewer interprets those patterns in her/his own way. This is consistent with the "immersive" approach to digital simulation (e.g., Allison 2008; Barceló et al. 2000; Favro 2006, 2012; Frischer 2008; Gill 2009; Goodrick and Gillings 2000; Maver 2001; Slator et al. 2001). Immersion is where the thing being simulated is just the ability to move around within a modified and appropriately textured virtual environment. We fill in the details of those textures and digitize objects/contexts that we know from the archaeological or historical records, and everything else is informed speculation. The goals of such simulations are much more about education, public outreach, and an articulation of technology, preservation, and visual interpretation than they are about explaining past mechanisms or developing hypotheses about the past.

There is no expectation that the speculative parts of the re-creation will ever be *objectively* evaluated for their accuracy. Authenticity is an intangible product of the visual realism of the textures, how convincing the context is to the viewers, and the qualitatively assessed accuracy of the archaeological or historical elements. The output is purely visual, though other senses are also occasionally employed; sound obviously, but even smell in analogue simulations (Shanks and Tilley 1987, p. 86). But these do not provide measurable data as an output. It is meant only to be experienced by the audience and the goal is to achieve a *sense* of reality, not an objective measure of it. It is the difference between witnessing an historical event and watching a film dramatization of it. Artistic license is to be expected.

The sense of reality, though, may be very powerful and convincing. But perhaps it is a false sense of reality despite the increased processing and rendering power of today's computers and modeling software. Although we may be quickly acquiring the ability to create more realistic textures and environments that can interactively simulate the past, the people we are studying are long gone and will always remain so. Their cognitive processes no longer exist and they cannot be re-created. They can *only* be simulated. The Battle of Gettysburg will never occur again, no new actual Clovis point can ever be made, only things which look like them or that we think look like them.

This is no small matter, as simulation at its most accurate may at best be considered only a tiny fragment of the entire long-gone cognitive processes involved. Even the most sophisticated immersive simulation is but a small window into the past. This is because it will only ever be the perspective of a single agent: the viewer (or more properly a combination of the viewer and the programmer who constructed it for the viewer to experience). Can we truly argue that a tiny fragment of anything represents it in its entirety? Or that one re-created agent's perception stands in for all the others? Every individual has a unique perspective, and you cannot simulate all of the perspectives of past people simultaneously, only the one you think is representative of the others.

Weather-forecasting simulations operate on the scale of supercomputers and arguably deal with far less complex processes and much less variability in their guiding rules or principles (Holton 2004; Molteni et al. 1999; Stensrud 2007; Zwieflhofer and Kreitz 2001). They are also without the individual and group concepts of limited knowledge, perception, choice, risk, and assessing future returns. Such simulations tend not to use ABM, or if they do, their agents are not thought of as cognitive ones. They can use a global frame of reference because the agent's information is not the basis of the decision topology, and they have no immersive perspective. You do not need to worry about whether a raindrop should or should not have the same knowledge as all of the other raindrops. Yet nearly imperceptible changes in the initial conditions will cause dramatic effects in the outcome and in no case could you ever re-create an exact historical weather pattern from identical inputs in a simulation even with a supercomputer.

This is even more so the case in archaeological situations. We cannot know that a complex simulated pattern represents the same *specific* behaviors as an archaeological one with any measurable level of certainty. We can only have a relative one based on our subjective confidence in it, that is, how well we think it represents the past or how convincing we think the rendering appears to be. But ultimately, an immersive reality-based re-creation can only be concerned with somewhat trivial sorts of patterns; like the placement of buildings, objects, trees, etc., or their stylistic appearances. This is because no larger explanatory questions are being asked. So the absence of a formal explanatory objective makes any attempt at statistical validation of re-creation or immersive reality type simulations entirely pointless. They are meant only to be experienced, not to explain.

It might also be useful to think about this using a metaphor. Imagine that we are faced with a series of archaeological sites found along a stretch of highway that consist of wrecked and discarded automobile parts scattered around from a long range of time and from numerous makes and models of vehicle. Naturally some portions of the vehicles are not there; that is, the perishable portions, or those which have rusted away. Some portions were also reused and deposited in sites or junkyards elsewhere. What engine parts we find are disarticulated, do not necessarily fit between different makes and models, and no longer function. We usually cannot rebuild any single accurate automobile from these parts.

But even if there were enough pieces from a site (say a junkyard) to complete a single automobile, it would not be an example of a vehicle that actually had a use-life of its own. It would be a replication (despite the original parts) of a vehicle in the same way that Civil War reenactors are re-creating the Battle of Gettysburg, or a computerized weather system is a simulation of something that looks like a hurricane. They are only intended to behave like the thing being simulated, or how we think it should behave. Our confidence in how accurate that simulation is would be entirely reliant on the availability of other examples to which we could compare it. If we re-created a 1932 Packard, we could only have confidence in its accuracy if we had another to compare it to. But if we had others to compare it to, then what purposes do we have for simulating it?

If we do re-create it and we have confidence in its authenticity, it still tells us very little about how such an automobile was used in the past, who drove it, where they drove it, for how long, and why. All of these are questions many processual archaeologists may be interested in asking. If we drove the re-created Packard around ourselves it might give us insight into what it feels like to drive that vehicle, but it doesn't tell us how past people felt while driving it or an objective insight into their contextual experience (only a subjective one). Such things might be the kinds of questions a post-processualist would ask. Without explanatory purpose the accuracy of simulations cannot be objectively evaluated, nor should they be. But a re-created Packard might give us insight into the operating parameters of such a vehicle and that might be very useful for developing explanatory objectives. I would consider this to be an aspect of data mining.

8.4.2 *Simulations as Data Mining*

In some cases the purpose of the simulation may be to explore the data and to develop new hypotheses. Again, no specific explanation is sought, only the potential to recognize spatial or other kinds of patterns and deduce from them hypotheses which may be tested further down the line. If so, this is essentially a form of data mining and is subject to the same kinds of biases and limitations of data mining in general, such as overfitting, pattern misinterpretation and issues of scale (Chen et al. 1996; Guo and Grossman 1999; Hastie et al. 2001; Nisbet et al. 2009).

One could argue that ABM and MAS (or even predictive modeling) are merely forms of data exploration or ways of experimenting with the data (Axelrod 2006; Phan and Varenne 2010; Tesfatsion and Judd 2006). That by using input data and simple decision rules, we can observe self-organizing behavior arise "organically" in the simulation. Variations in the input data will cause changes in the output to be observed, measured, and compared. Contrasting the observed output with what might be expected under other conditions will give us hypotheses for how past humans may have reacted in the same situations.

I agree that there is a lot of utility to this approach, and I believe it helps us to design hypotheses that bear further detailed examination. However, I also believe that there is a theoretical danger to simulating social systems in this way that cannot be understated. Digital simulations are *always* tiny abstractions of cultural dynamics; they have to be because we cannot digitally simulate entire systems on a 1:1 scale, nor can we always disentangle one system from another. But simple simulations are likely to lead to building simple hypotheses, and too much abstraction will always underestimate human complexity. Simple hypotheses may be very useful in understanding a system or elaborating upon it, but there is an inherent danger in assuming that the simple abstraction accurately represents the complex original.

Since ABM and MAS simulations are also typically a closed system (i.e., it cannot account for variables not included), it is inherently theoretically deterministic (Salmon 1998, pp. 145–147). This means that we should not always expect to recognize unusual or unpredictable phenomena with the data included in the simulation. Yet those may be the very things we are interested in. Sensitivity or uncertainty analysis in this context may help to determine whether or not there is too much variability, or flexibility, in our simulations but it will not necessarily lead toward a better fit with archaeological signatures or their explanatory relationships. That is a completely separate question and a by-product of the theoretical transition between the specifics of the archaeological record and the generalities of a simulated mechanism. Again, archaeological data is by definition limited in its extent, quality, and representation and there is only so much it will tell us.

Referring back to the metaphor, if we could simulate an internal combustion engine from piecing together specific bits and pieces of archaeological engine parts, it becomes something altogether different to extrapolate more generalized ideas about what they were doing with that engine. Taking the traditional material-oriented archaeological perspective, we would be limited to placing the simulation in context only with the materials and landscape that we found alongside the highway. A processual approach may be interested in understanding how market forces caused a change in the power and torque output of the engine, or its fuel consumption over time.

Examining and experimenting with the parameters of the engine simulation alone, even in the context of the highway and larger landscape, may give very little insight into developing hypotheses about larger economic forces though. This may be despite the fact that we may very well be able to reconstruct the power and torque of that particular engine. Likewise, a post-processual or phenomenological perspective may be interested in describing the experience of the wind in your hair as you drive the automobile down the highway. Again, these are not easily extrapolated from a simulation that examines only the archaeological parameters.

Using the reconstructed engine parameters as constraints in ABM or MAS simulations may lead to the development of explanatory questions or perhaps ways in which we might approach the testing of explanatory questions. But despite the potential for organically developing interesting patterns, data, or other outputs from ABM or MAS simulations, unless addressing those explanatory questions is the intended outcome, we cannot know that past human societies acted in the same ways. We can only identify those outputs as potential alternative models for human behavior in the past that must then be verified independently. Without a full understanding of the mechanisms by which the simulations operate or the limitations of the mathematical rules, principles, or formulas, there is no link between the inputs, the transformations, and their outputs.

Furthermore, ABM and MAS simulations typically treat the agents as having uniformly consistent access to information and always operating in the same ways. These ways may be guided by the operating rules, but those rules are almost always simplistic and applied homogenously between agents. There is generally no inclusion of different perceptions, heterogeneous information between agents, erroneous assessments, maladaptive and neutral behaviors, or fuzzy choices. This does not mean a useful simulation always has to include these things. But when you consider that simulation by definition must be a simplified abstraction of a much more complex system, then it is clear that ABM is, at best, only a starting point for understanding past human behavior.

8.4.3 Simulations as Explanatory Tools

Perhaps we want to use simulations to explain previously defined, or hypothesized, archaeological, or behavioral, spatial patterns. Here, a formal explanation is the required outcome; in the sense that the observed patterns were either expected or could be surmised, given the parameters of the simulation. Some explicit or implicit level of confidence must be applicable to the results. If so, then we need to consider the nature of explanation and its relationship to causality, particularly with respect to its application in archaeology.

But how do we use archaeological simulations to explain? It cannot be said that "explanation" is a concept that has been resolved. There is still a great deal of conflict over what constitutes sufficient explanatory understanding in archaeology (e.g., Alexandri et al. 2013; Gómez 2013; Hodder 2012; Kohler 2012; Krieger 2012; Schiffer 2013; Verhagen and Whitley 2012). The primary schools of thought follow the notion that an explanation either (1) predicts the phenomena under examination, given behavioral rules or tendencies (cf. Binford 1965, 1972, 1977; Flannery 1968; Hill 1977; Salmon 1982; Watson et al. 1971) or (2) describes it in some manner, such as from a sensory, pseudo-emic (phenomenological), or biased interpretive perspective (cf. Bender et al. 2007; Hodder 1989, 2012; Ingold 2007; Shanks 1992; Tilley 1990, 1991, 1994).

Neither approach sufficiently deals with causality though. The critical component is in testing. The positivist explanation is considered *refuted* by physical evidence that disproves it (it is technically never verified, but only generally accepted until proven otherwise). But statistical correlation with archaeological signatures is still thought of as the only valid method of testing in archaeology. Correlation is, though, completely distinct from, and may have no relation to, causality itself (Cox 1992; Pearl 2000; Salmon 1998). The phenomenological or "interpretive" explanation is untestable in a positivist framework, because it cannot be quantified or statistically assessed, and thus is inherently inconsistent with a demonstrated logical causality. It must be accepted only qualitatively, that is, subjectively. Though there are certainly ways in which some phenomenological attributes can be examined quantitatively (e.g., Gillings 2009, 2012; Gillings et al. 1999, 2008; Llobera 1996, 2001, 2012; McEwan and Millican 2012) and perhaps may at some point be incorporated into mechanistic simulations or causal/mechanical explanations.

Sticking with the positivist perspective, though, simulation inputs may be derived either inductively (from datasets of previously known archaeological sites) or deductively (from theories about human behavior), but the output is still almost always assessed through pattern recognition, iteration, and comparison with the known archaeological record (e.g., Barceló 2012; Barton et al. 2010; Campillo et al. 2012; Flores et al. 2011; Griffith et al. 2010; Janssen and Ostrom 2006; Kohler et al. 2012; Murphy 2012). Such tests usually rely on either explicit or implicit correlative evaluations with material from the archaeological record: site patterns, sites, features, and artifact distributions.

But this again is the basis for testing all archaeological hypotheses in a positivist framework: *correlation with archaeological signatures*. Generalization and reductionism in defining what those archaeological signatures actually represent is inherent in that process. This is particularly so if the initial inputs were derived inductively. It implies a normative, material culture-based perspective on all past behaviors and human activity *and it assumes all of the preexisting biases by which that material was preserved and collected*. Activity that does not create archaeological signatures is traditionally not considered *testable* from the perspective of hypothesis validation (or refutation) in a positivist framework *because there is nothing to measure in the archaeological record*.

The problem is, however, that this approach conflates correlation with causation, emphasizing the former and relying on a biased material culture that may not directly equate with the outputs of the simulated mechanism in the first place. The quantification of archaeological material does not directly equate with people, their behavior, or its intensity despite our tendency to treat it that way. How can we test a simulation by comparing it to something for which we are unsure of its meaning? It also confounds the specific (the archaeological record) with the general (the mechanisms that might explain it). If we want to test the general hypotheses, then the presence, nature, or location of specific phenomena in the archaeological record may, or may not, be appropriate data to support them.

Ultimately using the archaeological record to validate a simulation often fails to explicitly provide for the causality that is a key theoretical implication of the use of agents in the overall simulation. The archaeological materials used to test the simulation *must* be representative of the *same* causal processes that are built into the simulation itself, and those causal processes must be made explicit. This is not a component of the standard deductive-nomological (D-N) or inductive-statistical (I-S) models of explanation (Hempel 1965; Hempel and Oppenheim 1948; Salmon 1971, 1984, 1990).

In contrast to the D-N and I-S models, a causal/mechanical model of scientific explanation (Salmon 1984, 1990, 1998) explicitly requires the delineation of cause-and-effect relationships as the lynchpin to explanation. Only by defining causality in the form of logical relationships can one explain the phenomena under analysis. Correlation may or may not exist with physical evidence, but it is in no way required to refute or validate the hypothesis. Instead, the correlation of two things must be shown to have a common cause (Sklar 2000, p. 146). An explanation is considered on the basis of its probability and the *soundness* of those individual logical cause-and-effect relationships.

The nature of quantitative simulations in archaeology makes them extremely well suited to the purpose of defining these very logical relationships, and therefore a possible gateway to developing causal explanations. But they have to be considered from the perspective of the agents involved and have to incorporate dynamical phenomena on different levels. There will always be a level of subjectivity to such explanations. But this is archaeology we are talking about, subjectivity is intrinsic to the discipline because, as already mentioned, the past is gone and cannot be re-created, only simulated.

The goal is to present logically sound, sufficient, and comprehensive interpretations that other archaeologists can accept until something better comes along. Digital simulations are simply ways in which those ideas may be presented and examined in context. The simulations themselves are *logical* tests of the hypothetical causal relationships, but they cannot be independently validated merely by the presence or absence of archaeological material. There must be a causal relationship that is specified.

When we simulate nonhuman biological organisms in an ABM or MAS, we generally do not bother with the concept of perception, choice, spatially limited knowledge, or group-based decisions. Instead, we tend to use something known as "pattern-oriented" modeling (Grimm et al. 2005). That technique is intended to generalize between theories of adaptive behavior and system complexity. This is not because we believe nonhumans do not make perception-based decisions, but because we are more interested in their *general* responses to the environment, not their individual ones.

In essence, we are trying to find out what makes individual nonhuman organisms *similar* to each other and we assume their mechanistic decisions are biological imperatives, not cognitive, or preferential, ones. With human social simulations we are often more interested in what makes individuals, or groups of people, *different* from each other. In other words, we may be more interested in *specific* behavioral choices, not general patterns of them. The exception, naturally, tends to be with simulations of early hominid behavior. Simulating differences in behavior, though, requires thinking about the simulation's structure in different ways and could have very real consequences in how it may be interpreted.

To use the internal combustion engine metaphor one last time, if we simulate the internal combustion engine (so to speak) of a biological system, we often want to understand how that engine works for all similar species or for a species in many different contexts. We are looking for generalizations regardless of the context. Or if the context affects the operation of the engine, understanding that may be an objective in itself. But the destination of the "automobile" is assumed to be procreation and survival—it is embedded in the Darwinian framework. It is a generality, and observing the specific "places" that species (past or present) occur is intended to support, or test, hypotheses about those kinds of places. The occurrence of an individual, or group, can be equated with behavior because it is based on direct observation. The archaeological record is an *indirect* reference to human behavior, and therefore cannot be a statistical validation of it in the absence of a causal/mechanistic explanation for its presence.

For human systems we may be specifically interested in not just how the "engine" operates but specifically where the "automobile" was headed, how long it took to get there, why that route was chosen, and what kinds of music they played along the way. The "destinations" we are interested in are both specific (a place) and generalized (a kind of place). In fact, one could argue that the processual perspective in archaeology is merely a focusing on the generalities of humanity (the kinds of places we like to drive to), while the post-processual perspective is keyed to the specifics (where did past people actually drive to and what did they feel like getting there).

Neither is anything without the other and digital simulations must attempt to reconcile the articulation between the generalities of the simulated mechanism and the specifics of the archaeological record. This cannot be done without an understanding of their causal interplay. All of this is but one more perspective on the Middle Range Theory discussion (e.g., Binford 1977, 1982a, b; Kosso 1991; Raab and Goodyear 1984; Tschauner 1996). Thus, done properly, simulation could potentially be Middle Range Theory in action.

8.5 Conclusions

In summary, then, the purposes for why we might want to create a digital archaeological simulation are paramount to understanding how we should examine their accuracy. If we are interested only in creating an immersive simulation for the purpose of pedagogy, then we are typically not presenting new ideas but depicting existing ones in a way that the viewer can get a sense of them. No explanatory objectives are implied and the entire simulation is purely subjective and qualitative. No statistical measures of accuracy or sensitivity can, or even should, be applied.

If we want to explore the data we have on hand by experimenting with variable inputs, transformation routines and formulas, and comparing the outputs, then there may be many ways in which we can create useful simulations (particularly ABM or MAS ones). However, we need to be aware of what mechanisms these simulations are proxies for and why. If they are highly simplistic we may be implying much less complexity than may be suitable. Statistically evaluating the outputs may be possible in some situations but are very likely to be based on misleading correlative measures if cause-and-effect explanatory relationships are unclear. The typical focus of ABM and MAS modelers has been to evaluate them in the same ways in which we test simulations in natural systems and that may be completely missing the point.

Simulations that engage cognitive agency and that have defined explanatory objectives inherently invoke causality in the mechanism being examined. This means that *in addition to* any computational coherence and soundness, the simulation must be logically consistent throughout with respect to issues of cause-and-effect. Any correlation with archaeological components must explicitly situate them within the causal/mechanical model and cannot be considered a validation, or refutation, of the simulation in its absence. The simulation may predict a pattern of sites under given input conditions, but unless it can show that those sites are functionally representative of the behaviors being predicted, it is not an independent validation. Because such mechanisms are very complex and cannot be separated from other mechanisms in other systems, it makes them extremely difficult to simulate in a convincing manner.

Archaeological simulation then really should be focused on specific components of mechanistic complex decision-making, not its entirety. This means we cannot necessarily expect to predict archaeological signatures, since they may be the result of processes not considered, and are not proportionally indicative of human activity. But if the simulation logically resolves specific hypotheses of causality or illustrates the inputs, transformations, and outputs of a mechanism (which is always part of a larger one), then an explanation can be considered to have been proposed. Refuting that explanation would then require proposing alternate hypotheses that are also logically consistent, and can be shown to be more likely, or subjectively more acceptable. Likewise, implementing the full range of probable or possible input parameters for the constituent models within a simulation builds support for the ultimate conclusions. In this sense no one explanation is necessarily "proven" but all logically consistent alternatives can be compared and perhaps statistically evaluated from a probability perspective.

This brings us back to the testing paradigm in archaeology: the complete reliance on archaeological signatures for all hypothesis building or testing. Given a complex simulation that provides a clear, logical, and consistent causal/mechanical explanation for one (or more) phenomenon within a decision-making system, how can we find something archaeological to indicate its probability? What we consider to be the archaeological record is fragmentary, a palimpsest of behaviors, sometimes categorical in nature, and not directly proportional to human activity. How do we make a simulation relevant to what we do as field archaeologists? Many times these simulations use different scales of spatial data, operate on separate theoretical levels, and deal with diverse units of measure. How they are handled, what assumptions are made, and how the outputs feed back into each other are illustrated in different ways but often incompletely and without full disclosure.

When a full accounting of how each specific aspect of the simulation was developed (i.e., every decision criterion weighting, every transformation, and all of the agent input assumptions) is made, it becomes prohibitively large for publication or even understanding by the lay audience. It is exceedingly difficult to publish all of the functional attributes and operations of an internal combustion engine for example. Instead, the reader must usually "take it on faith" that the interpretations are accurate, and have been logically assessed, are consistent, and do not suffer from errors of scale and what not. Ironically, the more of the process that is fully described, the less likely the lay audience is to accept the conclusions uncritically.

Archaeologists, in particular, seem to be more willing to accept vague nonspecific generalized and qualitative models of human behavior than simulations based on concrete numerical assumptions and scale-dependent digital datasets. This is because there are very often too many arguments for alternative assumptions about the inputs for each model in the simulation. Faced with too much detail the reader is either overwhelmed by the information not knowing which assumptions to accept or not, or they are not confident in tracing all of the cause-and-effect relationships. It may be erroneously assumed that taking a vague and qualitative approach to archaeological model building avoids these pitfalls.

We inherently want to believe the simplest explanation possible. But mechanisms do not operate that way. They may be very complex, while their guiding principles are actually not. It is the obligation of the archaeologist to clarify both the operational structure of the mechanism and its guiding principles. An internal combustion engine is very complex to describe in detail, and it may have many different ways of operating. When we use digital simulations in archaeology we need to fully disclose all of these working parts in as much detail as we can. That does not mean that the lay audience will necessarily understand them all. But they should ultimately understand that an internal combustion engine operates in combination with other systems to facilitate movement of people or goods through the landscape for some purpose. The guiding principles can be simplified yet they still have causal relationships with the complex mechanisms by which they operate.

References

Agnew, V. (2005). Introduction: What is reenactment? *Criticism, 46*(3), 327–339.

Agnew, V. (2007). History's affective turn: Historical reenactment and its work in the present. *Rethinking History, 11*(3), 299–312.

Alexandri, A., Buchli, V., Carman, J., Hodder, I., Last, J., Lucas, G., et al. (Eds.). (2013). *Interpreting archaeology: Finding meaning in the past*. London: Routledge.

Allison, J. (2008). History educators and the challenge of immersive pasts: A critical review of virtual reality 'tools' and history pedagogy. *Learning, Media and Technology, 33*(4), 343–352.

Altschul, J. H., Sebastian, L., & Heidelberg, K. (2004). *Predictive modeling in the military. Similar goals, divergent paths*. Rio Rancho, NM: SRI Foundation.

Axelrod, R. (2006). Advancing the art of simulation in the social sciences. In J. P. Rennard (Ed.), *Handbook of research on nature inspired computing for economy and management*. Hersey, PA: Idea.

Axtell, R. L., Epstein, J. M., Dean, J. S., Gumerman, G. J., Swedlund, A. C., Harbuger, J., et al. (2006). Population growth and collapse in a multiagent model of the Kayenta Anasazi in Long House Valley. In J. M. Epstein (Ed.), *Generative social science* (pp. 117–129). Princeton, NJ: Princeton University Press.

Barber, K. S. (2007). *Multi-scale behavioral modeling and analysis promoting a fundamental understanding of agent-based system design and operation*. University of Texas at Austin, for the Defense Advanced Research Projects Agency. Final Technical Report: AFRL-IF-RS-TR-2007-58.

Barceló, J. A. (2012). Computer simulation in archaeology: Art, science or nightmare? *Virtual Archaeology Review, 3*(5), 8–12.

Barceló, J. A., Forte, M., & Sanders, D. H. (Eds.). (2000). *Virtual reality in archaeology* (British archaeological reports, International series, Vol. 843). Oxford, England: ArcheoPress.

Barton, C. M., Ullah, I., & Mitasova, H. (2010). Computational modeling and Neolithic sociological dynamics: A case study from Southwest Asia. *American Antiquity, 75*(2), 364–386.

Bartumeus, F. (2009). Behavioral intermittence, lévy patterns, and randomness in animal movement. *Oikos, 118*, 488–494.

Bender, B., Hamilton, S., & Tilley, C. (2007). *Stone worlds: Narrative and reflexivity in landscape archaeology*. Walnut Creek, CA: Left Coast Press.

Binford, L. (1965). Archaeological systematics and the study of culture process. *American Antiquity, 31*(2), 203–210.

Binford, L. (1972). *An archaeological perspective*. New York: Seminar Press.

Binford, L. (Ed.). (1977). *For theory building in archaeology*. Orlando, FL: Academic Press.

Binford, L. (1982a). Objectivity-explanation-archaeology 1981. In C. Renfrew, M. Rowlands, & B. Seagraves (Eds.), *Theory and explanation in archaeology* (pp. 125–138). New York: Academic Press.

Binford, L. (1982b). Meaning, inference and the material record. In C. Renfrew & S. Shennan (Eds.), *Ranking, resource and exchange* (pp. 160–163). Cambridge, MA: Cambridge University Press.

Boero, R., & Squazzoni, F. (2005). Does empirical embeddedness matter? Methodological issues on agent-based models for analytical social science. *Journal of Artificial Societies and Social Simulation, 8*(4), 6.

Bonatti, C., Díaz, L. J., & Viana, M. (2005). *Dynamics beyond uniform hyperbolicity: A global geometric and probabilistic perspective*. New York: Springer.

Bordes, F. (1950). Principes d'une méthode d'étude des techniques de débitage et de la typologie du Paléolithique ancien et moyen, L'Anthropologie t. 54.

Callahan, E. (1994). *Primitive technology: practical guidelines for making stone tools, pottery, basketry, etc. the aboriginal way; selected from rare and widely scattered publications*. Lynchburg, VA: Piltdown Productions.

Campillo, X. R., Cela, J. M., & Cardona, F. X. H. (2012). Simulating archaeologists? Using agent-based modeling to improve battlefield excavations. *Journal of Archaeological Science, 39*, 347–356.

Chen, M. S., Han, J., & Yu, P. S. (1996). Data mining: An overview from a database perspective. *IEEE Transactions on knowledge and Data Engineering, 8*(6), 866–883.

Clemons, L. (2008). *Branding Texas: performing culture in the Lone Star State*. Austin, TX: University of Texas Press.

Clemons, L. (2011). Present enacting past: The functions of battle reenacting in historical representation. In S. Magelsson & R. Justice-Malloy (Eds.), *Enacting history* (pp. 10–21). Tuscaloosa, AL: University of Alabama Press.

Cox, D. R. (1992). Causality: Some statistical aspects. *Journal of the Royal Statistical Society, Series A, 155*, 291–301.

Crabtree, D. (1972). *An introduction to flintworking*. Occasional Papers of the Idaho State University Museum, No. 28.

Crabtree, D., & Butler, B. R. (1964). Notes on experiments in flintknapping: 1. Heat-treatment of silica materials. *Tebiwa, 7*(1), 1–6.

Dalla Bona, L. (1994). *Ontario Ministry of Natural Resources archaeological predictive modeling project*. Thunder Bay, ON, Canada: Center for Archaeological Resource Prediction, Lakehead University.

Dean, J. S., Gumerman, G. J., Epstein, J. M., Axtell, R. L., Swedlund, A. C., Parker, M. T., et al. (2006). Understanding Anasazi culture change through agent-based modeling. In J. M. Epstein (Ed.), *Generative social science* (pp. 90–116). Princeton, NJ: Princeton University Press.

Deeben, J., Hallewas, D., Kolen, J., & Wiemer, R. (1997). Beyond the crystal ball: Predictive modeling as a tool in archaeological heritage management and occupation history. In W. Willems, H. Kars, & D. Hallewas (Eds.), *Archaeological heritage management in the Netherlands. Fifty years state service for archaeological investigations* (pp. 76–118). Amersfoort, The Netherlands: Rijksdienst voor het Oudheidkundig Bodemonderzoek.

Deeben, J., Hallewas, D. P., & Maarleveld, T. J. (2002). Predictive modeling in archaeological heritage management of the Netherlands: The indicative map of archaeological values (2nd generation). *Berichten van de Rijksdienst voor het Oudheidkundig Bodemonderzoek, 45*, 9–56.

Ejstrud, B. (2003). Indicative models in landscape management: Testing the methods. In J. Kunow & J. Müller (Eds.), *Symposium on the archaeology of landscapes and geographic information systems. Predictive maps, settlement dynamics and space and territory in prehistory* (pp. 119–134). Wünsdorf, Germany: Brandenburgisches Landesamt für Denkmalpflege und Archäologisches Landesmuseum.

Favro, D. (2006). In the eyes of the beholder: Virtual reality re-creations and academia. *Journal of Roman Archaeology Supplementary Series, 61*, 321–334.

Favro, D. (2012). Se non èvero, èben trovato (if not true, it is well conceived): Digital immersive reconstructions of historical environments. *Journal of the Society of Architectural Historians, 71*(3), 273–277.

Flannery, K. (1968). Archeological systems theory and early Mesoamerica. In B. J. Meggers (Ed.), *Anthropological archeology in the Americas* (pp. 67–87). Washington, DC: Anthropological Society of Washington.

Flores, J. C., Bologna, M., & Urzagasti, D. (2011). A mathematical model for the Andean Tiwanaku civilization collapse: Climate variations. *Journal of Theoretical Biology, 291*, 29–32.

Frischer, B. D. (Ed.). (2008). *Beyond illustration: 2d and 3d digital technologies as tools for discovery in archaeology*. Oxford, England: British Archaeological Reports.

George, A. L., & Bennett, A. (2005). *Case studies and theory development in the social sciences*. Cambridge, MA: MIT Press.

Gill, A. (2009). Digitizing the past: charting new courses in the modeling of virtual landscapes. In Flaten, A. and Gill, A (Eds.), Digital crossroads: new directions in 3D architectural modeling in the humanities, Special Issue, *Visual Resources: An International Journal of Documentation* 25, no. 4, pp. 313–32.

Gillings, M. (2009). Visual affordance, landscape and the megaliths of Alderney. *Oxford Journal of Archaeology, 28*(4), 335–356.

Gillings, M. (2012). Landscape phenomenology, GIS and the role of affordance. *Journal of Archaeological Method Theory, 19*(4), 601–611.

Gillings, M., Mattingly, D., & van Dalen, J. (1999). *Geographical information systems and landscape archaeology*. Oxford, England: Oxbow.

Gillings, M., Pollard, J., Wheatley, D., & Peterson, R. (2008). *Landscape of the megaliths*. Oxford, England: Oxbow Books.

Gómez, A. (2013). Archaeology and scientific explanation: Naturalism, interpretivism and 'A Third Way'. In H. Andersen, D. Dieks, W. J. Gonzalez, T. Uebel, & G. Wheeler (Eds.), *New challenges to philosophy of science: The philosophy of science in a European perspective* (Vol. 4, pp. 239–251). New York: Springer.

Goodrick, G., & Gillings, M. (2000). Constructs, simulations and hyperreal worlds: The role of virtual reality (VR) in archaeological research. In *On the theory and practice of archaeological computing* (pp. 41–58). Oxford, England: Oxbow.

Griffith, C. S., Long, B. L., & Sept, J. M. (2010). HOMINIDS: An agent-based spatial simulation model to evaluate behavioral patterns of early Pleistocene hominids. *Ecological Modeling, 221*, 738–760.

Grimm, V., Revilla, E., Berger, U., Jeltsch, F., Mooij, W. M., Railsback, S. F., et al. (2005). Pattern-oriented modeling of agent-based complex systems: Lessons from ecology. *Science, 310*(5750), 987–991.

Guo, Y., & Grossman, R. (Eds.). (1999). *High performance data mining: Scaling algorithms, applications and systems*. New York: Kluwer Academic.

Hájek, P. (1998). *Metamathematics of fuzzy logic*. Dordrecht, The Netherlands: Kluwer.

Hall, D. (1994). Civil War reenactors and the postmodern sense of history. *Journal of American Culture, 17*(3), 7–11.

Halpern, J. Y. (2003). *Reasoning about uncertainty*. Cambridge, MA: MIT Press.

Handler, R., & Gable, E. (1997). *The new history in an old museum: Creating the past at Colonial Williamsburg*. Durham, NC: Duke University Press.

Handler, R., & Saxton, W. (1988). Dyssimulation: Reflexivity, narrative, and the quest for authenticity in 'living history'. *Cultural Anthropology, 3*(3), 242–260.

Harris, T. M. (2006). Scale as artifact: GIS, ecological fallacy, and archaeological analysis. In G. Lock & B. L. Molyneaux (Eds.), *Confronting scale in archaeology. Issues of theory and practice* (pp. 39–53). New York: Springer.

Hart, R. (1981). Children's representation of the landscape: Lessons and questions from a field study. In L. S. Liben, A. H. Patterson, & N. Newcombe (Eds.), *Spatial representation and behavior across the life span*. New York: Academic Press.

Hartman, S. (1996). The world as a process. In R. Hegselmann, U. Müller, & K. Troitzsch (Eds.), *Modeling and simulation in the social sciences from the philosophy of science point of view* (pp. 77–100). Dordrecht, The Netherlands: Kluwer.

Hastie, T., Tibshirani, R., & Friedman, J. (2001). *The elements of statistical learning: Data mining, inference, and prediction*. New York: Springer.

Hempel, C. G. (1965). *Aspects of scientific explanation*. New York: Free Press.

Hempel, C. G., & Oppenheim, P. (1948). Studies in the logic of explanation. *Philosophy of Science, 15*(2), 135–175.

Hill, J. N. (1977). Systems theory and the explanation of change. In J. N. Hill (Ed.), *Explanation of prehistoric change* (pp. 433–450). Albuquerque, NM: University of New Mexico Press.

Hodder, I. (Ed.). (1989). *The meanings of things: material culture and symbolic expression*. London: Routledge.

Hodder, I. (2012). *Entangled: An archaeology of the relationships between humans and things*. New York: Wiley.

Holton, J. R. (2004). *An introduction to dynamic meteorology, Volume 1*. New York: Academic Press.

Hudak, G. J., Hobbs, E., Brooks, A., Sersland, C., & Phillips, C. (Eds.). (2002). *Mn/Model final report 2002: A predictive model of precontact archaeological site location for the state of Minnesota*. Minneapolis, MN: Minnesota Department of Transportation.

Humphreys, P. (2004). *Extending ourselves: Computational science, empiricism, and scientific method*. Oxford, England: Oxford University Press.

Ingold, T. (2007). Materials against materiality. *Archaeological Dialogues, 14*(1), 1–16.

Janssen, M. A., & Ostrom, E. (2006). Empirically based, agent-based models. *Ecology and Society, 11*(2), 37.

Jones, G.L. (2007). *Gut history: Civil War reenacting and the making of an American past*. PhD dissertation, Emory University, Atlanta, GA.

Judge, J. W., & Sebastian, L. (Eds.). (1988). *Quantifying the present and predicting the past: Theory, method and application of archaeological predictive modeling*. Denver, CO: U.S. Department of the Interior, Bureau of Land Management.

Kamermans, H., van Leusen, M., & Verhagen, P. (Eds.). (2009). *Archaeological prediction and risk management*. Leiden, South Holland: Leiden University Press.
Kitchin, R., & Blades, M. (2002). *The cognition of geographic space*. London: I.B. Taurus.
Kohler, T. A. (2012). Complex systems and archaeology. In I. Hodder (Ed.), *Archaeological theory today* (pp. 93–123). Cambridge, MA: Polity Press.
Kohler, T. A., Bocinsky, R. K., Cockburn, D., Crabtree, S. A., Varien, M. D., Kolm, K. E., et al. (2012). Modeling prehispanic Pueblo societies in their ecosystems. *Ecological Modeling, 241*, 30–41.
Kohler, T. A., & Parker, S. C. (1986). Predictive models for archaeological resource location. In M. B. Schiffer (Ed.), *Advances in archaeological method and theory* (Vol. 9, pp. 397–452). New York: Academic Press.
Kohler, T. A., & van der Leeuw, S. (Eds.). (2007). *Model-based archaeology of socionatural systems*. Santa Fe, NM: School of Advanced Research.
Kosso, P. (1991). Method in archaeology: Middle-range theory as hermeneutics. *American Antiquity, 56*(4), 621–627.
Krieger, W. H. (2012). Theory, locality, & methodology in archaeology: Just add water? *HOPOS: The Journal of the International Society for the History of Philosophy of Science, 2*(2), 243–257.
Kumar, K., & Prabhakar, T. V. (2010). Pattern-oriented knowledge model for architecture design. In *Proceedings of the 17th Conference on Pattern Languages of Programs* (pp. 23–32). New York: Association for Computing Machinery.
Kvamme, K. L. (1983). *A manual for predictive site location models: Examples from the Grand Junction District, Colorado*. Grand Junction District, CO: Bureau of Land Management.
Kvamme, K. L. (1984). Models of prehistoric site location near Pinyon Canyon, Colorado. In C. J. Condie (Ed.), *Papers of the Philmont Conference on the archaeology of Northeastern New Mexico* (pp. 349–370). Albuquerque, NM: New Mexico Archaeological Council.
Kvamme, K. L. (1985). Determining empirical relationships between the natural environment and prehistoric site locations: A hunter–gatherer example. In C. Carr (Ed.), *For concordance in archaeological analysis: Bridging data structure, quantitative technique, and theory* (pp. 208–238). Prospect Heights, CO: Waveland Press.
Llobera, M. (1996). Exploring the topography of mind: GIS, social space and archaeology. *Antiquity, 70*, 612–622.
Llobera, M. (2001). Building past landscape perception with GIS: Understanding topographic prominence. *Journal of Archaeological Science, 28*, 1005–1014.
Llobera, M. (2012). Life on a pixel: Challenges in the development of digital methods within an 'Interpretive' landscape archaeology framework. *Journal of Archaeological Method and Theory, 19*(4), 495–509.
Luhmann, N. (1975). Systemtheorie, Evolutionstheorie und Kommunikationstheorie. *Soziologische Gids, 22*(3), 154–168.
Maver, T. (2001). Virtual heritage: Reconstructing the past, reconfiguring the future. *Proceedings of the seventh international conference on virtual systems and multimedia (VSMM'01)* (pp. 168–176). Washington, DC: IEEE Computer Society.
McEwan, D. G., & Millican, K. (2012). In search of the middle ground: Quantitative spatial techniques and experiential theory in archaeology. *Journal of Archaeological Method and Theory, 19*(4), 491–494.
Molteni, F., Buizza, R., Palmer, T. N., & Petroliagis, T. (1999). The ECMWF ensemble prediction system: Methodology and validation. *Quarterly Journal of the Royal Meteorological Society, 122*(529), 73–119.
Murphy, J. T. (2012). Exploring complexity with the Hohokam water management simulation: A middle way for archaeological modeling. *Ecological Modeling, 241*, 15–29.
Niazi, M., & Hussain, A. (2011). Agent-based computing from multi-agent systems to agent-based models: A visual survey. *Scientometrics, 89*(2), 479–499.
Nisbet, R., Elder, J., & Miner, G. (2009). *Handbook of statistical analysis & data mining applications*. New York: Academic Press/Elsevier.

Pandey, V., Mourelatos, Z.P., & Castanier, M.P. (2013). *Decision topology assessment in engineering design under uncertainty*. Proceedings of IDETC/CIE 2014 ASME 2014 international design engineering technical conferences & computers and information in engineering conference, Buffalo, NY.

Parker, S. C. (1985). Predictive modeling of site settlement systems using multivariate logistics. In C. Carr (Ed.), *For concordance in archaeological analysis: Bridging data structure, quantitative technique, and theory* (pp. 173–207). Prospect Heights, CO: Waveland Press.

Parsons, T. (1978). *Action theory and the human condition*. New York: Free Press.

Pearl, J. (2000). *Causality: Models, reasoning and inference*. Cambridge, MA: Cambridge University Press.

Perony, N., Tessone, C. J., König, B., & Schweitzer, F. (2012). How random is social behavior? Disentangling social complexity through the study of a wild house mouse population. *PLoS Computational Biology, 8*(11), e1002786. doi:10.1371/journal.pcbi.1002786.

Phan, D., & Varenne, F. (2010). Agent-based models and simulations in economics and social sciences: From conceptual exploration to distinct ways of experimenting. *Journal of Artificial Societies and Social Simulation, 13*(1), 5.

Pillatt, T. (2012). Experiencing climate: Finding weather in eighteenth century Cumbria. *Journal of Archaeological Method Theory, 19*, 564–581.

Raab, L. M., & Goodyear, A. C. (1984). Middle-range theory in archaeology: A critical review of origins and applications. *American Antiquity, 49*(2), 255–268.

Salmon, W. (1971). *Statistical explanation and statistical relevance*. Pittsburgh, PA: University of Pittsburgh Press.

Salmon, M. H. (1982). *Philosophy and archaeology*. New York: Academic Press.

Salmon, W. (1984). *Scientific explanation and the causal structure of the world*. Princeton, NJ: Princeton University Press.

Salmon, W. (1990). *Four decades of scientific explanation*. Pittsburgh, PA: University of Pittsburgh Press.

Salmon, W. (1998). *Causality and explanation*. Oxford, England: Oxford University Press.

Schiffer, M. B. (2013). Science: A behavioral perspective. In M. B. Schiffer (Ed.), *The archaeology of science: Manuals in archaeological method, theory and technique* (Vol. 9, pp. 13–24). New York: Springer.

Schweitzer, F. (2003). *Brownian agents and active particles: Collective dynamics in the natural and social sciences*. Berlin, Germany: Springer.

Shanks, M. (1992). *Experiencing the past*. London: Routledge.

Shanks, M., & Tilley, C. Y. (1987). *Re-constructing archaeology: Theory and practice*. London: Routledge.

Sklar, L. (2000). *Explanation, law and cause*. New York: Taylor & Francis.

Slator, B.M., Clark, J.T., Landrum, J., Bergstrom, A., Hawley, J., Johnston, E., et al. (2001). Teaching with immersive virtual archaeology. *Proceedings of the seventh international conference on virtual systems and multimedia (VSMM'01)* (pp. 253–262). Washington, DC: IEEE Computer Society.

Stensrud, D. J. (2007). *Parameterization schemes: Keys to understanding numerical weather prediction models*. Cambridge, MA: Cambridge University Press.

Strogatz, S. H. (2001). *Nonlinear dynamics and chaos: With applications to physics, biology and chemistry*. New York: Perseus.

Tesfatsion, L., & Judd, K. L. (Eds.). (2006). *Handbook of computational economics* (Agent based computational economics, Vol. 2). Amsterdam, The Netherlands: Elsevier.

Tilley, C. (Ed.). (1990). *Reading material culture*. Oxford, England: Blackwell.

Tilley, C. (1991). *Material culture and text: The art of ambiguity*. London: Routledge.

Tilley, C. (1994). *A phenomenology of landscape*. London: Routledge.

Tschauner, H. (1996). Middle-range theory, behavioral archaeology, and postempiricist philosophy of science in archaeology. *Journal of Archaeological Method and Theory, 3*(1), 1–30.

van Leusen, M., & Kamermans, H. (Eds.). (2005). *Predictive modeling for archaeological heritage management: A research agenda*. Amersfoort, The Netherlands: Rijksdienst voor het Oudheidkundig Bodemonderzoek.

Verhagen, P. (2005). Prospection strategies and archaeological predictive modeling. In M. van Leusen & H. Kamermans (Eds.), *Predictive modeling for archaeological heritage management: A research agenda* (pp. 109–121). Amersfoort, The Netherlands: Rijksdienst voor het Oudheidkundig Bodemonderzoek.

Verhagen, P. (2007). Predictive models put to the test. In P. Verhagen (Ed.), *Case studies in archaeological predictive modeling* (pp. 115–168). Leiden, The Netherlands: Leiden University Press.

Verhagen, P., & Whitley, T. G. (2012). Integrating archaeological theory and predictive modeling: A live report from the scene. *Journal of Archaeological Method and Theory, 19*(1), 49–100.

von Bertalanffy, K. L. (1970). '... aber vom Menschen wissen wir nichts.' Flechtner, H. J. (translator). Düsseldorf: Econ Verlag GmbH.

Warren, K., Franklin, C., & Streeter, C. L. (1998). New directions in systems theory: Chaos and complexity. *Social Work, 43*(4), 357–372.

Watson, P. J., LeBlanc, S. A., & Redman, C. L. (1971). *Archaeological explanation*. New York: Columbia University Press.

Wescott, D. (2011). *Primitive technology: A book of earth skills*. Rexburg, ID: Society for Primitive Technology.

Whitley, T. G. (2004a). Causality and cross-purposes in archaeological predictive modeling. In Fischer Ausserer, A., Börner, W., Goriany, M., & Karlhuber-Vöckl, L. (Eds.) *[Enter the past]: the e-way into the four dimensions of cultural heritage: CAA 2003: Computer applications and quantitative methods in archaeology: Proceedings of the 31th Conference, Vienna, Austria, April 2003* (pp. 236–239). Oxford, England: Archaeopress.

Whitley, T. G. (2004b). *Risk, choice, and perception: Elements of an immersive GIS*. Paper prepared for the 69th Annual Meeting of the Society for American Archaeology, Montreal, Quebec, March 31–April 4, 2004.

Whitley, T. G. (2005). A brief outline of causality-based cognitive archaeological probabilistic modeling. In M. van Leusen & H. Kamermans (Eds.), *Predictive modeling for archaeological heritage management: A research agenda* (pp. 123–138). Amersfoort, The Netherlands: Rijksdienst voor het Oudheidkundig Bodemonderzoek.

Winsberg, E. (2009). A tale of two methods. *Synthese, 169*(3), 575–592.

Yager, R. R., & Filev, D. P. (1994). *Essentials of fuzzy modeling and control*. New York: Wiley.

Zadeh, L. A. (1965). Fuzzy sets. *Information and Control, 8*(3), 338–353.

Zwieflhofer, W., & Kreitz, N. (Eds.). (2001). *Developments in teracomputing: Proceedings of the ninth ECMWF Workshop on the use of high performance computing in meteorology*. London/Singapore: European Centre for Medium Range Weather Forecasts/World Scientific Press.

Chapter 9
Uncertainties

Sander van der Leeuw

9.1 Introduction

The current volume is a very welcome addition to the literature on modeling. I very much agree with its authors and editors that far too little attention has been given in archaeology to the reduction, at the greatest extent possible, of the uncertainties that are generated by the activity of modeling itself, and more specifically by Agent-Based Modeling (ABM) or Micro-Simulation. The book attempts to fill some of that gap by discussing, in particular, Sensitivity Analysis (SA) as one approach to reduce and assess uncertainty generated by modeling.

But let us put that uncertainty, and more generally the kinds of modeling that the book is discussing, in a somewhat wider context. I would like to begin by referring to the work of Henri Atlan, a neurosurgeon and philosopher on cognition. In a relatively unknown paper (Atlan 1992, p. 58), he poses the question of the relationship between theories and observations in terms of the following example:

> Imagine five traffic lights, which individually can assume three states (red, orange, green). As a group, these traffic lights can assume $3^5 = 243$ states (combinations of colors). But the number of potential connections between these traffic lights that could potentially explain the states that they can assume is in the order of 3^{25}, that is, about a thousand billion.

Atlan draws an interesting conclusion from this, that—no matter what—*any theory we might have* (in this case a schema or blueprint of connections between the lights) *is actually underdetermined by our observations*, simply because we can never hope to make the thousand billion observations necessary to be able to

S. van der Leeuw (✉)
Schools of Sustainability and Human Evolution and Social Change, ASU-SFI Center for Biosocial Complexity, Arizona State University, Tempe, AZ, USA

Santa Fe Institute, Santa Fe, NM, USA
e-mail: vanderle@asu.edu

M. Brouwer Burg et al. (eds.), *Uncertainty and Sensitivity Analysis in Archaeological Computational Modeling*, Interdisciplinary Contributions to Archaeology, DOI 10.1007/978-3-319-27833-9_9

systematically eliminate all configurations except one. Of course, the (huge) uncertainty of any proposed theory can be reduced by having sequential observations, and by increasing the observation density, but we will never be able, Atlan argues, to have enough observations to analytically come up with the "correct" theory about the configuration of connections.

The traffic lights example constitutes a very simple and mechanical system. How much more valid is Atlan's conclusion for the kind of very complex socio-natural systems we are actually studying in archaeology! All of us are aware of the fact that our ideas about the past are based on relatively scant data and therefore reflect major uncertainties, but this example, to my mind, does something more: it gives a sense of the width of the gap involved—one of many hundreds of orders of magnitude. This raises some doubts about whether we can analytically reconstruct the past at all.

Yet, even with this limitation to our cognitive system, we are able as human beings to function relatively well in the environments we have chosen or created for ourselves. Why? On the one hand because we do not, every time, try and create an appropriate theory to determine our actions. That has an important implication: *our theories are to a high degree determined by our prior experiences, applied without analytical thought*. On the other hand, we learn in a feedback cycle that often begins with a "rough" or approximate response that is subsequently refined by experience. One could compare that to learning in a "fuzzy set" approach (e.g., Zadeh 1975). And that, in turn, points to an important justification for modeling, the fact that it allows one to refine a theory by testing some of its implications "in silico," which can then be compared with real-life observations, leading to the refinement of the theory.

But there is another limitation to our capacity to know the "world out there"—the fact that our Short Term Working Memory, the part of our brain that processes information to act, cannot deal with the interactions between more than a limited number of dimensions or sources of information (generally estimated at somewhere between six and eight; Read and van der Leeuw 2009, 2015). As a result, as individuals, *we always act upon a very heavily reduced perception of the dynamics we are involved in*. But as our actions affect a much larger number of dimensions of those dynamics, they create many "unintended," "unconsidered' or "unanticipated" consequences. Over time, in the process of gaining knowledge about socio-environmental dynamics, the result is that we extensively modify these dynamics so that our knowledge is in effect more and more inadequate.

Why am I pointing all this out? First of all, because I think that a general issue in dealing with uncertainty in archaeological modeling is that there are different kinds of uncertainty and that these are all too often lumped together, or at least not sufficiently distinguished. Moreover, I would argue that in dealing with the uncertainties involved in our model building, we also need to consider (a) the ontological uncertainties of our perception of the past, (b) the path-dependency of our model construction procedures that influences the interpretative choices that we make, and (c) the interaction between these two factors. The answers to these issues have relevance for the role and value of our ways of reducing uncertainty in our models. Fundamentally, the underlying dilemma could be framed as: "When we explain archaeological observations, are we explaining the past or the present?" That is a question that most archaeologists do not consider, probably because it leads one into uncharted territory that is more the domain of philosophers and historians, a terrain that is brilliantly mapped by Olivier (2011). In what follows, I have avoided the complexities of this body of literature by referring to the work of several historians who have exposed some of the issues with greater clarity than I could possibly have done.

And that brings me to an interesting aspect of the role of modeling in archaeology in general, which is also observable in this book and has important implications for the way we do things as modelers. Traditionally, prehistoric archaeology is driven by our interest in discovering our *origins*, whether as human beings, or as farmers, or as members of a particular group, society, or nation. In essence, therefore, the discipline *looks back* into the past; it takes an "ex post" approach to the relationship between past and present. But when designing and using models, archaeologists use an "ex ante" approach, *looking forward* to try and understand how certain effects result from assumptions about initial conditions, structures, and dynamics of socio-natural processes.

This distinction has its echoes in the contrast between our traditional, reductionist science and the relatively novel "Complex Systems" science of the last quarter of the last century (Mitchell 2011). This contrast has its roots in the beginnings of the natural sciences, under the auspices of the Royal Society in eighteenth century Britain. Its fundamental tenet was that every step of a scientific argument had to be proven. Now, as one can only prove things about the past and/or the present, but not about the future, this led to a science that fundamentally focused on the relationship between past and present, with an emphasis on explaining the present either in terms of a causal narrative or in terms of mathematical relationships. Complex Systems science does the opposite. It adopts an "ex ante" perspective, focusing on the emergence of novelty. As a discipline that focuses entirely on the (mostly distant) past, this approach has not received much attention from archaeology (but see van der Leeuw and McGlade 1997) and that is one of the reasons, in my opinion, for some of the issues encountered about uncertainty in modeling.

Contrary to what we were taught in the 1970s by certain philosophers of science ("explanation = prediction"; see Watson et al. 1971), the "ex post" and the "ex ante" approaches are fundamentally different in their logic and assumptions. Whereas the former generally results in causal narratives that *reduce* the dimensionality of the phenomena studied beyond the reduction that is inherent in the limitations of our cognitive capacity, the latter aims to investigate multiple possibilities, probabilities, and trajectories in terms of uncertainties, in fact *enhancing* the number of dimensions that are considered. It is as if while the discipline as a whole traditionally looks *against* the arrow of time, the modeler looks *along* that arrow. And that, in my mind, causes all kinds of confusions that we'd be better off knowing about and making explicit.

Each of these two approaches has its own way of dealing with uncertainties. In the former case (ex post), there are (a) ontological uncertainties (uncertainties about how the past will evolve that are inherent in the fact that any socio-environmental system is a complex, and therefore unpredictable, system) and (b) uncertainties that derive from the fact that our information about that past is fragmentary. Both kinds of uncertainties are commingled and downplayed (or even ignored) in the "explanatory" causal narratives that link past and present. The fact that they are implicit is one of the important reasons that these uncertainties, in such a narrative, are not quantified (or indeed quantifiable). The resulting narrative leans heavily on the path-dependency of our experience in interpreting the past.

In the case of the "ex ante" (modeling) approach, both the above uncertainties exist, of course, just like in the "ex post" case. The uncertainties deriving from the fragmentary nature of our data are not explicitly dealt with any differently than in the "ex post" case. But the models do attempt to explicate the ontological uncertainties because they dynamically model the relationship between initial conditions and outcomes. And that adds data points and/or information that enable us in some cases to better match theory (the model) and the archaeological data and thus reduce, indirectly, the uncertainties due to the fragmentary archaeological record. But in the process, the modeling adds a third category of uncertainties—those that derive from the way in which the model was constructed. And those are the uncertainties that much of this book constructively tries to assess and reduce by applying SA and other techniques.

To conclude my argument thus far, I would argue that the uncertainties inherent in the fragmentary nature of our information about the past are such that we have no other way to reduce them than to collect more archaeological data, but these uncertainties can never be reduced to the point that we can be confident about our vision of the past. In the historian Barraclough's words (1955) (cited in Carr 1967, p. 8): "History, though based on facts, is, strictly speaking, not factual at all, but a series of accepted judgments." Archaeology is, in my opinion, no different.

This fundamentally limits the accuracy of archaeological theories or models, and to my mind makes it in most instances relatively useless to try and create dynamical models that are thought to reflect "past realities." I do therefore side with those who see the use of modeling more in extrapolating the consequences of (dynamical) theories about the past, in order to clarify our thinking. Once dynamical models (whether differential equation models or agent-based models) have served to clarify our thinking, we should then throw them away, keeping what we learned in order to make a new, better model. In archaeology, modeling helps us develop "tools for thought" (Collingwood 2014) rather than (decision-support style) models of reality.

In choosing this approach, a major advantage is that we can usually keep the models simple, and thus relatively easy to understand, so that we can limit the introduction of technical uncertainties in the models. But such models generally only represent a (small) part of the dynamics involved, and one needs to juxtapose a number of models to gain a more encompassing perspective on the dynamics at hand. In effect, one assembles what I call a "bee's eye view," referring to the fact that many insects have facetted eyes that simultaneously project slightly different perspectives on the retina, which are then assembled into a complete picture in the brain.

But let me be crystal clear, that does not in any way reduce the value of modeling in archaeology, on the contrary! Modeling is an essential tool in developing fragments of "ex ante" understanding of past processes, helping us to deal with "the tension between a view of history having the centre of gravity in the past and a view having the centre of gravity in the present" (Carr 1967, p. 23). This tension has often been overlooked in archaeology. To incorporate it into our thinking, we should begin by according modeling its correct role, as a tool to further "ex ante" thinking, rather than perpetuate the confusion between "ex post" and "ex ante" approaches to understanding the past (van der Leeuw 2014). In a number of disciplines, this difference between "ex post" and "ex ante" thinking has by now penetrated much of the work being done, mainly under the impact of Complex Systems science. It is thus in my opinion an important advance, stimulated by the archaeological modeling community, that some archaeologists now explicitly focus on emergence, equifinality, and holistic approaches to our understanding of socio-environmental dynamics. But in this respect, archaeology still has some catching up to do.

Next, I want to briefly highlight some points from the individual chapters of this volume, without pretense of completeness, and taking as a given that the general remarks made thus far are relevant to the issues raised in those chapters, but need no further attention here.

9.2 Chapter Synthesis

One of the important technical issues raised by Brouwer Burg et al. in Chap. 1 is the need to strike a balance between, on the one hand, the important advantage of coupling agent-based models with sufficiently detailed geo-referenced models of the environmental conditions in which human decision-making plays, so that the agent-based models of behavior are constrained by reality; and on the other hand, the difficulty—whether by coupling the two models via data transfer, or by subsuming one model into the other—of doing so in current modeling practice. Such models tend to become overly complex and difficult to assess. This point is a general one: we should keep our models simple and move away from constructing them ad hoc.

Brouwer Burg et al.'s chapter rightly draws attention to the need to develop a modular modeling approach such as is being done by the OpenABM site that is part of the CoMSES network. This has several advantages. For one, such modules, if applied in different circumstances as part of different models, are subjected to more rigorous testing than can be achieved by applying them to single situations. As importantly, this brings the modeling community closer together around a limited set of modeling routines, and will therefore favor discussions and collaborations.

Another important point made here is that most of the geographical approaches widely use ground truthing and various kinds of stratified sampling methods to ground their (exploratory) models in the relevant environmental parameters. The best way to implement this in archaeology is to integrate repeated surveys of the environment with modeling so that an iterative learning process is set in motion that reduces, step by step, some of the uncertainties inherent in the landscape and other environmental circumstances. Stratification of the sampling strategies on the basis of geography, environmental characteristics, and frequency of occurrence of archaeological remains then helps close the gap between models and reality, especially if the sampling strategy is based on the accrual of novel information.

A last point of this chapter that I would like to draw attention to is the importance of expert opinion, which is found to be more effective than quantitative analysis in ecological modeling, especially when models are relatively complex. This is clearly a consequence of the human capacity to deal with complex situations that cannot analytically be comprehended, and refers to prior experience as outlined at the beginning of this chapter. Due attention should be given to such expert opinion in our efforts to reduce uncertainties and noise.

One of the points emphasized by Lovis (Chap. 2) is the fact that ABMs are used both deductively and heuristically by archaeologists. Again—I cannot insist on this enough—both these uses are in themselves legitimate provided they are made explicit in the research design. All too often, there is a degree of confusion between inductive versus deductive strategies, ex-ante versus ex-post strategies or top-down (allocative) versus bottom-up (aggregative) strategies. All combinations of these approaches occur, but should explicitly be distinguished. The structure of ABMs (in terms of parameters of behavior that can be drawn from "real life") makes them particularly suitable as bridges between theory and data (van der Leeuw 2004).

As a result, "The internal relationships of different model variables, and the nature of their interaction, can generally be defined as a multivariate suite of linked hypothesized 'if: then' statements. The internal model structure can therefore *sometimes* be couched as inferential hypotheses, but most often these are inductively originated exploratory devices querying the effects of changes in one or more characteristic [variables] of a system on another, that is, operationalizing the exploratory model as a heuristic device." (Lovis, Chap. 2: 25).

Lovis continues: "Sensitivity Analysis is often associated with predictive computational models including ABMs, although it is arguable that it may be most strongly tied to theory-driven models engaged in exploration of system dynamics (Kyle Bocinsky, personal communication), as well as being a central component of decision allocations and outcomes in Artificial Intelligence (AI). It is one component of several verification processes situated early in most research design and which collectively result in model validation" (Lovis, Chap. 2: 22). These processes are directed at assessing the scope of the following uncertainties inherent in the model construction (and not in the archaeological information or the dynamics of the system): (1) input data errors, (2) "model choice," and (3) potential fits to known input–output data. They also relate directly to the choice of the model's resolution—which should on the one hand relate to the spatio-temporal scale of the data, and on the other to the scale of the phenomena questioned.

A last point to highlight from Lovis' chapter is the fact that many ABMs do not result in quantitative elements of prediction. Qualitative conclusions, however, can be as useful in making decisions about potential consequences of the modeled dynamics! But that does have consequences for SA, which is aimed at exact, quantitative replication between deterministic models and observed information. Lovis discusses these consequences in terms of Multi-Criteria Decision-Making, Exploratory Data Analysis, and Knowledge Discovery in Databases. All these techniques are employed prior to the construction of the models to help select the appropriate information to be included in them. In that selection, archaeologists need to be aware that not all environmental information can be captured based on uniformitarian principles. It is important for both the environmental and the behavioral parts of the dynamic to "… systematically break down embedded decisions into their constituent logical units. Such precision as it relates to social behavioral rules can subsequently in turn be employed as bridging information for the formation processes of the archaeological record and how that record will be manifested, that is, expectations of what the archaeological record should look like without background 'noise' (Lovis, Chap. 2, 30)."

Peeters and Romeijn (Chap. 3) make an interesting distinction between statistical uncertainties and model uncertainties. Model uncertainties are fundamental, concerning the conceptualization of agents' relationships to the environment. How do we assess and control the model uncertainties involved? The authors explore three approaches: (1) statistical model selection, (2) robustness analysis, and (3) the use of measures of informativeness and surprise. I want to go into their approach at some length because "… the uncertainty that pertains to the model itself does not normally come into view in […] statistical approaches" (Peeters and Romeijn, Chap. 3, 37). Moreover, "… mistakes in the modeling assumptions have comparatively large effects on the model output (Peeters and Romeijn, Chap. 3: 37)." Lastly, there is a potentially vicious circle involved, as the model that is confronted with the data is to a possibly large extent derived from the same data! Hence, a very different approach is needed.

In the first approach, statistical model selection, one tries to fit models to data, converting model uncertainty into statistical uncertainty, taking models as hypotheses, and evaluating them according to their respective fit with the data, or according to other data-related quality criteria. However, the under-determination of our theories by our observations implies that there may be models that are completely different from the ones we have chosen as alternatives, which nevertheless might fit the data, but are so far outside our conception of reality that they are not likely to be tested. Hence statistical testing is not enough.

Next, the authors try robustness analysis. They conclude that "Most importantly, if we select a single model in response to model uncertainty, or average over a number of models, we seem to cover up something that may in fact be highly informative, namely that the models have certain qualitative features in common (Peeters & Romeijn Chap. 3: 55)." True, but this focus on commonalities (and neglect of differences) reinforces the path-dependent nature of model selection. Rather than evaluating the nature and role of the models chosen and their uncertainties against completely different models, it tests for the internal consistency of a set of related models and their sensitivity to changes in environmental conditions, but not for the ontological uncertainties of the models' representation of reality.

What robustness analysis usefully does do is point to the fundamental mismatch between the environmental and behavioral parts of the model, casting doubt on the modeling assumptions and inviting substantial revisions of the model. These revisions, however, have to come from the field of theory, and there we are back to the minefield that I began this paper with: the inadequacy of our observations if we want to challenge prior experience in interpreting the data involved.

The suggestion of Peeters and Romeijn is interesting, though not very well developed—to select for measures of informativeness and surprise, asking: "What do we learn from the model that adds new information to our knowledge?" which brings us back to the notion that models serve best as tools for learning rather than as representation of reality.

Brouwer Burg (Chap. 4) deals with GIS-based modeling of archaeological dynamics that incorporates empirically based paleo-ecological reconstructions. She explores the weaknesses and strengths of these techniques with regard to the propagation of uncertainty and error and examines the utility of SA. Her model is a two-tiered, multi-criteria decision model, in which one tier inductively generates ecological models of past landscapes from empirical data, and the other explores the differential suitability of the landscape given a range of past behavioral processes, informed by ethnographic data from boreal and temperate forest hunter-gatherers. Thus, she hopes "to heuristically investigate the many different natural and cultural parameters that consciously and unconsciously affect socio-natural behavioral processes." (Brouwer Burg, Chap. 4: 63).

The main weaknesses of the model are first its static and additive nature so that initial errors in geographical model definition are propagated and compounded by layers concerning the vegetation, animal life, etc. As a result, there is important error propagation when moving from the static to the dynamic version of the model. Other uncertainties are introduced in the assumptions and choices detailing model construction. In this case, these were identified as the more likely location of uncertainty production. Thirdly, the scarcity and survival bias of archaeological data introduces further uncertainties in ground truthing.

On the other hand, this approach allows for more precise detailing of the environmental data than ABM does, and thus for improved testing of particular models of socio-environmental interactions. Potentially, this approach can provide a firm and relatively accurate foundation upon which to model nuanced nonlinear behavioral processes of hunter-gatherers, as well as serve heuristic purposes.

Interestingly, the model's hierarchical, multi-criteria approach elaborates four orders of parameters, including (1) the most basic model inputs such as suitability distributions of fauna, themselves based on the parameters of food distribution and cover/shelter, (2) the parameters derived from the above that partially underpin decision-making criteria for resource acquisition choices, (3) parameters based more concretely on the presence/absence of landscape features, and (4) decision-making criteria for settlement choices given a selected strategy for resource acquisition and mobility.

My main regret on this paper is that it does not consider the uncertainties involved in creating decision trees modeling the populations' criteria determining their behavior. That is the elephant in the room—the major challenge that we are now facing. *We need to find ways to shift from an environmentally constrained perspective to a human-constrained one because, in the end, humans define their environments, the challenges they observe in them as well as the opportunities they afford them, and the ways they interact with them.* That involves thinking about a completely different set of uncertainties!

To some extent, this issue is approached in the next chapter (Chap. 5) by Jon Carroll, who looks at uncertainties in building ABM models and thus adopts an "ex ante" perspective focusing on the emergence of behavior rather than the "ex post" perspectives on the past that underpinned the chapters so far that focused on explaining observed behavior. It will not surprise those that know me a little better that I favor such an approach as it enables us not only to learn from the past about the present (= explaining the present) but also to learn from both past and present *for the future*.

The role of modeling is thus different—it encourages the researcher to pose questions that can only be explored through simulation. In this case, that concerns different ideas about communication and information transfer that might explain different rates of cultural transmission. The author does this by exploring links between individuals, geography, and aggregation. In the description of the model, one immediately notices a major advantage of this approach: it can assign to each individual rules drawn from real life that can be understood without either statistics or complex reasoning. Moreover, the fact that the model is driven bottom-up by interaction between individuals enables it to generate unexpected patterns rather than focus on the explanation of imputed patterns.

The way in which the author approaches uncertainties and verification is also very different—it moves from code verification to ensure that the model would do what it was intended, to a form of SA aiming to see if the performance of the model is sensitive to the assumptions made in building it. That stage serves to identify nonlinearities in the model that could be caused by unintended interactions between different feedback loops, but could also be part of the intended behavior of the model. The final phase of this process is validation, evaluating whether the model approximates a realistic target behavior. This is where the degree of abstraction in the model becomes important; if the model is too complex (with too much detail to approximate "reality"), validation is almost impossible due to the large number of uncertainties.

Carroll concludes "… sensitivity analysis is included as part of the development process, providing an enhanced understanding of model behaviors that might otherwise go unnoticed, and this has resulted in greater understanding of the explanatory capabilities of computational methods such as ABM." (Chap. 5: 89).

Watts (Chap. 6) focuses on the quantitative aspect of dealing with uncertainties in ABMs: How many time steps? How many simulations? How many agents? Often these topics are dealt with on the basis of expediency, but that invalidates the fact that there may be aspects of the dynamics themselves (and thus of the results) that are impacted by choices in these domains. In particular, such scale questions should be included in the verification and validation phases of ABMs because they are fundamental structural features of all models. Moreover, they have the potential of economizing the collection of data from large simulation models.

Watts argues that "… storing simulation output data in a matrix (often a similarity matrix comparing the agents or aggregates of agents at different scales), and calculating correlations between the matrices with Mantel tests […] is a useful way to summarize similarities between simulations that have a large amount of output from many different agents or over long simulations" (Watts Chap. 6: 93). This will give a sense of how long a simulation has to run, or how many simulations are necessary before the amount of information acquired by each new time step or run levels off, an indication that longer or more is not always helpful. Thus it enables one to make data-driven decisions about sampling strategies, including about how many agents should figure into the model, for example.

In Chap. 7, White moves in a similar direction, but focuses on one, more specific, relationship, that between "demographic characteristics and the strength of the population stabilizing mechanism in a model hunter-gatherer system (White Chap. 7: 113)." This is achieved by using an ABM model so that the outcome is an emergent feature of the parameters of the model, in this case individual interactions and decisions, combined with stochastic processes such as the probability of death or the fertility rate. In the model, "... experimental data were generated to explore the relationships between the strength of the mortality-based feedback mechanism and a variety of demographic outcomes" (White Chap. 7: 121).

A SA was then done that related the mortality-based feedback mechanism to the demographic characteristics of the population, showing in particular that a stronger feedback causes higher variability in small-scale populations. But "... the summary results from the experiments do not allow extensive investigation of how the various demographic outcomes are related in small populations. There are weak/moderate correlations among mean household size, adult mortality, male age at marriage, and the percentage of polygynous marriage but further work will be required to understand the specific cause-effect relationships that drive these correlations (White Chap. 7: 129)." The lesson from the project is that initially unexpected but apparently realistic results can emerge from the SA of models.

As behooves a concluding chapter (Chap. 8), Whitley looks more in general at the relationship between archaeological simulation, reality, and testing. He carefully establishes the fact that archaeological simulations involve a cognitive dimension that reflects on the modeler's attempt to recreate ancient decision-making. From this follow a number of assumptions. These derive directly from Atlan's (1992) idea that our perception and decision-making are underdetermined by our observations and overdetermined by prior experience, asserting that decision-making is never ad hoc, but implies a systematic framework, within which decisions are made by an iterative process or mechanism that involves learning and improvement.

The chapter then introduces the interesting concept of "decision topology," referring to the search space within which individual decisions are made. Such decision topologies are impacted by communication and information processing between individuals and thus by their proximity (both spatial and non-spatial), and by the ways in which social (rather than cultural!) groupings are defined. But even within such groupings, there is place for equifinality, as people may arrive at the same conclusions by following different paths. Making decisions involves choosing between different alternatives within the topology, based on relative probabilities, and thus on multiple inputs. In evaluating those alternatives, the perspective of the decision-maker (agent) is the one to be modeled. This perspective will be contextual, often incomplete or even inaccurate. To model decisions in a computer simulation, they have to be quantified, even when they are originally analog. Decision-making is best described by Bayesian functions, according to the weighted-additive definition.

The author next asks: "What is the purpose of our simulations?" Is it recreation of some aspect of the past, immersing the modeler in that past so that she can explore it? Or is the purpose to explore the data to develop new hypotheses or explain previously defined, or hypothesized, archaeological or behavioral spatial patterns? In that case, the modeling serves as a kind of data-mining, generating new data from among the inputs of the model.

From my point of view, the most interesting use of simulations is, however, to explain previously defined or hypothesized archaeological or behavioral patterns. Here, a formal explanation is the required outcome in the sense that the observed patterns were either expected, or could be surmised, given the parameters of the simulation. Some explicit or implicit level of confidence must be applicable to the results. If so, then we need to consider the nature of explanation and its relationship to causality, particularly with respect to its application in archaeology.

I have argued earlier that I do not follow either of the two dominant schools of thought on explanation. Explanation does not in itself predict, nor is it sufficient to describe, the phenomena concerned in a way that appeals to one's sensory, phenomenological, or personally biased perspective. Whitley agrees, but adduces very different, interesting arguments:

> The critical component is in testing. The positivist explanation is considered *refuted* by physical evidence that disproves it (it is technically never verified, but only generally accepted until proven otherwise). But statistical correlation with archaeological signatures is still thought of as the only valid method of testing in archaeology. Correlation is, though, completely distinct from, and may have no relation to, causality itself [...]. The phenomenological or "interpretive" explanation is untestable in a positivist framework, because it cannot be quantified or statistically assessed, and thus is inherently inconsistent with a demonstrated logical causality. It must be accepted only qualitatively, that is, subjectively (Whitley Chap. 8: 146).

The problem here is that correlation is not the same as causation. As we saw in our example of traffic lights, simulating the 243 states of the system in a correct manner does not at all provide us with an understanding of the actual causation of the simulated dynamic among the potential billions.

To be used in an explanatory manner, a correlation is considered on the basis of its probability and the soundness of its logical cause-and-effect relationships. This explicitly requires the delineation of cause-and-effect relationships as the lynchpin to explanation. Only by defining causality in the form of logical relationships can one explain the phenomena under analysis. But that causality must be seen to be that of the individual agents looking at the information available—it cannot be *our* sense of causality.

How to achieve this? It seems to me that to move in that direction, we need to introduce the concept of "risk" and distinguish it from "uncertainty" and "variability." In the economics literature, which deals with the society–environment interface, the three concepts are distinguished in the following manner. *Variability* is the natural state of a complex system, which has unpredictable dynamics that set the context within which any society must function. Whereas *uncertainty* deals with the perception of possible, but unknown, outcomes of this social–environmental dynamic, and *risk* explicitly relates uncertainty to loss, and therefore to human values whether material or social.

Introducing risk and risk perception might shift the balance in Whitley's dilemma because it creates a new, nonrandom link among the cause-and-effect relationships perceived by the agents looking at the decision. It directly links their perception of the future to their perception of the past. That relationship can to some extent be quantified by relating the probabilities of uncertain outcomes to the damage that can be done to the investment in a society's values. Moreover, in a more general sense, distinguishing between these three terms, and using each in its appropriate context, would also help clarify the arguments in several of the other chapters in this volume.

9.3 Conclusion

To conclude this long paper, I want to leave the reader with one of the biggest and most challenging questions facing us as archaeologists: understanding the transitions between major kinds of social structures in ways that are more realistic than the simple evolutionary "progress" schemas that have been the staple of our education as anthropologists and archaeologists.

That requires thinking in terms of "tipping points." I have argued in an earlier paper (2012) directed at a sustainability audience, rather than archaeologists, that one could consider such tipping points as temporary incapacities of a society's information-processing system to deal with the dynamics it is involved in. These incapacities occur when there is an accumulation of unintended consequences of that society's earlier actions. The basic idea behind this is that over the long term, every solution that a society implements to deal with a challenge will trigger future challenges, which then need to be dealt with in turn. Due to the over-determination by past experience of the society's ideas, over time the society thus builds an ever-denser scaffolding structure of related and interacting institutions. In the process, it deals with the most frequent of the challenges first, and in doing so, shifts its risk spectrum from frequent and known challenges to unknown challenges more distant in time. Ultimately, these unknown challenges will collide and create a situation in which the society does not know how to deal with all of the unintended consequences simultaneously. It will experience that as a "crisis," and try to overcome it by fundamentally changing its structures. From an external perspective, this crisis can be considered a "tipping point."

How could modeling contribute to our understanding of this process? Once one sees models as tools to explicate the consequences of certain decisions, in principle they allow comparison between alternative decisions and their consequences, including so-called *unintended* ones. That would allow the comparison, from the perspective of the potential consequences of decisions, between options chosen and potentially available options that were not chosen. I realize that this may sound far-fetched, especially after what I have said about the difficulties of relating our visions of the past to the information that is available about it. But I would expect the introduction of risk perception and the evaluation of it by comparing options chosen to those available but not chosen in terms of the consequences of these options to be an interesting challenge for the next generation of models.

References

Atlan, H. (1992). Self-organising networks: Weak, strong and intentional. The role of their under-determination. *La Nuova Critica Nuova Seria, 19–20*, 51–70.
Barraclough, G. (1955). *History in a changing world*. Oxford, England: Blackwell.
Carlson, T. (1982). *Time resources, society and ecology: On the capacity for human interaction in space and time* (Vol. 2). London: Unwin Hyman.
Carr, E. H. (1967). *What is history?* London: Vintage Books.
Collingwood, R. G. (2014). *The idea of history*. London: Martino Fine Books (Original Published 1946).
Mitchell, M. (2011). *Complexity: A guided tour*. Oxford, England: Oxford University Press.
Olivier, L. (2011). *The dark abyss of time*. Lanham, MD: Altamira Press.
Read, D. W., & van der Leeuw, S. E. (2009). Biology is only part of the story.... In A. C. Renfrew & L. Malafouris (Eds.), *Sapient mind* (pp. 33–49). Oxford, England: Oxford University Press.
Read, D. W., & van der Leeuw, S. E. (2015). The extension of social relations in time and space during the Palaeolithic. In F. Coward, R. Hosfield, M. Pope, & F. Wenban-Smith (Eds.), *Settlement, society and cognition in human evolution* (pp. 31–53). Cambridge, MA: Cambridge University Press.
van der Leeuw, S. E. (2004). Why model? *Cybernetics and Systems: An International Journal, 35*, 117–128.
van der Leeuw, S. E. (2012). Global systems dynamics and policy: Lessons from the distant past. *Complexity Economics, 1*(2012), 33–60.
van der Leeuw, S. E. (2014). Transforming lessons from the past into lessons for the future. In A. F. Chase & V. Scarborough (Eds.), *The resilience and vulnerability of ancient landscapes: Transforming Maya archaeology through IHOPE* (Archeological Papers of the American Anthropological Association, Vol. 24, pp. 215–231). New York: Wiley.
van der Leeuw, S. E., & McGlade, J. (1997). *Archaeology: Time, process and structural transformations*. London: Routledge.
Watson, P. J., LeBlanc, S., & Redman, C. L. (1971). *Explanation in archaeology: An explicitly scientific approach*. New York: Columbia University Press.
Zadeh, L. A. (1975). Calculus of fuzzy restrictions. In L. A. Zadeh, K. S. Fu, K. Tanaka, & M. Shimura (Eds.), *Fuzzy sets and their applications to cognitive and decision processes* (pp. 1–39). New York: Academic Press.

Index

M. Brouwer Burg et al. (eds.), *Uncertainty and Sensitivity Analysis in Archaeological Computational Modeling*, Interdisciplinary Contributions to Archaeology, DOI 10.1007/978-3-319-27833-9

B

C

D

E

F

G

H

MIX
Papier aus verantwortungsvollen Quellen
Paper from responsible sources
FSC® C105338

If you have any concerns about our products,
you can contact us on
ProductSafety@springernature.com

In case Publisher is established outside the EU,
the EU authorized representative is:
Springer Nature Customer Service Center GmbH
Europaplatz 3, 69115 Heidelberg, Germany

Printed by Libri Plureos GmbH
in Hamburg, Germany